A Longman Cultural Edition

D0645804

JULIUS CAESAR

William Shakespeare

Edited by

Oliver Arnold
Princeton University

Longman

New York   San Francisco   Boston
London   Toronto   Sydney   Tokyo   Singapore   Madrid
Mexico City   Munich   Paris   Cape Town   Hong Kong   Montreal

Senior Sponsoring Editor: Virginia L. Blanford
Editorial Assistant: Rosie Ellis
Executive Marketing Manager: Joyce Nilsen
Production Coordinator: Scarlett Lindsay
Project Coordination, Text Design, and Electronic Page Makeup: Grapevine
  Publishing Services, Inc.
Cover Designer/Manager: John Callahan
Cover Art: © Getty Images
Photo Researcher: Rebecca Karamehmedovic
Senior Manufacturing Buyer: Alfred C. Dorsey
Printer and Binder: Courier Corporation-Westford
Cover Printer: Coral Graphics Services, Inc.

For permission to use copyrighted material, grateful acknowledgment is made to the
copyright holders on p. ix, which are hereby made part of this copyright page.

Library of Congress Cataloging-in-Publication Data

Shakespeare, William, 1564–1616.
    [Julius Caesar]
    William Shakespeare's Julius Caesar / edited by Oliver Arnold.
        p. cm. — (A Longman cultural edition)
    Includes bibliographical references and index.
    ISBN-13: 978-0-321-20943-6 (alk. paper)
    ISBN-10: 0-321-20943-5 (alk. paper)
        1. Caesar, Julius—Assassination—Drama. 2. Brutus, Marcus Junius, 85?–42 B.C.—
Drama. 3. Rome—History—Civil War, 43–31 B.C.—Drama. I. Arnold, Oliver,
1962– II. Title.

PR2808.A2A76 2009
822.3'3—dc22
                                                                          2008039874

1 2 3 4 5 6 7 8 9 10—CRW—12 11 10 09

Longman
is an imprint of

ISBN 13: 978-0-321-20943-6
ISBN 10:   0-321-20943-5

www.pearsonhighered.com

This book is for Daisy and her mother, Susan Maslan,
and grandmother, Patricia Arnold —
Portia has nothing on them for fortitude,
but they have bigger hearts.

Contents

Republicanism, Popular Politics, and the Rhetoric of Liberty in 1599   160

Further Reading   209

List of Illustrations

p. xvi. Silver denarius of Julius Caesar (44 BCE). © Yale University Art Gallery / Art Resource, NY.

p. xvii. James I gold "laurel" coin (1619–25). By permission of National Museums and Galleries of Wales, Cardiff.

p. xviii. Sandro Botticelli, detail of an illustration for Dante's *Inferno*, Canto XXXIV (1480–1500). Staatliche Museen, Berlin. By permission of Bildarchiv Preussischer Kulturbesitz/Art Resource, New York.

p. 112. Michelangelo Buonarotti. Bust of Brutus (1540). By permission of Museo Nazionale del Bargello, Scala/Art Resource, New York.

p. 131. Title page of Leonard Digges' *A Prognostication everlasting of right good effect* (1585). By permission of British Museum Library, London.

p. 185. "Los Angeles to Outdo World in Tribute to the Bard of Avon." *Los Angeles Times*, April 16, 1916. By permission of the Los Angeles Times Corporation, Los Angeles.

About Longman Cultural Editions

Inspired by the innovative *Longman Anthology of British Literature*, the Longman Cultural Editions are designed to illuminate the lively, ever variable intersections of literature, tradition, and culture. In each volume, a work or works of literary imagination gather new dimensions from materials that relate to informing traditions and debates, to contemporary conversations and controversies, and to later eras of reading and reaction. While the nature of the contexts vary from volume to volume, the reliable constants (in addition to handsome production and affordable pricing) are expert editing and helpful annotation throughout; a stimulating introduction; a table of dates to track composition, publication, and reception in relation to biographical, cultural, and historical events; illustrations guaranteed to spark conversation; and a guide for further browsing and study. Whether you are reading this volume along with the *Anthology*, or in a different or more specialized kind of course, or reading independently of any coursework, we hope you'll encounter much to stimulate your attention, curiosity, and pleasure.

SUSAN J. WOLFSON
General Editor, Longman Cultural Editions
Professor of English, Princeton University

About This Edition

At least three presses publish editions aiming to introduce readers to
the contexts that shaped the writing, performance, and reception of
individual plays by Shakespeare, but Pearson Longman is the first to
bring out such an edition of *Julius Caesar*. Still very widely read in
American high schools, a fixture in undergraduate Shakespeare sur-
veys, and frequently staged, *Caesar* is, by leaps and bounds, the
most familiar English Renaissance representation of the classical
world. But perhaps the play has struck editors as an unlikely candi-
date for the work-in-context treatment: the political struggles at the
heart of the play—the attempt to preserve republican institutions
and freedoms in the face of Caesar's desire to transform Rome into
a monarchy—do not seem very resonant for Shakespeare's England,
where kings and queens had reigned for many hundreds of years
and monarchy remained the unquestioned, unchallenged system of
governance. Yet the Roman world that Shakespeare fashions is
haunted by questions that were deeply important to Elizabethans:
What is the meaning of sacrifice? How should one interpret
dreams? Should the warnings of ghosts be heeded? Is divine will revealed by signs? Even the apparently exotic politics of Rome in 44
BCE would have sparked flashes of recognition in many Elizabethan
playgoers. By the time *Caesar* was first performed in 1599, English
historians, political thinkers, members of Parliament, and others
routinely drew analogies between the Roman Republic—with its
powerful consuls, patrician senators, and tribunes of the people—
and England's "mixed-estate" of monarch, House of Lords, and
House of Commons. Moreover, Brutus and Cassius's rhetoric of liberty may well have struck a chord—a complexly twangy rather than
unproblematically sympathetic chord—with the first audiences of

Caesar: one of the most powerful articulations of national identity in early modern England reconciled loving devotion to the monarch and a deep belief that, whereas the subjects of all other monarchs were slaves, English subjects were free.

How did Elizabethan practices and beliefs shape both Shakespeare's creation of *Caesar* and its impact on early modern spectators? The literary works, political tracts, theological discourses, treatises on ghosts and dreams, and other cultural documents gathered together in the Contexts section of this volume will help the reader ponder this question and develop a range of responses. Reconstructing the contexts within which a work of art is created and experienced can be a tricky business: the great Renaissance scholar Harry Berger once defined a "text" as something that opens up a space for interpretation and a "context" as something that fixes meaning, that closes up the space of interpretation. My approach to choosing, excerpting, and presenting Elizabethan writings that complicate and deepen our understanding of *Caesar* has been guided, above all, by a desire to make these selections function as texts, in Berger's sense of the word. To that end, I have given the reader more than he or she needs to read *Caesar* as I read it or as other scholars have read it. Editors must make choices, but I have tried not to limit the reader's interpretive potential with brief, narrowly circumscribed excerpts that "back up" a particular interpretation of a line, scene, or key issue in the play. Lengthier selections open up more room for novel interpretations and have the added benefit of serving not only as illuminations of a single play but also as substantial introductions to important aspects of Elizabethan culture.

I have edited the punctuation and modernized the spelling of the selections in the Contexts section, many of which have not been reprinted since Shakespeare's own day; I have, however, reproduced titles in all their early modern glory. The text of *Caesar* was established by David Bevington for *The Complete Works of Shakespeare* (Pearson Longman, 6th Edition). Bevington's excellent notes in *The Complete Works* have, for the most part, been reproduced here; I have omitted a few dozen of Bevington's notes and added several dozen new notes of my own. The textual history of *Caesar* is very straightforward (especially by Shakespearean standards): the play was first printed in the 1623 First Folio, and all subsequent printings of the play derive from the First Folio text. Almost all scholars agree that the First Folio text was set up from a "fair copy" of Shakespeare's manuscript and is free of major problems. For a brief account of the editorial puzzle that has attracted the most interest, see Bevington's note to 4.3.180–94.

I am very grateful to the unfailingly helpful staffs at Art Resource, the Yale University Art Gallery, the National Museums and Galleries of Wales, the Staatliche Museen, the Museo Nazionale del Bargello, the British Museum Library, and the *Los Angeles Times*. The Johns Hopkins University Press generously allowed me to draw on materials in "'Caesar is turn'd to hear': Theater, Popular Dictatorship, and the Conspiracy of Republicanism in *Julius Caesar*" (*The Third Citizen: Shakespeare's Theater and the Early Modern House of Commons*, pp. 140–178, © 2007 The Johns Hopkins University Press). Pearson Longman has been a splendid partner in the project, and I am grateful to Rosie Ellis, Abby Lindquist, Joyce Nilsen, and, especially, Dianne Hall. My crack copyeditor Chrysta Meadowbrooke and my proofreader Leslie Ballard saved me from all sorts of blunders and infelicities, and my research assistants Elizabeth Melly and Scott Francis gave me invaluable assistance.

I have been thinking and writing about *Julius Caesar* for a long, long time; among the many loved ones and colleagues who have listened to me chatter about the play, I want to thank, in particular, Michael Goldman, Stephen Greenblatt, Martin Harries, Jeffrey Knapp, and Susan Maslan for inspiration, sharp comments, and wise advice. It is a pleasure to acknowledge two special debts. I have taught *Caesar* in lecture courses, undergraduate seminars, and graduate seminars at Princeton University and in seminars at the Bread Loaf School of English. I have learned an awful lot from my students, both about the play and about how to teach it—I am very grateful to them. For the last fifteen years, it has been my great good luck to have Susan Wolfson as a compassionate and intellectually generous colleague. Before I began to work on this volume, I knew that Susan was not just a brilliant Romanticist but a formidable Shakespearean. As I worked with her in the development of this book, I discovered that she is also an extraordinarily gifted and dedicated editor.

OLIVER ARNOLD
Princeton University

Introduction

When the first audiences of *Julius Caesar* arrived at the Globe in 1599, they must have anticipated a play of epic striving, a play that captured something of the extravagant grandeur of Roman history and its most famous protagonist. Caesar loomed even larger in the Renaissance imagination than he does in ours: Alexander the Great's only rival for martial genius, a brilliant politician, an orator second only to Cicero, a gifted writer whose enduring works were read in Elizabethan grammar schools, and a famous lover to boot (Caesar was in Cleopatra's arms long before Antony). Shakespeare's contemporaries looked back to Rome for models of excellence in war, love, government, and art; they found all of those gifts flowering in Julius Caesar—he was a Renaissance man. Caesar was, moreover, a particularly resonant figure in England: according to Elizabethan historians, Caesar's two incursions into Britain in 55 and 54 BCE were the first successful invasions of the island. The Tower of London itself, some believed, had been built by Caesar, and material reminders of the island's 300-year subjection to Roman rule—roads, walls, ruins, coins turned up in country gardens—were part of everyday life.

Caesar's star power made him an exceptionally appealing subject for a commercial theater, but to represent Caesar's rise and fall was also to participate in an important intellectual tradition: from 44 BCE on, Caesar's ambition and the conspirators' assassination had been touchstones for political debates about monarchy, tyranny, and republicanism and for moral debates about personal loyalty and civic duty. In Dante's *Inferno*, beyond the lowest circle, Satan gnashes Brutus, Cassius, and Judas—the three most egregious exemplars of betrayal—in his teeth; in *The Mirror for Magistrates*, Caesar's shade acknowledges that his death wounds were

Silver denarius of Julius Caesar (44 BCE).

"just revenge" for the bloody carnage produced by his desire to "have renowne and rule above the rest";[1] when James VI of Scotland became King James I of England in 1603, some poets tried to win his favor by comparing him to Caesar, a model of strong but just rule; but other early modern English writers figured Caesar as the tyrannical oppressor of both ancient Britain and his fellow Romans. For Shakespeare's England, Julius Caesar was more than a surpassingly exciting figure from the distant past; he remained a vital and controversial subject.

The year 1599 was a propitious one for Shakespeare to bring to life a titan such as Caesar—"the noblest man / That ever lived in the tide of times" (3.1.258–59), according to Antony. Shakespeare and several other leading members of the Lord Chamberlain's Men (the playing company of which Shakespeare was a member and part

---

[1]William Baldwin, John Higgins, et al., *The Mirror for Magistrates*, ed. Lily B. Campbell. Cambridge: Cambridge University Press, 1938, p. 198.

James I gold "laurel coin (1619–25).

owner) had just built the Globe, a splendid playhouse whose vast dimensions suited larger-than-life characters. In *Henry V*, which also played at the Globe in 1599, Shakespeare seems to test himself in the context of his new venue: the play explores the charisma of a nearly mythic hero-king and the capacity of theater to reproduce charismatic enchantment. *Caesar* was staged within months of the first performances of *Henry V*, and we might expect Shakespeare's play about Rome's most storied man and his play about England's most celebrated king to share a fundamental approach to representing greatness. The two plays, however, could hardly be more different: with more than 1,000 lines to speak, Henry V thoroughly dominates the stage from the second scene to the final curtain; Caesar speaks only 135 lines—Brutus has 728, Cassius 525, Antony 329, and Casca 133—and dies before the play is half over. All of Shakespeare's other great tragic protagonists, including Brutus and Cassius, die in Act 5.

Why does Shakespeare show us so little of Caesar, and why, during his fleeting moments on stage, is he such a shadow of the

Sandro Botticelli, detail of an illustration
for Dante's *Inferno*, Canto XXXIV (1480–1500).

colossus we encounter in classical and other renaissance texts? After all, we see nothing—and hear next to nothing—of Caesar's military, political, and amorous triumphs, nor can we hear in his speeches the rhetorical sparks or keen intelligence that won the historical Caesar so many admirers. William Hazlitt is only the most famous of the many critics who have been disappointed in Shakespeare's apparent fumbling of the dramatic opportunities Caesar offered: "We do not much admire the representation here given of Julius Caesar, nor do we think it answers to the portrait given of him in his Commentaries. He makes several vapouring and rather pedantic speeches, and does nothing. Indeed, he has nothing to do."[2] Hard words, and hard words from one of the nineteenth century's most enthusiastic readers of Shakespeare at that.

Hazlitt finds the play empty at its center, but we may see Shakespeare's decentering as an ambitious strategy rather than a defect. Some critics have argued, for example, that Shakespeare steals some of the spotlight for Brutus, Cassius, and Antony in order to reproduce for the stage the experience of reading Plutarch, the principle source for *Caesar*. As the title of his profoundly influential *The Parallel Lives of the Greeks and Romans* suggests, Plutarch explores character by juxtaposing an eminent Greek and an eminent Roman; according to some scholars, *Caesar* succeeds as a penetrating study of character precisely because our experience of each of the four principal protagonists is shaped and complicated by Plutarchan juxtapositions with the other three. This approach has many merits, but it neglects the most astonishingly novel aspects of Shakespeare's representation of Caesar and his downfall; these radical departures from tradition turn on a redistribution of dramatic energy from Caesar not only to other great patricians but also to the tribunes and the common people of Rome.

Shakespeare is more interested in Caesarism—a political strategy, an ideology, a movement in history—than in Caesar himself; and, as we shall see, even his interest in the man turns on what Caesarism demands of Caesar. Caesarism, as Shakespeare conceives of it, institutes a particular relation between governing authority and the people of Rome: Caesar's power, according to his

[2]William Hazlitt, *Characters of Shakespear's Plays*. London: Taylor and Hessey, 1818, p. 238.

detractors, depends on his great popularity; and the people love Caesar because he submits himself—or, at least, pretends to submit himself—to their will. In Plutarch, by contrast, the people hate Caesar at the time of his death. Plutarch, like other ancient authorities, assigns very little political importance to Caesar's unpopularity; neither he nor the men who strike him down take the people's desires into account in their political calculations. In Shakespeare's play, by contrast, Caesar, Brutus, Cassius, Antony, and the tribunes all treat popular support as the positive condition of power and political success: thus, the tribune Flavius figures the "vulgar" people—rather than loyal army veterans or patrician followers—as the "growing feathers" that threaten to raise Caesar "above the view of men" (1.1.70–74); and Brutus, Cassius, and Antony fret endlessly about how to win the people's support.

In the rest of this Introduction, I focus on the political dynamics of *Julius Caesar* and Shakespeare's idiosyncratic departures from Plutarch, but in the Contexts section of this volume, readers will find discussions of the supernatural phenomena—signs from heaven, ghosts, and a prophetic dream—that figure so prominently in *Caesar*; the relation between Shakespeare's representation of Roman politics and Elizabethan political culture; and the ways in which stage performances and films of *Caesar* have reflected contemporary political and cultural concerns.

Caesarism and Popular Power

Julius Caesar begins with a confrontation between the plebeians and their tribunes: the people have flooded the streets to celebrate Caesar's victory over Pompey's sons in the last great battle of the civil war that Caesar and Pompey the Great waged for supremacy in Rome; Flavius and Murellus, who supported Pompey, admonish the people for rejoicing in the defeat of their fellow Romans.

FLAVIUS   Hence! Home, you idle creatures, get you home!
   Is this a holiday?

                    *   *   *   *   *

   But wherefore art not in thy shop today?
   Why dost thou lead these men about the streets?

COBBLER   Truly, sir, to wear out their shoes, to get myself into more
work. But indeed, sir, we make holiday to see Caesar and to rejoice in his triumph.

(1.1.1–2, 27–31)

After he scolds the people off the stage, Flavius tells Marullus to re-
move the crowns and other "trophies" that Caesar's supporters
have placed on his statues:

MARULLUS   May we do so?
You know it is the Feast of Lupercal.[3]
FLAVIUS   It is no matter. Let no images
Be hung with Caesar's trophies. I'll about
And drive away the vulgar from the streets;
So do you too, where you perceive them thick.
These growing feathers plucked from Caesar's wing
Will make him fly an ordinary pitch,
Who else would soar above the view of men
And keep us all in servile fearfulness.

(1.1.66–75)

At the very beginning of his play, Shakespeare wants to establish
two features of the political landscape of Rome: Caesar enjoys a secure place in the affections of a cobbler and his fellow "mechani-
cals"; and the people's support for Caesar breeds enmity between
them and their own tribunes, whom they have elected and who are
charged with representing the people's interests.

Thomas North's English translation of Jacques Amyot's French
translation of Plutarch's *Lives of the Ancient Greeks and Romans*
was the principal source for *Caesar*, but Shakespeare turns
Plutarch's account of Roman politics at the time of Caesar's death
on its head: in Plutarch, the people have come to hate Caesar, once
their great favorite, and the triumph that he celebrates over Pompey's sons "did as much offend the Romans, and more, than any
thing that ever he had done before";[4] when Plutarch's tribunes re-

[3]See p. 105 for an account of the Lupercalia.
[4]*Shakespeare's Plutarch, Being a Selection from the Lives in North's Plutarch*, ed.
Walter William Skeat. London and New York: Macmillan and Co., 1892, p. 92. All
subsequent parenthetical page references to North's Plutarch follow this edition.

move "diadems" from the "images of Caesar," "the people followed them rejoicing at it, and called them Brutes, because of Brutus, who had in old time driven the kings out of Rome, and that brought the kingdom of one person unto the government of the Senate and the people" (96). (For selections from North's Plutarch, see pp. 97–127.)

The conflict that Shakespeare invents between the people and their tribunes is a symptom of the way Caesar's populism—his cultivation of the people, his direct appeals for their support—unsettles the tribunes' traditional role as the people's delegates and the brokers of their power. Caesar hopes to transcend all other constituted authorities by appealing directly to the people's judgment, and the people, in turn, directly exercise power over Caesar. From the tribunes' perspective, then, Caesarism is a double assault on republican order: Caesar's desire to usurp all political power and the people's unmediated participation in the empowerment of Caesar pose equally devastating threats to the function and authority of the tribunes.

The first scene foregrounds the unfolding of the conspiracy in popular politics and forces the audience to consider any action against Caesar as an attack on the people. The second scene seems to restart the play: the tribunes, having displaced the people from the stage, are themselves displaced by Cassius, Brutus, and the patrician politics that overwhelmingly dominate ancient accounts of Caesar's fall. In his famous attempt to recruit Brutus, Cassius never appeals to the general good of Rome; instead, he invokes the patrician origins of the Republic, urges the affront Caesar's ascendance gives to his patrician peers, and assures Brutus that "many of the best respect in Rome" (1.2.59) look to him for deliverance. Brutus, however, seems indifferent to this distinctly elitist rhetoric: as his brother-in-law engages him in intimate conversation, Brutus is repeatedly distracted by, and more deeply moved by, the sound of "the people" shouting offstage. While Cassius and Brutus speak, we later discover, Antony and Caesar are staging a little drama before the crowds gathered to celebrate the Lupercalia and Caesar's triumph over Pompey: Antony offers Caesar a crown three times, which Caesar rejects three times. Each time Caesar refuses the crown, the common people roar their approval. Like the audience in Shakespeare's theater, Brutus does not see the pantomime but only hears the crowd's shouts, which he misinterprets: "I do fear," he tells Cassius after the first shout, "the people / Choose Caesar for their king" (1.2.79–80). After the second shout, Brutus wonders, "[a]nother general shout! / I do believe that these applauses are / For some new honors that are heaped on Caesar" (1.2.132–34). "General" is an extraordinarily important word in Brutus's political vocabulary: he has just warned Cassius that he will entertain action against Caesar only if the cause is "the general good" (1.2.85); later, as he ponders joining the plot, Brutus will muse, "I know no personal cause to spurn at [Caesar] / But for the general" (2.1.11–12); and, after the assassination, he will assure Antony that he acted out of "pity to the general wrong of Rome" (3.1.172). Yet Brutus first begins to invoke "the general good" at precisely the moment he believes the people are, by *general* acclamation, *choosing* Caesar for their king. Brutus, that is, begins to elaborate a populist justification for the assassination of Caesar (1.2.85) at the same instant he fears the people have willingly acclaimed Caesar their king (1.2.79–80).

Brutus quickly discovers that he has mistaken the meaning of the people's exclamations; a few moments after the shouting subsides, Casca, who will soon join the conspiracy, recounts the thwarted crowning:

CASCA . . . there was a crown offered him; and, being offered him, he put it by with the back of his hand, thus, and then the people fell a-shouting.

BRUTUS What was the second noise for?

CASCA Why, for that too.

CASSIUS They shouted thrice. What was the last cry for?

CASCA Why, for that too.

BRUTUS Was the crown offered him thrice?

CASCA Ay, marry, was't, and he put it by thrice, every time gentler than other, and at every putting-by mine honest neighbors shouted.

(1.2.221–31)

We might expect Brutus to seize happily upon this reassuring evidence that the people do not, after all, want to make Caesar king, but instead he has some trouble digesting the error he has made. His persistent questioning of Casca suggests, to be sure, that he is carefully verifying his mistake, but when Brutus asks, "Was the crown offered him thrice?" immediately after Casca has indicated that Caesar "put . . . by" the crown a third time, his obsession with Antony's offering of the crown begins to sound willfully obtuse. The point, Casca reiterates, is not simply that Caesar was offered the crown thrice; it is also that "he put it by thrice" in deference to the people's will.

Caesar, of course, is anything but deferential to the senators and patricians, but he consistently submits himself to the people. Trailed by an entourage and a "throng" of people (1.2.21), Caesar first appears on stage immediately after the confrontation between the tribunes and the people. The dictator converses with his family and friends, but as he is instructing Antony to "touch Calphurnia" as he runs the Lupercalian circuit, the Soothsayer cries out.

SOOTHSAYER Caesar!
CAESAR Ha? Who calls?
CASCA Bid every noise be still. Peace yet again!
CAESAR Who is it in the press that calls on me?
  I hear a tongue shriller than all the music
  Cry "Caesar!" Speak. Caesar is turned to hear.
SOOTHSAYER Beware the ides of March.
CAESAR   What man is that?
BRUTUS A soothsayer bids you beware the ides of March.
                                                          (1.2.12–19)

Someone from the crowd calls out Caesar's name, and the master of the world turns around to answer. The contrast between the anonymity of the hailer and the fame of the hailed is striking. Both before and after he turns, Caesar does not know who has called out his name: "Who calls?" "Who is it in the press that calls on me?" "What man is that?" Caesar recognizes the authority of the hailer without knowing him: to be Caesar is to be subject to a nobody, to anyone, to everyone. Caesar's tendency to refer to himself in the third person may strike us monomaniacal, but he first speaks his own name ("Caesar is turned to hear") only after he is named by an unfamiliar voice calling out from "the press." Caesar belongs so little to himself that his proper name seems the possession of anyone who speaks it.

Caesar is so wholly the people's creature that he cannot, at least in public, even acknowledge that there is anything left of the private man. Thus, Artemidorus's attempt to inform Caesar of the plot fails because he appeals to Caesar's personal interests:

ARTEMIDORUS Hail, Caesar! Read this schedule.
DECIUS Trebonius doth desire you to o'erread,
At your best leisure, this his humble suit.
ARTEMIDORUS O Caesar, read mine first, for mine's a suit
That touches Caesar nearer. Read it, great Caesar.
CAESAR What touches us ourself shall be last served.

(3.1.3–8)

Caesar cannot act for himself because his identity as "Caesar" requires that he always turn away from himself to hear the other. In North's Plutarch, by contrast, Caesar is intensely interested in Artemidorus's letter about "matters of great weight" that "touch [him] nearly": "Caesar took it of him, but could never read it—though he many times attempted it—for the number of people that did salute him" (99).

Brutus and the People

Brutus's rhetoric of subordinating his personal interests to the general interest would seem to make him Caesar's twin, but Brutus's relationship with the people is not at all like Caesar's: before the Forum scene, we never witness or even hear reports of direct encounters between Brutus and the Roman people. Brutus's experience of the people is indirect. He hears their shouts; he listens to Casca's report of their behavior; and he decides to kill Caesar after he reads an anonymous note purporting to express the will of "Rome." The note has been forged by Cassius: when his appeal to elite opinion—"many of the best respect in Rome" (1.2.59), he tells Brutus, want him to bring down Caesar—falls flat, Cassius decides to fabricate public opinion. "I will this night," he tells Cinna,

In several hands in at his windows throw,
As if they came from several citizens,
Writings, all tending to the great opinion
That Rome holds of his name, wherein obscurely
Caesar's ambitions shall be glancèd at.

(1.2.316–20)

Cassius's scheme to win Brutus over to the conspiracy seems to establish Brutus's integrity as a public man: the plan to write a series of notes in "several" hands suggests that Brutus will act only if he believes that Rome wants him to act.[5] But, of course, Cassius simultaneously assumes—justly, as it happens—that Brutus may well conclude from a mere handful of notes that Rome wills Caesar's death. This is an especially telling assumption because the day's events have afforded such ample evidence of the people's attitude toward Caesar. The people do not wish to make Caesar king, but neither do they wish his death: Casca tells Brutus and Cassius that when Caesar "perceived the common herd was glad he refus'd the crown . . . [he] plucked me ope his doublet and offered them his throat to cut" (1.2.263–66). There are no takers, but perhaps this is mere posturing: would Caesar actually allow the people to strike him down? In any event, Antony's offering of the crown certainly does not diminish the people's affection for Caesar. After Caesar swoons and begs the people's indulgence, "[t]hree or four wenches where I stood," Casca reports, "cried, 'Alas, good soul!' and forgave him with all their hearts. But there's no heed to be taken of them; if Caesar had stabbed their mothers they would have done no less" (1.2.271–75).

The image of Caesar offering his throat to the people in a public place haunts the moment when Brutus, alone at night in his orchard, constructs Rome's will out of a seventeen-word note. Brutus's servant Lucius finds the paper while "searching the window for a flint" (2.1.36), and reading the letter out loud to himself fires Brutus's growing inclination to the plot:

"Brutus, thou sleep'st. Awake, and see thyself!
Shall Rome, etc. Speak, strike, redress!"
"Brutus, thou sleep'st. Awake!"
Such instigations have been often dropped
Where I have took them up.

---

[5]Cassius later enlists Cinna's help:
  Good Cinna, take this paper,
  And look you lay it in the praetor's chair
  Where Brutus may but find it. And throw this
  In at his windows. Set this up with wax
  Upon old Brutus' statue. All this done,
  Repair to Pompey's porch, where you shall find us.

  (1.3.142–47)

"Shall Rome, etc." Thus must I piece it out:
Shall Rome stand under one man's awe? What, Rome?
My ancestors did from the streets of Rome
The Tarquin drive, when he was called a king.
"Speak, strike, redress!" Am I entreated
To speak and strike? O Rome, I make thee promise,
If the redress will follow, thou receivest
Thy full petition at the hand of Brutus.

(2.1.146–58)

Only hours before Brutus reads the letter, Cassius had asked him to "see" himself as Rome's elite see him—as the Republic's savior. Brutus warns him, "you would have me seek into myself / For that which is not in me?" (1.2.64–65). Brutus's motive for striking down Caesar must not be personal, it must not be "in" him; rather, it must come from some external source. The letter, echoing Cassius, asks Brutus to "see" himself, but it also asks him to assume the voice of Rome—to become a vessel for "that which is not in" him. Reading the letter aloud necessarily requires Brutus to articulate the words of the other. "Brutus, thou sleep'st. Awake,": thus, Brutus addresses himself in Rome's voice, and performing the other—playing Rome—is the positive condition for becoming himself. Cassius's letter, then, brilliantly seizes on Brutus's rhetoric of the general good and urges him toward the moment of representation: the crucial gap in "Shall Rome, etc." invites Brutus not to mouth Rome's words but to put words in Rome's mouth. "Shall Rome, etc. Thus must I piece it out": to piece out that "etc." Brutus must speak not in his own person but as Rome. Thus, Brutus's anxiety about Caesar's ambition—"He would be crowned" (2.1.12)—fills up the empty content of Rome's rhetorical question to Brutus: "Shall Rome, etc." becomes "Shall Rome stand under one man's awe?" When Brutus supplies "Rome" with those words, he fulfills the letter's second command ("Speak"); and once he has spoken as a Rome that rejects Caesar, the striking and redressing follow inevitably. As he reaches the end of his soliloquy, Brutus brings, in a wondrously balanced sentence, both Rome and himself into being: "O Rome, I make thee promise, / If the redress will follow, thou receivest / Thy full petition at the hand of Brutus." Brutus hails Rome—"O Rome"—precisely as the Brutus whom Rome has hailed ("Brutus, thou sleep'st"). (Now we can no longer fully distinguish between internal and external, between "that which is not" in Brutus and that which is him.) Put another way, Brutus hails precisely the Rome that hails precisely this Brutus. It is at this moment that Brutus, for the first time in the play, refers to himself in the third person.

Brutus's ventriloquizing of Rome is an act of bad faith, but it is not merely bad faith. Immediately before he reads the letter, Brutus is mulling over the bloody course of action he expects Cassius to propose: "It must be [Caesar's] death. And for my part / I know no personal cause to spurn at him, / But for the general" (2.1.10–12). Taken individually, Brutus's claims of selflessness can look like exercises in spin control: "I slew my best lover for the good of Rome" (3.2.44–45), Brutus tells the crowd in the Forum; "pity to the general wrong of Rome" forced his hand, he assures Antony (3.1.172); only "the general good" is a sufficient cause for action, he warns Cassius (1.2.85). But in the orchard scene Brutus's only audience is himself; this is a story he tells himself and tells himself in private, too. To act, he must believe that he represents, that he acts for the people of Rome. (For a discussion of the Elizabethan contexts that shape Brutus's claims to speak and act for the people, see pp. 166–71 and 179–80.)

The Politics of Sacrifice

In the famous Forum scene, Brutus finally faces the people themselves: after the news of the assassination spreads, the people gather to demand an explanation from the conspirators ("We will be satisfied!" [3.2.1]), and Brutus promises them that "public reasons shall be renderèd / Of Caesar's death" (3.2.7–8). We might expect Brutus's performance to go badly; after all, Caesar was the people's darling, whereas Brutus almost invariably misjudges the people's mood. In fact, Brutus's speech about the "public reasons"—that is, reasons articulated in a public forum and reasons pertaining to the public interest—for the assassination produces a remarkable effect: although Brutus has just struck down their beloved Caesar, the people hail him as a new Caesar. How does Brutus do it? Brutus wins over the hostile crowd by representing Caesar's death as a sacrifice.

Brutus has, from the beginning, hoped to convince the people that killing Caesar is a sacrificial act rather than a mere murder. Brutus rejects Cassius's suggestion that Antony die with Caesar, for example, because additional bloodshed would undermine his plan to spin the assassination:

> Our course will seem too bloody, Caius Cassius,
> To cut the head off and then hack the limbs,
> Like wrath in death and envy afterwards;
> For Antony is but a limb of Caesar.
> Let's be *sacrificers*, but not butchers, Caius.
> We all stand up against the spirit of Caesar,
> And in the spirit of men there is no blood.
> Oh, that we then could come by Caesar's spirit
> And not dismember Caesar! But, alas,
> Caesar must bleed for it. And, gentle friends,
> Let's kill him boldly, but not wrathfully;
> Let's carve him as a *dish fit for the gods*,
> Not hew him as a carcass fit for hounds.
> And let our hearts, as subtle masters do,
> Stir up their servants to an act of rage
> And after seem to chide 'em. This shall make
> Our purpose necessary, and not envious;
> Which so appearing to the common eyes,
> We shall be called purgers, not murderers.
>
> (2.1.163–81; emphasis added)

Brutus aims to figure Caesar's death not merely as a sacrifice—a ritual killing meant to propitiate a divine power—but as a communal sacrifice: a sacrifice, that is, that benefits and reflects the will of the entire community rather than particular persons. If Brutus can persuade the people that they have profited from the sacrificing of Caesar, they would hardly wish to take revenge against his killers. Indeed, a properly executed public sacrifice makes "revenge" impossible. Because the entire community understands itself to have approved the sacrificial slaughter, particular persons cannot be held accountable for the killing: if everyone has a hand on the knife, no one is left to avenge the victim.

When Brutus appears in the Forum, his first theme is sacrifice:

> If there be any in this assembly, any dear friend of Caesar's, to him I say that Brutus' love to Caesar was no less than his. If then that friend demand why Brutus rose against Caesar, this is my answer: not that I loved Caesar less, but that I loved Rome more.
>
> (3.2.17–22)

Loving Rome more than Caesar, Brutus suggests, entails loving the general good more than personal good, for slaying Caesar required a personal sacrifice: "I slew my best lover for the good of Rome" (3.2.44–45). But how can Brutus figure Caesar as a *public* sacrifice? After all, he and six other men stab Caesar in the privacy of the Senate House. Brutus audaciously seeks to create an illusion of communal participation *after* Caesar has been killed. Brutus begins by asking the people to identify themselves as the sacrificial beneficiaries of Caesar's spilt blood: "Had you rather Caesar were living and die all slaves," Brutus asks the crowd, "than that Caesar were dead, to live all free men?" (3.2.22–24). The first part of Brutus's question is straightforward enough: would you prefer that Caesar were now alive even though he would enslave you and thus make your lives living death? Caesar *is* dead; thus, the proposition in Brutus's question is expressed as counter-factual. The analogies that Brutus draws between death and slavery, on the one hand, and life and freedom, on the other, depend upon and promote a sacrificial logic: to embrace freedom and life is to embrace Caesar's death as a liberating, life-giving sacrifice. The second part of Brutus's question—"[Or] had you rather . . . that Caesar were dead, to live all free men?"—is puzzling. Caesar *is* dead at the time of Brutus's utterance, but Brutus renders the proposition "Caesar is dead" as counter-factual. It is impossible to yoke the two parts of Brutus's question into a coherent whole, but the (irrational) effect of Brutus's utterance is to suggest that Caesar's life is in the people's hands; Brutus is asking his audience to turn their thumbs up or down over a corpse. Brutus does not want to establish the people as accessories after the fact; he wants them to think of themselves as accomplices in the doing of the deed.[6] Brutus's motivation is both personal and general: if the entire community shares the guilt for Caesar's death, seeking revenge against Brutus would violate the very sacrificial logic that makes Caesar's death meaningful and beneficial to them (they will "*live* all free men" [emphasis added] rather than "die all slaves" only if Caesar's death is sacrificial).

Brutus ends his speech with a first-rate imitation of Caesar's own mode of self-sacrifice: "With this I depart, that, as I slew my best lover for the good of Rome, I have the same dagger for myself when it shall please my country to need my death" (3.2.44–47). This ritual subjection to the people's will repeats Caesar's sacrificial gesture after the thwarted crowning: "he plucked me ope his doublet, and offered them his throat to cut" (1.2.264–66). And what worked for Caesar works for Brutus: rejecting his offer to sacrifice himself, the people erupt in raucous celebration.

ALL   Live, Brutus, live, live!
FIRST PLEBEIAN   Bring him with triumph home unto his house.
SECOND PLEBEIAN   Give him a statue with his ancestors.
THIRD PLEBEIAN   Let him be Caesar.
FOURTH PLEBEIAN   Caesar's better parts
   Shall be crowned in Brutus.

                                        (3.2.48–53)

When the Third Plebeian proposes that Brutus "be Caesar," he in no way suggests that Brutus become king; similarly, the Fourth Plebeian wants to crown in Brutus not Caesar's monarchic ambitions but instead his willingness to bow to the people's desire that he *refuse* the crown. Brutus becomes Caesar at precisely the moment he finally subjects himself not to a Rome of his own imagining, but to the Roman people in their own persons. When he is theirs, he becomes a second Caesar—a great man, that is, whose greatness depends in part on his willingness to subject himself to

[6]René Girard argues that Brutus's hope that "immediately after the murder, the conspiracy will dissolve into the restored unanimity of the Roman people, *its* sacrificial unanimity" is "sound" sacrificial thinking (212). I am arguing, by contrast, that Brutus's sacrifice is defective precisely because it seeks unanimity *after* the sacrificial act has already been performed.

the people. In the same moment, Brutus's sacrificial logic is fulfilled: by granting Brutus life, the people simultaneously reciprocate his sacrificial gesture—Brutus kills his "best lover" that they might "live all free men"—and thereby establish (however briefly) the killing of Caesar as a communal sacrifice that arrests violence and secures "[p]eace, freedom, and liberty" (3.1.111).

Following Brutus's triumph seems an unenviable position; when Antony first mentions Brutus's name, the Fourth Plebeian says ominously, "'Twere best he speak no harm of Brutus here" (3.2.70). Antony, however, manages to whip up the plebeians into a murderous rage against Brutus and the other conspirators. Many critics read the rapid shifts in the people's allegiance—from the dead Caesar to Brutus and back to Caesar and his eulogist Antony all in a few minutes—as evidence of Shakespeare's horror of the mob or, at the very least, his belief that the lower orders are too fickle to participate in political life. To condemn the people as nothing more than a wild-eyed mob is to adopt the tribunes' and patricians' account of the people. At the beginning of the Forum scene, the plebeians are eminently calm and sensible: they demand an explanation of the assassination (3.2.1); when Brutus announces that he and Cassius will deliver speeches simultaneously, the plebeians divide themselves into two groups and agree to "compare [Brutus's and Cassius's] reasons / When severally we hear them rendered" (3.2.9–10); and, even after Brutus has won them over, they agree to give Antony a careful hearing. To be sure, first Brutus and then Antony succeed in winning the people over to positions that they had, only moments earlier, rejected, but both men must work to produce these changes. To miss precisely how Brutus's and Antony's performances persuade and move the plebeians is to miss much of the play's meaning.

So how does Antony turn the crowd against Brutus? He reminds the people of Caesar's selflessness, of his sacrifices for Rome and its people; he hints that Caesar's will includes generous bequests to the plebeians; and he challenges Brutus's claim that Caesar aimed at kingship, at *personal* glory or gain. Antony begins by answering Brutus's indictment of Caesar's self-serving ambition:

He hath brought many captives home to Rome,
Whose ransoms did the general coffers fill.

Did this in Caesar seem ambitious?
When that the poor have cried, Caesar hath wept;
Ambition should be made of sterner stuff.

* * * * *

You all did see that on the Lupercal
I thrice presented him a kingly crown,
Which he did thrice refuse. Was this ambition?

(3.2.90–94, 97–99)

Antony's Caesar wants nothing for himself, and the selfless concern
for the people that animated his life, Antony later claims, finds its
fulfillment in a will that, far from seeking to establish a family dy-
nasty, confers much of Caesar's private property on the public: "he
hath left you all his walks, / His private arbors, and new-planted
orchards, / On this side Tiber; he hath left them you, / And to your
heirs forever—common pleasures, / To walk abroad and recreate
yourselves" (3.2.248–52).

Antony's vision of a Caesar who sacrifices all and asks for nothing in return begins to turn the crowd against Brutus and the conspirators, but Antony fully achieves his purpose only when he con-
ducts a clinical yet emotional reconstruction of Caesar's death:

If you have tears, prepare to shed them now.
You all do know this mantle. I remember
The first time ever Caesar put it on;
'Twas on a summer's evening in his tent,
That day he overcame the Nervii.
Look, in this place ran Cassius' dagger through.
See what a rent the envious Casca made.
Through this the well-belovèd Brutus stabbed,
And as he plucked his cursèd steel away,
Mark how the blood of Caesar followed it,

* * * * *

Oh, now you weep, and I perceive you feel
The dint of pity. These are gracious drops.
Kind souls, what weep you when you but behold
Our Caesar's vesture wounded? Look you here,
Here is himself, marred as you see with traitors.

(3.2.170–79, 194–98)

Brutus's decision to let Antony bring the body to the Forum is an astonishing miscalculation. Antony's post-mortem of Caesar's butchered corpse is spectacularly affective and effective:

FIRST PLEBEIAN   Oh, piteous spectacle!
SECOND PLEBEIAN   O noble Caesar!
THIRD PLEBEIAN   Oh, woeful day!
FOURTH PLEBEIAN   Oh, traitors, villains!
FIRST PLEBEIAN   Oh, most bloody sight!
SECOND PLEBEIAN   We will be revenged.
ALL   Revenge! About! Seek! Burn! Fire! Kill!
     Slay! Let not a traitor live!

(3.2.199–206)

The unanimous cry for "Revenge!" is the unmistakable sign that the illusion of sacrifice has been shattered. Brutus sought to implicate the people in Caesar's death precisely because the universally shared guilt of a communal sacrifice makes revenge impossible and unnecessary. Now Antony has set in motion the cycle of reciprocal violence that will consume Rome in civil war.[7]

Brutus tries to turn Caesar's blood into a symbol, a sign of freedom and liberating sacrifice: "Stoop, Romans, stoop," Brutus instructs the other conspirators,

And let us bathe our hands in Caesar's blood
Up to the elbows and besmear our swords.
Then walk we forth even to the marketplace,
And, waving our red weapons o'er our heads,
Let's all cry "Peace, freedom, and liberty!"

(3.1.106–11)

Caesar's blood already stains the conspirators. Why, then, should they cover themselves in more blood? Before the assassination, as we

---

[7]Antony's skeptical analysis of Brutus's motives, his recollections of Caesar's self-lessness, and his claim that the dictator's will names the people as heirs certainly move his audience (3.2.79–147): the Fourth Plebeian calls the conspirators "traitors" (3.2.155), and the Second Plebeian charges them as "murderers" (3.2.157). When the Second Plebeian decides that the conspirators are murderers rather than sacrificers, we can see that Brutus's enterprise is collapsing, but I would argue that Antony's post-mortem is quite distinctly the *coup de grace* (or *theatre*): there is no talk of revenge—and revenge is what Antony seeks—until the people see the body.

have seen, Brutus himself was very concerned that the conspirators appear less bloody. Brutus turns Caesar's real blood into a stage prop, into makeup. The blood that splatters on the conspirators' swords and arms as they stab Caesar and the blood Brutus smears on his sword and arms signify two quite different things. The former is the blood of an especially messy and violent murder; the latter, Brutus hopes, in both its excess and its odd precision ("Up to the elbows"), will give the appearance of orderly sacrifice, of carving rather than hewing. The theatrical action Brutus gives his fellows—waving their red swords with their red hands and forearms—and the accompanying line he supplies produces a spectacle that conflates Caesar's blood and the benefits of sacrifice—"Peace, freedom, and liberty."

Antony's autopsy reconnects the blood on Brutus's "cursed steel" to the wounds in Caesar's "vesture" and his body. The "piteous spectacle" of Caesar's body reveals that he has died of particular but random wounds inflicted haphazardly by a handful of men; it is impossible to read sacrifice—at least of the sort Brutus aims at—from this corpse. But the effect of Antony's post-mortem on the people exceeds the effect of forensic evidence on a jury. The mere presence and familiarity of Caesar's corpse must recall to the people their affection for the man. We should remember that the popular enmity toward Caesar that Brutus very briefly produces is an aberration in Shakespeare's Rome: Antony triumphs over Brutus simply by reviving the feelings the people have expressed throughout the play.[8] But Caesar's fragile, mortal, vulnerable body also reminds the people of the power they once enjoyed in relation to Caesar: the body they see before them is the body that Caesar offered to them after the thwarted crowning; the conspirators have usurped the role that Caesar once offered them. The sight of the body, then, opens the people's ears to Antony's suggestion that they held a kind of communal property in Caesar: the body before them, Antony tells the people, was "our Caesar"; and the outrage against "our Caesar" is an outrage against the people and all of Rome:

> Even at the base of Pompey's statue,
> Which all the while ran blood, great Caesar fell.

---

[8]Richard Wilson argues provocatively that "Antony's anatomy lesson . . . turns desire in the mob to authoritarian ends" (59), but Antony's goals in the Forum seem to me more modest.

> Oh, what a fall was there, my countrymen!
> Then I, and you, and all of us fell down,
> Whilst bloody treason flourished over us.
>
> (3.2.189–93)

The death of Caesar is a universal loss rather than a universal bless-
ing; the assassination is treason against the community, against us,
rather than treason against Caesar alone.

Antony must unravel Brutus's construction of Caesar as communal sacrifice before he can move the people to reclaim Caesar as
their Caesar, but creating a sense of community in Caesar does not
desacralize Caesar himself. Antony begins his post-mortem by having the people "make a ring about the corpse," and in the center of
this ritual circle he resacralizes Caesar's blood even as he insists
that the blood on Brutus's sword and hands is merely the blood of
murder: "Let but the commons hear [Caesar's] testament," he pre-
dicts, "And they would go and kiss dead Caesar's wounds / And
dip their napkins in his sacred blood, / Yea, beg a hair of him for
memory" (3.2.132, 134–36). The forming of the ring marks a distinct shift in Antony's oration. Antony has been speaking from the
rostrum, but now he asks permission to descend: "You will compel
me then to read the will? / Then make a ring about the corpse of
Caesar, / And let me show you him that made the will. / Shall I descend? And will you give me leave?" (3.2.158–61). "All" respond
"Come down" (3.2.162). This is Antony's Caesarean moment: the
future master of half the world asks the people's leave to descend.
Once Antony is among the people, the forming of the ring becomes, for several moments, the center of our attention:

FOURTH PLEBEIAN   A ring; stand round.
FIRST PLEBEIAN   Stand from the hearse. Stand from the body.
SECOND PLEBEIAN   Room for Antony, most noble Antony!
ANTONY   Nay, press not so upon me. Stand farre off.
ALL   Stand back! Room! Bear back!

> (3.2.165–69)

The exact nature of the sacredness Antony attributes to Caesar is
somewhat uncertain: does the memorial hair suggest to a Christian
audience sainthood or perhaps even Christ's martyrdom? Or do the
dipping of the napkin and Antony's later image of "put[ting] a

tongue / In every wound of Caesar" (3.2.229–30) also suggest the totem meal of primal pagan sacrifice? What seems certain is that the invitation to share out Caesar's blood and hair among the people is part of Antony's attempt to create a ritual experience of community in Caesar's death. Antony, then, does not simply erase communal sacrifice; the "gracious drops" he wins from the people reconsecrate and regenerate—see *OED* 6 for this meaning of "gracious"—Caesar's bloody corpse as sacred victim. Perhaps, then, Antony rewrites Caesar's death as a very particular kind of failed sacrifice—a sacrifice that creates community but also produces a Judas. Thus, the sacredness of Caesar and the necessity of revenge are continuous rather than opposed: "We'll burn his body in the holy place / And with the brands fire the traitors' houses" (3.2.255–56). The same fire that deifies the sacrificial Caesar will be used to enact revenge on his killers.

Theater and Politics

In 1599, theater historians believe, *Henry V*, *As You Like It*, and *Julius Caesar* were all performed for the first time. The newly opened Globe seems to have inspired some of Shakespeare's most sustained meditations on the nature of theater and theatricality: in *Henry V*, the Prologue and Chorus articulate a complex theory of the imaginative labor necessary to theater; in *As You Like It*, Jaques elaborates his famous conceit, "All the world's a stage, / And all the men and women merely players" (2.7.139–40).[9] Political ideas and struggles so dominate *Caesar* that we may miss how often Shakespeare's Romans invoke theater and theatricality; indeed, the way the various protagonists conceive theater often illuminates—is often continuous with—the way they conceive politics.

The conspirators frequently invoke theater and deploy theatrical metaphors, but the first association of theater and the plot against Caesar suggests that the conspiracy is, in a sense, antitheatrical. Before the conspirators call on Brutus, they meet at Pompey's Theater "after midnight" (1.3.163), when "there is no stir or walking in the streets" (1.3.127). The conspiracy is hatched in an

---

[9]All quotations from and references to Shakespeare's works follow *The Complete Works of Shakespeare*, ed. David Bevington. New York: Pearson Education, Inc., 2009.

empty theater. In Elizabethan and Jacobean culture, the theater was a byword for publicness: alarmingly crowded, disturbingly open to anyone who could pay, theaters—especially amphitheaters like the Globe—scandalously subjected the most private affairs and thoughts of both kings and clowns to the light of day and to the scrutiny of popular audiences. The conspirators, then, transform Pompey's Theater into its own antithesis; the conspiracy is a betrayal of theater—of openness and community.

The conspirators turn a theater into a secret meeting place, and they think of theatricality as a mode of conspiracy—that is, as a technique of concealment. Brutus, for example, explicitly identifies theater as a model for conspiratorial dissimulation: "Let not our looks put on our purposes, / But bear it as our Roman actors do, / With untired spirits and formal constancy" (2.1.226–28). Later, however, Brutus and Cassius hope that, once the plot has been accomplished, theater will play an important role in public affirmations of the conspirator's liberation of Rome:

CASSIUS   How many ages hence
   Shall this our lofty scene be acted over
   In states unborn and accents yet unknown!
BRUTUS   How many times shall Caesar bleed in sport,
   That now on Pompey's basis lies along
   No worthier than the dust!
CASSIUS   So oft as that shall be,
   So often shall the knot of us be called
   The men that gave their country liberty.

                                             (3.1.112–20)

If Brutus and Cassius, with Caesar dead at their feet, seem here to conceive theater in more positive terms, as something more than deception, their account of theater remains impoverished. Cassius is not concerned with aesthetic judgments; he anticipates instead that theatergoers will perpetually ratify the conspirators' actions by constructing those actions on the conspirators' terms: to accept them as "the men that gave their country liberty" is to accept their killing of Caesar as a sacrifice.

Why do Brutus and Cassius anticipate only approving audiences? Theatergoers, as Casca reminds us, both clap and hiss. Cassius's anticipation of universal and eternal approval depends on a vision of history and a theory of theater. Brutus and Cassius expect that the death of Caesar and the restoration of the republic will bring political history to an end: reenactments of their restoration of the republic will never be hissed because they will always be staged in republican states before audiences of confirmed republicans. In this republican future, Cassius assumes, dramatizations of the conspiracy will never contest its motives or results because history totalizes theater. Thus, republicanism models both Brutus's ersatz sacrifice and Cassius's defanged theater. Brutus's performance in the Forum creates the illusion of communal judgment even as it makes the people's authority and power to judge secondhand, marginal, belated. We need only recall the moment when Caesar bears his throat to the people's knives to see that the scene of popular judgment Brutus stages in the Forum is an empty illusion. Similarly, in Cassius's theater, the audience acts out an empty exercise in affirmation; in Elizabethan and Jacobean theater, by contrast, audiences composed of humble "Car-m[e]n and Tinker[s] . . . sit to give judgment on the plaies life and death."[10] The function of theater in the static republican future will be to bear witness to and celebrate history rather than to act in history. Theater here is not a place of presence and action; the theatrical is merely a sign of things already done.

The mere presence of Shakespeare's audience subverts Brutus and Cassius's dream of an eternal and universal republic even as they dream it: Elizabeth I's subjects at the Globe did not need to wait for Act 5 and Antony and Octavian's triumph at Philippi to know that the conspirators lose the battle for history. Losing in history need not, of course, entail losing on the stage: though Brutus and Cassius cannot imagine a negative representation of the republican conspiracy being staged in a republic, anyone not committed to their totalizing account of the relation between politics and culture can imagine a dramatic valorization of republicanism in a monarchic state. Indeed, Brutus loses on Shakespeare's stage not because Shakespeare must, as a good Elizabethan subject, endorse Caesar's monarchism; Shakespeare's critique of Brutus's republicanism is radical rather than conservative. In the name of republicanism, Brutus kills Caesar at the height of his popularity and then tries to convince the people that this

[10]*The Non-Dramatic Works of Thomas Dekker*, ed. Alexander Grossart, 5 vols. (1885; rpt. New York: Russell and Russell, 1963), 2.246–47.

usurpation of their power was a life-giving sacrifice that enacted rather than subverted the general will. Brutus loses at the Globe not only because his republicanism is antipopulist but also because his fabrication of sacrifice—his attempt to obscure his antipopulism—has been undermined by Shakespeare's lifting of the veil.

Before we see Brutus's triumph in the Forum, we see an impromptu trial run of his performance fail miserably. Brutus's first audience is Antony, who returns to the Senate House just as the conspirators, newly made up in Caesar's blood, are leaving for the marketplace. Antony immediately remarks the conspirators' "swords . . . rich / With the most noble blood of all this world" (3.1.157–58) and their "purpled hands" (160). When Brutus realizes how moved Caesar's friend is, he tries to contextualize the bloody spectacle by giving Antony a preview of the sacrificial rhetoric he will later deploy in the Forum: "pity to the general wrong of Rome— . . . / Hath done this deed on Caesar" (3.1.172–74); "I, that did love Caesar when I struck him, / Have thus proceeded" (3.1.184–85). Brutus's words fall flat. Even in the presence of the men he fears may kill him, Antony cannot fully suppress his revulsion: "Shall it not grieve thee," Antony says to the dead Caesar, "To see thy Antony making his peace, / Shaking the bloody fingers of thy foes— . . . here thy hunters stand, / Signed in thy spoil, and crimsoned in thy lethe" (3.1.198–200, 207–8). The effect of the very display Brutus has designed to pass the conspirators off as "sacrificers . . . not butchers" is almost comically disastrous: "Oh, pardon me, thou bleeding piece of earth," Antony begs his dead friend as soon as the conspirators have departed, "That I am meek and gentle with these butchers" (3.1.256–57).

Antony is, to be sure, a biased audience, but his devastating deflation of Brutus's spectacular and rhetorical devices nonetheless makes it extraordinarily difficult for any member of Shakespeare's audience—wherever his or her emotional and political sympathies may lie—to accept the spin Brutus puts on Caesar's death. When Antony calls the conspirators "butchers," we are reminded—even if we approve of the assassination—that Brutus is, at that very moment, trying to create an *appearance* of sacrifice that will obscure butchery. When Brutus speaks to the people in the Forum, his sacrificial gambit has already been emptied out for Shakespeare's audience. The undoing of Brutus's attempt to stage sacrifice, then, begins in Shakespeare's theatricalizing of conspiracy: seeing the bloody swords and arms is not quite the same when one has first witnessed Brutus calculating their effect.

Julius Caesar does offer an alternative account of theater and politics. In Casca's summing up of the thwarted coronation, the actor is the explicit figure for Caesarism: "If the tag-rag people did not clap him and hiss him, according as he pleased and displeased them, as they use to do the players in the theater, I am no true man" (1.2.258–61). When Brutus hears the "applauses" (1.2.133) ringing out offstage, he hears the people expressing their approval *as an audience* of Caesar's refusal of the crown; their theatrical authorization of this particular ending to the play Antony and Caesar enact is identical to their unwillingness to make Caesar king. In *Caesar*, the people of Rome are like a theatrical audience when—and only when—they retain their power rather than delegate their authority to others. In early modern parliamentary elections, voters typically voted by voice and often celebrated the moment of election by shouting and throwing their hats into the air. In the crowning scene, these traditional signs of empowerment signal instead the withholding of the suffrage Caesar seeks: "he put it the third time by, and still *as he refused it*, the rabblement hooted and clapped their chapped hands, and threw up their sweaty night-caps, and uttered such a deal of stinking breath because Caesar refused the crown that it had almost choked Caesar" (1.2.243–48). Republican politics and republican theatricality, as Brutus conceives them, manage the people and appropriate their power to judge; in Shakespeare's theater, democracies, and popular dictatorships, by contrast, the people never fully and irrevocably yield their power to judge.

The Politics of Suicide

I want to conclude this introduction by revisiting the moment when Brutus offers himself as a sacrifice to the Roman people: "With this I depart, that, as I slew my best lover for the good of Rome, I have the same dagger for myself when it shall please my country to need my death" (3.2.44–47). Brutus has borrowed this grand gesture from Casca's report of Caesar's performance in the marketplace: "he plucked me ope his doublet, and offered them his throat to cut" (1.2.264–66). But Brutus does not get Caesar's sacrificial submission quite right: Caesar offers his throat to the people's knives; Brutus offers to kill himself with his own dagger if the people will it. Caesar submits himself to a mass communal bloodletting; Brutus proposes that he will sacrifice himself. This conflation of suicide and sacrifice suggests that Brutus cannot properly conceive sacrifice because he cannot imagine the people acting out their own will in their own persons. The defect in Brutus's sacrificial thinking, that is, is simply the representationalism that governs all of Brutus's thinking: Brutus imagines that he will function as the instrumental agent of the general will at the moment he kills himself. Brutus the representative/artificial person—the man who hails himself in Rome's voice—will kill Brutus the individual/natural person. Brutus's construction of suicide as sacrifice is, moreover, entirely consistent with his habitual rhetoric: killing himself would simply be an extreme case of subordinating the personal to the general. The rhetoric of representation is always a sacrificial rhetoric. In the event, when Brutus learns how Antony has "moved" the people in the Forum, he does not cut his own throat; instead, he and Cassius "rid[e] like madmen through the gates of Rome" (3.2.270). Brutus has always counted on speaking the general will in the absence of the people themselves; he has always been able to count, that is, on the not entirely surprising coincidence between his personal will and the general will as he articulates it. Once the people speak their own will ("Revenge!"), Brutus decides that he would prefer not to enact it.

Brutus's claim that he speaks and acts for Rome does not give the people themselves much to do. Their role in the self-sacrifice he proposes would be identical to the role he gave them in Caesar's death: they will be the agents of his death; his death will fulfill their will; but they will have no hand in his slaughter. They will be alienated from their own agency. This is the essence of political representation and the antithesis of both Caesar's popular dictatorship and theatrical relations of power. Caesar never proposes to speak for the people nor to determine the common good; rather, he submits himself directly to the people's judgment and to their knives. Caesar, for all his absorption in his singular role of "Caesar," is, in his utter subjection to the audience, the political equivalent of the actor.

Brutus's odd notion that he could end his life by playing the roles of both sacrificial victim and sacrificial agent deepens the pathos of his death. In the Forum, Brutus cannot quite conceive of

putting the dagger in the hands of the people, but when he gives up
the ghost at Philippi, he wants someone else to hold the fatal sword:

BRUTUS   Sit thee down, Clitus. Slaying is the word.
  It is a deed in fashion. Hark thee, Clitus.
                                              [*He whispers*]
CLITUS   What, I, my lord? No, not for all the world.
BRUTUS   Peace then. No words.
CLITUS   I'll rather kill myself.
BRUTUS   Hark thee, Dardanius.   [*He whispers*]
DARDANIUS   Shall I do such a deed?
        [*Dardanius and Clitus move away from Brutus*]
CLITUS   Oh, Dardanius!
DARDANIUS   Oh, Clitus!
CLITUS   What ill request did Brutus make to thee?
DARDANIUS   To kill him, Clitus.

                                              (5.5.4–12)

Brutus next appeals to Volumnius: "I prithee / Hold thou my
sword-hilts, whilst I run on it" (5.5.27–28). Volumnius refuses,
and, finally, Brutus turns to Strato:

BRUTUS   Hold then my sword, and turn away thy face,
  While I do run upon it. Wilt thou, Strato?
STRATO   Give me your hand first. Fare you well, my lord.
BRUTUS   Farewell, good Strato.

                                              (5.5.47–50)

In the Forum, Brutus imagines that he can play two roles at once,
but his end at Philippi seems a cruel reversal of this fantasy: now
Brutus discovers that he cannot commit suicide without the help of
another set of hands. Later, while Antony and Octavian gaze at
Brutus's corpse, Strato manages both to tell a sweet lie about his
master's end and to report it truly: "Brutus only overcame himself, /
And no man else hath honour by his death" (5.5.56–57).

Table of Dates

The Rise and Fall of the Roman Republic

753 BCE   According to legend, Romulus founds Rome.

753–509   Rome is ruled by kings.

509   The Roman Republic is born when Tarquin (Lucius Tarquinius Superbus), the last king of Rome, is forced into exile. According to Livy (Titus Livius) and other historians, the revolt against the tyrannical Tarquin was precipitated by his son Sextus's rape of Lucretia, a Roman matron. After Lucretia committed suicide, Lucius Junius Brutus's public display of her body "so moved" the people that "with one consent and a general acclamation the Tarquins were all exiled, and the state government changed from kings to consuls" (Shakespeare, "The Argument" of *The Rape of Lucrece*).

494   Frustrated by the Senate's failure to curb aristocratic excess, Rome's plebeians abandon the city. They return only after the Senate grants them the right to elect tribunes to protect their interests. The Roman Republic now consists of three principal political institutions: the tribunes of the people, the Senate, and the consuls (two men of senatorial rank elected by the Senate and approved by the plebeians). (Shakespeare represents the establishment of the tribunate in *Coriolanus* [c. 1608].)

451–449   The *decemviri* (the ten men), who had been elected to draw up a new legal code, suspend republican freedoms and institutions, including the tribunate. In 449, Appius

Claudius, the leader of the *decemviri*, instructs his crony Marcus Claudius to claim that Virginia, the daughter of a republican-minded centurion, is the child of one of Marcus's household slaves and thus his property. Appius plans to rape Virginia as soon as Marcus takes possession of her. To prevent this defilement, Virginius murders his daughter; Virginius and Virginia's betrothed, Icilius, then lead a popular uprising that restores the tribunate and republican freedoms. (In the final act of *Titus Andronicus*, Titus alludes to Virginia.)

81–79   Sulla (Lucius Cornelius Sulla Felix) rules Rome as dictator. In 81, Sulla amends the constitution, increasing the power of the Senate and diminishing the power of the tribunate. Sulla retires from public life in 79.

60–59   Pompey the Great (Gnaeus Pompeius Magnus), Crassus (Lucius Licinius Crassus), and Julius Caesar (Gaius Julius Caesar) form an alliance, govern Rome, and curb the power of both the Senate and the tribunate.

49   The struggle between Caesar and Pompey for supremacy in Rome erupts into open conflict; Caesar, serving as the governor of Gaul, invades Italy, and Rome is plunged into a full-scale civil war. Pompey and his forces abandon Rome. Caesar is appointed dictator.

48   Caesar defeats Pompey at the Battle of Pharsalus.

45   Caesar is appointed dictator for life.

44   Caesar is assassinated. Brutus (Marcus Junius Brutus), Cassius (Gaius Cassius Longinus), and the other conspirators abandon Rome after they fail to secure sufficient support. Rome is again consumed by civil war, with the conspirators leading one faction and Antony (Marcus Antonius) and Octavian (Gaius Julius Caesar Octavianus—Caesar's great-nephew and the future emperor Augustus) leading the other.

42   Antony, Octavian, and Lepidus (Marcus Aemilius Lepidus) are appointed triumvirs; they order mass proscriptions to consolidate their control of Italy.

Antony and Octavian defeat Brutus and Cassius at the Battle of Philippi.

32–31   Octavian and Antony's always fragile power-sharing arrangement completely collapses in 32, and the resulting civil war—Rome's third such catastrophe in less than 20 years—ends in 31 with Antony's defeat at the Battle of Actium. Soon thereafter, Antony and Cleopatra commit suicide.

27–14   Augustus Caesar rules Rome. The Age of the Caesars stretches to 476 CE, when Odovacar, leader of the Goths, deposes Romulus Augustulus.

Roman Britain

55 BCE   Julius Caesar leads Rome's first expedition to Britain.

54   In Caesar's second invasion, Roman forces defeat British tribes, but Rome does not colonize Britain.

5 CE   Rome recognizes Cymbeline as king of Britain.

43–51   Caratacus, leader of British resistance to Roman rule, refuses to pay annual tribute to Rome. After nearly 100 years of exercising only loose control over Britain, Rome invades with the aim of fully integrating the island into the empire. Caratacus is defeated in 51 and brought to Rome. (In *Cymbeline* [c. 1609], Shakespeare's eponymous protagonist combines aspects of the historical Cymbeline and Caratacus. In Shakespeare's play, the British refuse to pay tribute, defeat the invading Roman army, and then agree to resume payment of the tribute.)

75–77   Rome completes its conquest of Britain. The island remains under firm Roman control for more than 300 years.

303   The emperor Diocletian resolves to suppress Christianity. The persecution of British Christians is widespread and brutal.

407–8   As the empire comes under increasing pressure from the Goths, Roman legions withdraw from Britain; Roman occupation ends.

Shakespeare's England

1485 CE   Henry Tudor, Earl of Richmond, defeats Richard III at Bosworth Field. Henry assumes throne as Henry VII; the Tudors rule England until 1603. In 1486, the marriage of Henry and Elizabeth of York unites the houses of Lancaster and York, the two great branches of England's royal family who had waged civil war for much of the fourteenth century.

1509   Henry VII dies; his son is crowned Henry VIII.

1517   The Protestant Reformation begins.

1533   Henry VIII divorces Catherine of Aragon and marries Anne Boleyn. Pope Clement VII excommunicates Henry. In August, Anne gives birth to a daughter, the future Elizabeth I.

1534   The Act of Supremacy establishes Henry VIII as the supreme head of the Church of England.

1536   Anne Boleyn is beheaded; Henry VIII marries Jane Seymour.

1547   Henry VIII dies; his son by Jane Seymour is crowned Edward VI. During Edward's brief reign, his leading councilors strengthen Protestantism's status as the state religion.

1553   Edward VI dies; after the nine-day reign of Lady Jane Grey, Mary, the daughter of Henry VIII and Catherine of Aragon, becomes queen. Over the next two years, Mary I returns England to Roman Catholicism and orders the persecution of Protestants.

1558   Mary dies; Elizabeth, Henry VIII and Anne Boleyn's daughter, is crowned Elizabeth I. Elizabeth's government immediately begins the process of restoring Protestantism.

1563   The Convocation of the Church establishes the Thirty-nine Articles, which define Anglican doctrine. By Act of Parliament, adherence to the Thirty-nine Articles becomes law in 1571.

1564   William Shakespeare, son of John Shakespeare and Mary Arden Shakespeare, is christened at Holy Trinity Church in Stratford-upon-Avon on April 26. April 23 is, by tradition, Shakespeare's birthday.

1567   Mary, Queen of Scots, marries James Hepburn, Earl of Bothwell, after the murder of her first husband Lord Darnley (perhaps at Bothwell's hands). After marrying Bothwell, Mary is imprisoned and forced to abdicate by a group of powerful Scottish noblemen. Mary's son by Darnley becomes James VI of Scotland.

1568   Mary escapes and flees to England, seeking Elizabeth's aid.

        John Shakespeare is elected bailiff (mayor) of Stratford.

1571–72 The Ridolfi plot to depose Elizabeth and install Mary, Queen of Scots, is thwarted. The plot involved Roberto di Ridolfi, a Florentine banker living in England; Thomas Howard, duke of Norfolk; papal officials; and Spain.

1575–76 After a steady decline in his fortunes, John Shakespeare retires from public life.

1576   James Burbage erects The Theatre, England's first purpose-built commercial theater.

1582   William Shakespeare marries Anne Hathaway; she is pregnant at the time.

1583   Francis Throckmorton, an English catholic, conspires with Spanish operatives to put Mary on the throne. Throckmorton is executed in 1584.

        William and Anne's daughter Susanna is baptized in Holy Trinity Church.

        Queen Elizabeth establishes a playing company, The Queen's Men, by royal order.

1585   William Parry, who enjoyed sufficient patronage to get himself elected to the House of Commons, is executed for conspiring against Elizabeth.

Shakespeare's twin son and daughter, Hamnet and Judith, are baptized in Holy Trinity Church.

1586   Sir Francis Walsingham uncovers the Babington plot, named for Antony Babington, who conspired with John Ballard, a catholic priest, to kill Elizabeth and install Mary.

1587   Mary, Queen of Scots, is executed. Spain declares war on England.

1588   The Spanish Armada is defeated by the English fleet. Spain and England remain at war until 1603.

1592   Shakespeare is now established in London as a playwright and actor. Shakespeare's theatrical career in London may well have been launched as early as 1587.

c. 1593–94 *Titus Andronicus* is first performed.

1594   *The Rape of Lucrece* is published.

1595   Shakespeare becomes a member of and sharer in the newly formed Lord Chamberlain's Men, one of London's two leading acting companies.

1596   Hamnet dies.

1597   Shakespeare purchases New Place, one of the most important private dwellings in Stratford.

1599   The Globe, of which Shakespeare is a part owner, opens on the Bankside. *Henry V* and *Julius Caesar* are staged at the Globe.

1601   On February 7, Robert Devereaux, Earl of Essex, is summoned to court; the next day he locks up four emissaries from the court, including the Earl of Worcester, who had come for an explanation of his failure to answer the summons. On February 8, Essex and a band of 300 men, including nearly a dozen noblemen, march into London. London's citizens ignore Essex's attempt to rally them to his cause; the Essex Rebellion fails miserably, and the earl retreats to Essex House. After a brief siege, Essex and his remaining followers surrender to the queen's troops. Essex is found guilty of treason and beheaded on February 25. Essex had for many years been Elizabeth's great favorite, but his fortunes suffered many blows between 1598 and 1601: in 1598, he nearly drew his sword on the queen, who had struck him for impudent behavior; he was given a chance to redeem himself in 1599 when the queen dispatched him to put down an Irish rebellion, but he made truce with the rebels that Elizabeth and his fellow privy councilors considered treasonous; and in 1600 Elizabeth's refusal to renew his right to collect taxes on wine—easily his most important source of revenue—left him in the desperate state that led to his ill-conceived march into the streets of London.

1601   John Shakespeare dies.

1603   Elizabeth dies; James VI of Scotland is crowned James I of England.

Shakespeare's company, the Lord Chamberlain's Men, is reorganized as the King's Men. Shakespeare and the other members are now entitled to wear the royal livery.

c. 1607   *Antony and Cleopatra* is first performed.

1607   Shakespeare's daughter Susanna marries John Hall.

1608   Shakespeare and six others become the administrators of the Blackfriars Theatre. The Blackfriars had been used by companies of boy actors, but, in 1609, the King's Men began to play at the Blackfriars in winter and the Globe in summer. The Blackfriars quickly becomes London's most important indoor theater.

Mary Arden Shakespeare dies.

c. 1608   *Coriolanus* is first performed.

1609   *The Sonnets* is published.

c. 1610   *Cymbeline* is first performed.

1611–13   Shakespeare retires to New Place.

1616   Shakespeare dies; he is buried in Holy Trinity Church.

1623   William Jaggard publishes *Mr. William Shakespeare's Comedies, Histories, & Tragedies*, a folio volume of 36 plays. The production of the folio—known as the First Folio—is overseen by John Heminges and Henry Condell, members of the King's Men.

Rome on the English Stage, 1559–1642[1]

c. 1559–67 *Apius and Virginia*, R. B. An interlude—a brief dramatic piece, often performed at a banquet or as one of a series of entertainments—mixing figures from a key episode in republican history and the abstractions (e.g., Justice, Memory, Rumor) typical of morality plays.

c. 1586–91 *The Wounds of Civil War*, Thomas Lodge. Sulla's rise to power at the expense of republican liberties.

1592   *Antonius*, Mary Sidney Herbert, countess of Pembroke. Translation of Robert Garnier's *Marc Antoine* (1578), a play about the struggle between Octavian and Antony. Sidney added several thinly veiled references to contemporary anxieties about the possibility that Elizabeth's death would spark a civil war. *Antonius* is a closet drama—that is, a play meant to be read rather than staged.

c. 1592–96 *The Tragedie of Caesar and Pompey. Or Caesars Revenge*, Anonymous. A compact history of the end of the republic: Caesar's victory over Pompey; the assassination of Caesar; Antony and Octavian's victory over Brutus and Cassius. Staged in 1607 by the students of Trinity College, Oxford.

1593   *The Tragedie of Cleopatra*, Samuel Daniel. Cleopatra's final days, after the death of Antony. Figures Octavian

---

[1]Dates are for first performances; for plays not known to have been performed, I have supplied the date of publication. This list represents only a selection of the many Elizabethan, Jacobean, and Caroline plays set in ancient Rome or one of its provinces.

as a villain who engineers the murder of Cleopatra's son by Julius Caesar.

1594   *Cornelia*, Thomas Kyd. A translation of Robert Garnier's *Cornélie*, in which Cornelia, the second wife of Pompey the Great, endures her husband's defeat at Caesar's hands and witnesses his death. Cornelia's father now resists Caesar and commits suicide after he is defeated. No record of a performance.

c. 1602   *Caesar and Pompey*, George Chapman. Celebrates Pompey as a selfless defender of the Republic.

1603   *Sejanus, His Fall*, Ben Jonson. After rising to prominence as the emperor Tiberius's right-hand man, Sejanus is denounced by his patron and murdered by a mob.

c. 1606–8   *The Rape of Lucrece*, Thomas Heywood.

1607   *Julius Caesar*, William Alexander, Earl of Stirling. A closet drama, dedicated to James I.

c. 1607   *Claudius Tiberius Nero*, Anonymous. The lurid reign of the emperor who, famously, fiddled while Rome burned.

c. 1610–15 *The Valiant Welshman*, Robert Armin. The eponymous hero tries to free ancient Britain from its Roman oppressors.

1611   *Cataline, His Conspiracy*, Ben Jonson. In 63 BCE, Cataline, with the approval of Caesar and Crassus, plotted to assassinate Cicero and overthrow the government. After the plot was exposed, government troops defeated Cataline and his followers.

c. 1611   *Bonduca*, John Fletcher. Bonduca, cousin of Caratch (i.e., Caratacus), leads a rebellion against the Romans; after their defeat, Bonduca and her daughters commit suicide rather than be taken captive.

1622   *The Virgin Martyr*, Thomas Dekker and Phillip Massinger. Although set in Caesarea (now Armenia) during the time of Diocletian's campaign against Christianity, the play strikingly invokes ancient Britain's subjection to Rome:

a British slave heroically resists his Roman masters, and Theophilus fondly recalls torturing British Christians.

c. 1624–34 *Appius and Virginia*, John Webster. A dramatization of Appius's attempt to rape Virginia; see the events described earlier for 451–449 BCE in "The Rise and Fall of the Roman Republic."

1626   *The Roman Actor*, Philip Massinger. Domitia, empress of Rome, engineers the assassination of her husband Domitian, a monstrous tyrant who has murdered her lover Paris, Rome's most celebrated actor.

1633   *Fuimus Troes, Being a Story of the* Britaines *Valour at the Romanes First Invasion*, Jasper Fisher. The British heroically resist Julius Caesar. Performed at Magdalen College, Oxford University.

1635   *Hannibal and Scipio*, Thomas Nabbes. Scipio defeats Hannibal, completing Rome's decisive victory over Carthage in the second Punic War (202 BCE) and establishing its empire as the greatest Mediterranean power.

JULIUS CAESAR

by William Shakespeare

JULIUS CAESAR

[*Dramatis Personae*

JULIUS CAESAR
CALPURNIA, *Caesar's wife*
MARK ANTONY,
OCTAVIUS CAESAR, } *triumvirs after Caesar's death*
LEPIDUS,

MARCUS BRUTUS
PORTIA, *Brutus's wife*
CAIUS CASSIUS,
CASCA,
DECIUS BRUTUS,
CINNA, } *conspirators with Brutus*
METELLUS CIMBER,
TREBONIUS,
CAIUS LIGARIUS,

CICERO,
PUBLIUS, } *senators*
POPILIUS LENA,
FLAVIUS,
MARULLUS, } *tribunes of the people*

SOOTHSAYER
ARTEMIDORUS, *a teacher of rhetoric*
CINNA, *a poet*
Another POET

LUCILIUS,
TITINIUS,
MESSALA,
YOUNG CATO,
VOLUMNIUS,
VARRO,   *officers and soldiers in the army*
CLAUDIUS,   *of Brutus and Cassius*
CLITUS,
DARDANIUS,
LABEO,
FLAVIUS,

PINDARUS, *Cassius's servant*
LUCIUS,   *Brutus's servants*
STRATO,
Caesar's SERVANT
Antony's SERVANT
Octavius's SERVANT

CARPENTER
COBBLER
Five PLEBEIANS
Three SOLDIERS *in Brutus' army*
Two SOLDIERS *in Antony's army*
MESSENGER

GHOST *of Caesar*

Senators, Plebeians, Officers, Soldiers, and Attendants

SCENE: *Rome; the neighborhood of Sardis; the*
neighborhood of Philippi]

ACT 1
SCENE 1

Location: Rome. A street.

Enter Flavius, Marullus, and
certain commoners over the stage

FLAVIUS Hence! Home, you idle creatures, get you home!
Is this a holiday? What, know you not,
Being mechanical,° you ought not walk
Upon a laboring day without the sign°
Of your profession?—Speak, what trade art thou?   5
CARPENTER Why, sir, a carpenter.
MARULLUS Where is thy leather apron and thy rule?
What dost thou with thy best apparel on?—
You, sir, what trade are you?
COBBLER Truly, sir, in respect of a fine workman,° I am but, as   10
you would say, a cobbler.°
MARULLUS But what trade art thou? Answer me directly.
COBBLER A trade, sir, that I hope I may use with a safe
conscience, which is indeed, sir, a mender of bad soles.°
FLAVIUS
What trade, thou knave? Thou naughty knave, what trade?   15
COBBLER Nay, I beseech you, sir, be not out° with me. Yet if
you be out,° sir, I can mend you.°
FLAVIUS
What mean'st thou by that? Mend me, thou saucy fellow?
COBBLER Why, sir, cobble you.°
FLAVIUS Thou art a cobbler, art thou?   20

---

3 mechanical of the artisan class   **4 sign** garb and implements   **10 in . . . workman**
(1) as far as skilled work is concerned (2) compared with a skilled worker
11 cobbler (1) one who works with shoes (2) bungler   **14 soles** (with pun on
"souls")   **16 out** out of temper   **17 out** having worn-out shoes | **mend you** (1) cure
your bad temper (2) repair your shoes   **19 cobble you** mend your shoes (the
meaning "to pelt with stones" also suggests itself here, though perhaps it was not in
general use until later in the seventeenth century)

COBBLER Truly, sir, all that I live by is with the awl.° I meddle
with° no tradesman's matters nor women's matters, but
withal° I am indeed, sir, a surgeon to old shoes.
When they are in great danger, I recover° them. As proper° men as ever
trod upon neat's leather° have gone upon my handiwork.   25
FLAVIUS But wherefore art not in thy shop today?
Why dost thou lead these men about the streets?
COBBLER Truly, sir, to wear out their shoes, to get myself into
more work. But indeed, sir, we make holiday to see Caesar
and to rejoice in his triumph.°   30
MARULLUS Wherefore rejoice? What conquest brings he home?
What tributaries° follow him to Rome
To grace in captive bonds his chariot wheels?
You blocks, you stones, you worse than senseless° things!
O you hard hearts, you cruel men of Rome,   35
Knew you not Pompey?° Many a time and oft
Have you climbed up to walls and battlements,
To towers and windows, yea, to chimney tops,°
Your infants in your arms, and there have sat
The livelong day, with patient expectation,   40
To see great° Pompey pass the streets of Rome.
And when you saw his chariot but appear,
Have you not made an universal shout,
That Tiber° trembled underneath her banks
To hear the replication° of your sounds   45
Made in her concave° shores?
And do you now put on your best attire?
And do you now cull° out a holiday?
And do you now strew flowers in his way

21 **awl** (punning on *all*) 21–2 **meddle with** (1) have to do with (2) have sexual intercourse with 23 **withal** yet (with pun on *with awl*) 24 **recover** (1) resole (2) cure | **proper** fine, handsome 24–5 **as . . . leather** (proverbial; *neat's leather* is cowhide) 30 **triumph** triumphal procession (Caesar had overthrown the sons of Pompey the Great in Spain at the Battle of Munda, 17 March, 45 BCE; the triumph was held in October); in Plutarch, the people revile Caesar for celebrating his victory over Pompey's sons; see 103–4, below 32 **tributaries** captives who will pay ransom (tribute) 34 **senseless** insensible like stone (hence, unfeeling) 36 **Pompey** (Caesar had overthrown the great soldier and onetime triumvir at the Battle of Pharsalus in 48 B.C.; Pompey fled to Egypt, where he was murdered) 37–8 **battlements . . . chimney tops** (the details are appropriate to an Elizabethan cityscape) 41 **great** (alludes to Pompey's epithet, *Magnus*, "great") 44 **Tiber** the Tiber River 45 **replication** echo 46 **concave** hollowed out, overhanging 48 **cull** pick

That comes in triumph over Pompey's blood?°   50
Begone!
Run to your houses, fall upon your knees,
Pray to the gods to intermit° the plague
That needs must light on this ingratitude.
FLAVIUS Go, go, good countrymen, and for this fault   55
Assemble all the poor men of your sort;°
Draw them to Tiber banks, and weep your tears
Into the channel, till the lowest stream
Do kiss the most exalted shores of all.°
                      Exeunt all the commoners
See whe'er their basest mettle be not moved.°   60
They vanish tongue-tied in their guiltiness.
Go you down that way towards the Capitol;
This way will I. Disrobe the images°
If you do find them decked with ceremonies.°
MARULLUS May we do so?   65
You know it is the Feast of Lupercal.°
FLAVIUS It is no matter. Let no images
Be hung with Caesar's trophies.° I'll about°
And drive away the vulgar° from the streets;
So do you too, where you perceive them thick.   70
These growing feathers plucked from Caesar's wing
Will make him fly an ordinary pitch,°
Who else° would soar above the view of men
And keep us all in servile fearfulness.   *Exeunt*

---

50 Pompey's blood (1) Pompey's offspring (2) the blood of the Pompeys **53 intermit** suspend **56 sort** rank **58–9 till . . . all** until even at its lowest reach the river is filled to the brim **60 See . . . moved** See how even their ignoble natures can be appealed to (*mettle* and *metal* are interchangeable, meaning both "temperament" and the natural substance; a base *metal* is one that is easily changed or *moved*, unlike gold; compare 1.2.304–6) **63 images** statues (of Caesar in royal regalia, set up by his followers) **64 ceremonies** ceremonial trappings **66 Feast of Lupercal** a feast of purification (*Februa*, whence *February*) in honor of Pan, celebrated from ancient times in Rome on February 15 of each year (historically, this celebration came some months after Caesar's triumph in October of 45 B.C.; the celebrants, called *Luperci*, raced around the Palatine Hill and the Circus carrying thongs of goatskin, with which they lightly struck those who came in their way; women so touched were suppposed to be cured of barrenness; hence Caesar's wish that Antony would strike Calpurnia, 1.2.6–9) **68 trophies** spoils of war hung up as memorials of victory | **about** go around the other way **69 vulgar** commoners, plebeians **72 pitch** highest point in flight (a term from falconry) **73 else** otherwise

❖

ACT 1
SCENE 2

Location: A public place or street,
perhaps as in the previous scene.

Enter Caesar, Antony for the course, Calpurnia,
Portia, Decius, Cicero, Brutus, Cassius, Casca, a
Soothsayer; after them, Marullus and Flavius;
[citizens following]

CAESAR Calpurnia!

CASCA   Peace, ho! Caesar speaks.

CAESAR   Calpurnia!

CALPURNIA Here, my lord.

CAESAR Stand you directly in Antonio's° way
When he doth run his course. Antonio!

ANTONY Caesar, my lord?   5

CAESAR Forget not, in your speed, Antonio,
To touch Calpurnia; for our elders say
The barren, touchèd in this holy chase,
Shake off their sterile curse.°

ANTONY   I shall remember.
When Caesar says "Do this," it is performed.   10

CAESAR Set on,° and leave no ceremony out.   *[Flourish]*

SOOTHSAYER Caesar!

CAESAR Ha? Who calls?

CASCA Bid every noise be still. Peace yet again!
                                        [The music ceases]

CAESAR Who is it in the press° that calls on me?   15
I hear a tongue shriller than all the music
Cry "Caesar!" Speak. Caesar is turned to hear.

SOOTHSAYER Beware the ides of March.°

CAESAR   What man is that?

0.1 *for the course* stripped for the race, carrying a goatskin thong   3 **Antonio's**
(here and occasionally elsewhere Shakespeare employs Italian forms of Latin proper
names, perhaps for metrical reasons)   9 **sterile curse** curse of barrenness   11 **Set on**
proceed   15 **press** throng   18 **ides of March** March 15

BRUTUS   A soothsayer bids you beware the ides of March.°
CAESAR   Set him before me. Let me see his face.   20
CASSIUS Fellow, come from the throng. [*The Soothsayer comes
         forward*] Look upon Caesar.
CAESAR   What say'st thou to me now? Speak once again.
SOOTHSAYER   Beware the ides of March.
CAESAR   He is a dreamer. Let us leave him. Pass.
                    Sennet.° Exeunt. Manent° Brutus and Cassius
CASSIUS Will you go see the order of the course?°   25
BRUTUS   Not I.
CASSIUS I pray you, do.
BRUTUS   I am not gamesome.° I do lack some part
    Of that quick spirit that is in Antony.
    Let me not hinder, Cassius, your desires;   30
    I'll leave you.
CASSIUS Brutus, I do observe you now of late.
    I have not from your eyes that gentleness
    And show of love as I was wont° to have.
    You bear too stubborn and too strange a hand°   35
    Over your friend that loves you.
BRUTUS   Cassius,
    Be not deceived. If I have veiled my look,°
    I turn the trouble of my countenance
    Merely° upon myself. Vexèd I am
    Of late with passions of some difference,°   40
    Conceptions only proper to° myself,
    Which give some soil,° perhaps, to my behaviors.
    But let not therefore my good friends be grieved—
    Among which number, Cassius, be you one—
    Nor construe any further my neglect   45
    Than that poor Brutus, with himself at war,
    Forgets the shows of love to other men.

19 A . . . March for Roman and Elizabethan accounts of soothsaying, see 130–46,
below   24.1 *Sennet* trumpet call signaling the arrival or departure of a dignitary |
Manent They remain on stage   25 order of the course ritual and progress of the
race   28 gamesome fond of sports, merry   34 wont accustomed   35 You . . . hand
you behave too stubbornly and in too unfriendly a manner (the metaphor is from
horsemanship)   37 veiled my look been introverted, seemed less friendly   39 Merely
entirely   40 passions of some difference conflicting emotions   41 only proper to
relating only to   42 soil blemish

CASSIUS Then, Brutus, I have much mistook your passion,
By means whereof this breast of mine hath buried
Thoughts of great value,° worthy cogitations.   50
Tell me, good Brutus, can you see your face?
BRUTUS No, Cassius, for the eye sees not itself
But by reflection, by some other things.
CASSIUS 'Tis just.°
And it is very much lamented, Brutus,   55
That you have no such mirrors as will turn
Your hidden worthiness into your eye,
That you might see your shadow.° I have heard
Where many of the best respect° in Rome,
Except immortal Caesar, speaking of Brutus   60
And groaning underneath this age's yoke,
Have wished that noble Brutus had his eyes.°
BRUTUS Into what dangers would you lead me, Cassius,
That you would have me seek into myself
For that which is not in me?   65
CASSIUS Therefore, good Brutus, be prepared to hear;
And since you know you cannot see yourself
So well as by reflection, I, your glass,°
Will modestly discover to yourself
That of yourself which you yet know not of.   70
And be not jealous on° me, gentle° Brutus.
Were I a common laughter,° or did use°
To stale° with ordinary° oaths my love
To every new protester;° if you know
That I do fawn on men and hug them hard   75
And after scandal° them, or if you know
That I profess myself° in banqueting
To all the rout,° then hold me dangerous.
Flourish,° and shout

49–50 By . . . value because of which misunderstanding (my assuming you were displeased with me) I have kept to myself important thoughts   54 just true   58 shadow image, reflection   59 best respect highest repute and station   62 had his eyes (1) could see things from the perspective of Caesar's critics, or (2) could see better with his own eyes   68 glass mirror   71 jealous on suspicious of | gentle noble   72 laughter laughingstock, as at 4.3.114; or perhaps *laugher,* a shallow fellow who laughs at every jest | did use were accustomed   73 stale cheapen, make common | ordinary (1) commonplace (2) customary (3) tavern   74 protester one who protests or declares friendship   76 after scandal afterwards slander   77 profess myself make declarations of friendship   78 rout mob   78.1 *Flourish* fanfare for a dignitary

BRUTUS   What means this shouting? I do fear the people
Choose Caesar for their king.°
CASSIUS   Ay, do you fear it?   80
Then must I think you would not have it so.
BRUTUS   I would not, Cassius, yet I love him well.
But wherefore do you hold me here so long?
What is it that you would impart to me?
If it be aught toward the general good,   85
Set honor in one eye and death i'th'other
And I will look on both indifferently;°
For let the gods so speed me° as I love
The name of honor more than I fear death.
CASSIUS   I know that virtue to be in you, Brutus,   90
As well as I do know your outward favor.°
Well, honor is the subject of my story.
I cannot tell what you and other men
Think of this life; but, for my single self,
I had as lief° not be as live to be   95
In awe of such a thing as I myself.°
I was born free as Caesar, so were you;
We both have fed as well, and we can both
Endure the winter's cold as well as he.
For once, upon a raw and gusty day,   100
The troubled Tiber chafing with her shores,
Caesar said to me, "Dar'st thou, Cassius, now
Leap in with me into this angry flood
And swim to yonder point?" Upon the word,
Accoutred° as I was, I plungèd in   105
And bade him follow; so indeed he did.
The torrent roared, and we did buffet it
With lusty sinews, throwing it aside
And stemming° it with hearts of controversy.°
But ere we could arrive the point proposed,   110
Caesar cried, "Help me, Cassius, or I sink!"

79–80 What . . . king Brutus' fear is misplaced; the people have applauded Caesar's
(reluctant) *refusal* of kingship (see 1.2.215–231)   **87 indifferently** impartially
88 speed me make me prosper   **91 favor** appearance   **95 as lief not be** just as soon
not exist   **96 such . . . myself** a fellow mortal   **105 Accoutred** fully dressed in
armor   **109 stemming** making headway against | **hearts of controversy** hearts fired
up by rivalry

Ay, as Aeneas,° our great ancestor,
Did from the flames of Troy upon his shoulder
The old Anchises bear, so from the waves of Tiber
Did I the tirèd Caesar. And this man   115
Is now become a god, and Cassius is
A wretched creature and must bend his body°
If Caesar carelessly but nod on him.
He had a fever when he was in Spain,
And when the fit was on him I did mark   120
How he did shake. 'Tis true, this god did shake.
His coward lips did from their color° fly,
And that same eye whose bend° doth awe the world
Did lose his° luster. I did hear him groan.
Ay, and that tongue of his that bade the Romans   125
Mark him and write his speeches in their books,
Alas, it cried, "Give me some drink, Titinius,"
As a sick girl. Ye gods, it doth amaze me
A man of such a feeble temper° should
So get the start of° the majestic world   130
And bear the palm° alone.   *Shout. Flourish*
BRUTUS Another general shout!
I do believe that these applauses are
For some new honors that are heaped on Caesar.
CASSIUS Why, man, he doth bestride the narrow world   135
Like a Colossus,° and we petty men
Walk under his huge legs and peep about
To find ourselves dishonorable graves.
Men at some time are masters of their fates.
The fault, dear Brutus, is not in our stars,   140
But in ourselves, that we are underlings.
"Brutus" and "Caesar." What should be in that "Caesar"?
Why should that name be sounded more than yours?

---

112 Aeneas hero of Virgil's *Aeneid*, the legendary founder of Rome (hence *our great ancestor*), who bore his aged father Anchises out of burning Troy as it was falling to the Greeks **117 bend his body** bow **122 color** (1) normal healthy hue (2) military colors, flag (the lips are personified as deserters) **123 bend** glance, gaze **124 his** its **129 temper** constitution **130 get . . . of** gain ascendancy over **131 palm** victor's prize **136 Colossus** (a 100-foot-high bronze statue of Helios, the sun god, one of the seven wonders of the ancient world, was commonly supposed to have stood astride the entrance to the harbor of Rhodes)

Write them together, yours is as fair a name;
Sound them, it doth become the mouth as well;   145
Weigh them, it is as heavy; conjure with 'em,
"Brutus" will start° a spirit as soon as "Caesar."
Now, in the names of all the gods at once,
Upon what meat doth this our Caesar feed
That he is grown so great? Age, thou art shamed!   150
Rome, thou hast lost the breed of noble bloods!°
When went there by an age since the great flood°
But it was famed° with more than with one man?
When could they say, till now, that talked of Rome,
That her wide walks encompassed but one man?   155
Now is it Rome indeed, and room° enough,
When there is in it but one only man.
Oh, you and I have heard our fathers say
There was a Brutus° once that would have brooked°
Th'eternal devil to keep his state° in Rome   160
As easily as a king.°
BRUTUS   That you do love me, I am nothing jealous.°
What you would work° me to, I have some aim.°
How I have thought of this and of these times
I shall recount hereafter. For this present,   165
I would not, so with love I might entreat you,°
Be any further moved.° What you have said
I will consider; what you have to say
I will with patience hear and find a time
Both meet° to hear and answer such high things.   170
Till then, my noble friend, chew upon this:
Brutus had rather be a villager

---

147 start raise (perhaps the crowd is heard to shout a third time at this point, or
somewhere else in this conversation; at line 226 below, we are told that "They
shouted thrice")   **151 the breed . . . bloods** the bloodline of men of noble stock and
valiant spirit   **152 flood** the classical analogue of Noah's flood, in which all
humanity was destroyed except for Deucalion and his wife Pyrrha   **153 famed with**
famous for   **156 Rome, room** (pronounced alike)   **159 Brutus** Lucius Junius
Brutus, who expelled the Tarquins and founded the Roman republic (c. 509 BCE);
in his poem *The Rape of Lucrece* [c. 1594], Shakespeare treats the events that
precipitated the revolt against the Tarquins I **brooked** tolerated   **160 keep his
state** set himself up in majesty   **161 As . . . king** as readily as he would tolerate a
king   **162 nothing jealous** not at all doubtful   **163 work** persuade I **aim** inkling
166 so . . . you if I might entreat you in the name of friendship   **167 moved** urged
170 meet fitting

Than to repute himself a son of Rome
Under these hard conditions as this time
Is like° to lay upon us.   175
CASSIUS I am glad that my weak words
Have struck but thus much show of fire from Brutus.

                    Enter Caesar and his train° [Brutus and
                    Cassius continue to confer privately]

BRUTUS The games are done, and Caesar is returning.
CASSIUS As they pass by, pluck Casca by the sleeve,
And he will, after his sour fashion, tell you   180
What hath proceeded worthy note today.
BRUTUS I will do so. But look you, Cassius,
The angry spot doth glow on Caesar's brow,
And all the rest look like a chidden train.°
Calpurnia's cheek is pale, and Cicero°   185
Looks with such ferret° and such fiery eyes
As we have seen him in the Capitol,
Being crossed in conference° by some senators.
CASSIUS Casca will tell us what the matter is.
CAESAR Antonio!   190
ANTONY Caesar?
CAESAR Let me have men about me that are fat,
Sleek-headed men, and such as sleep o' nights.
Yond Cassius has a lean and hungry look.
He thinks too much. Such men are dangerous.   195
ANTONY Fear him not, Caesar, he's not dangerous.
He is a noble Roman, and well given.°
CAESAR Would he were fatter! But I fear him not.
Yet if my name were liable to fear,
I do not know the man I should avoid   200
So soon as that spare Cassius. He reads much,
He is a great observer, and he looks

---

175 like likely   **177.1** *train* retinue (see 1.2.0.1–4 for the names of those in the procession)   **184 a chidden train** scolded followers   **185 Cicero** Marcus Tullius Cicero; senator, famous orator, and prolific author, deeply revered in Shakespeare's England; although he was not among the conspirators, Cicero applauded the assassination of Caesar; Antony eventually marked Cicero for execution, and he met his death in 43 BCE   **186 ferret** ferretlike, small and red   **188 crossed in conference** opposed in debate   **197 given** disposed

Quite through° the deeds of men. He loves no plays,
As thou dost, Antony; he hears no music.°
Seldom he smiles, and smiles in such a sort°   205
As if he mocked himself and scorned his spirit
That could be moved to smile at anything.
Such men as he be never at heart's ease
Whiles they behold a greater than themselves,
And therefore are they very dangerous.   210
I rather tell thee what is to be feared
Than what I fear, for always I am Caesar.
Come on my right hand, for this ear is deaf,
And tell me truly what thou think'st of him.

Sennet. Exeunt Caesar and his train
[Casca remains with Brutus and Cassius]

CASCA   You pulled me by the cloak.° Would you speak with   215
me?
BRUTUS   Ay, Casca. Tell us what hath chanced° today,
That Caesar looks so sad.°
CASCA   Why, you were with him, were you not?
BRUTUS   I should not then ask Casca what had chanced.   220
CASCA   Why, there was a crown offered him; and, being offered
him, he put it by with the back of his hand, thus, and then
the people fell a-shouting.
BRUTUS   What was the second noise for?
CASCA   Why, for that too.   225
CASSIUS   They shouted thrice.° What was the last cry for?
CASCA   Why, for that too.
BRUTUS   Was the crown offered him thrice?
CASCA   Ay, marry,° was't, and he put it by thrice, every time
gentler than other, and at every putting-by mine honest°   230
neighbors shouted.
CASSIUS   Who offered him the crown?
CASCA   Why, Antony.
BRUTUS   Tell us the manner of it, gentle° Casca.

---

203 **through** into the motives of   204 **hears no music** (regarded as a sign of a
morose and treacherous character)   205 **sort** manner   215 **cloak** (Elizabethan
costume; see also *sleeve,* line 179, and *doublet,* line 262; the Roman toga was
sleeveless)   217 **chanced** happened   218 **sad** serious   226 **thrice** (see note at
1.2.147)   229 **marry** indeed (originally, "by the Virgin Mary")   230 **honest**
worthy (said contemptuously)   234 **gentle** noble

CASCA   I can as well be hanged as tell the manner of it. It was   235
mere foolery; I did not mark it. I saw Mark Antony offer him
a crown—yet 'twas not a crown neither, 'twas one of these
coronets°—and, as I told you, he put it by once; but for all
that, to my thinking, he would fain° have had it. Then he
offered it to him again; then he put it by again; but to my   240
thinking he was very loath to lay his fingers off it. And then
he offered it the third time. He put it the third time by, and
still as he refused it the rabblement hooted and clapped their
chapped hands, and threw up their sweaty nightcaps,° and
uttered such a deal of stinking breath because Caesar refused   245
the crown that it had almost choked Caesar, for he swooned
and fell down at it. And for mine own part I durst not laugh
for fear of opening my lips and receiving the bad air.

CASSIUS   But soft,° I pray you. What, did Caesar swoon?

CASCA   He fell down in the marketplace, and foamed at mouth,   250
and was speechless.

BRUTUS   'Tis very like. He hath the falling sickness.

CASSIUS   No, Caesar hath it not, but you and I,
And honest Casca, we have the falling sickness.°

CASCA   I know not what you mean by that, but I am sure   255
Caesar fell down. If the tag-rag° people did not clap him and
hiss him, according as he pleased and displeased them, as
they use° to do the players in the theater, I am no true man.

BRUTUS   What said he when he came unto himself?

CASCA   Marry, before he fell down, when he perceived the   260
common herd was glad he refused the crown, he plucked
me ope° his doublet° and offered them his throat to cut.
An° I had been a man of any occupation,° if I would not
have taken him at a word, I would I might go to hell among
the rogues. And so he fell. When he came to himself again,   265
he said if he had done or said anything amiss, he desired
Their Worships to think it was his infirmity. Three or four

---

238 coronets chaplets, garlands   **239 fain** gladly   **244 nightcaps** (scornful allusion
to the *pilleus,* a felt cap worn by the plebeians on festival days)   **249 soft** wait a
minute   **254 falling sickness** epilepsy (but Cassius takes it to mean "falling into
servitude")   **256 tag-rag** ragtag, riffraff   **258 use** are accustomed   **261–2 plucked
me ope** pulled open (*me* is used colloquially)   **262 doublet** Elizabethan upper
garment, like a jacket   **263 An** if | **man . . . occupation** (1) working man (2) man
of action

wenches where I stood cried, "Alas, good soul!" and
forgave him with all their hearts. But there's no heed to be
taken of them; if Caesar had stabbed their mothers they   270
would have done no less.

BRUTUS And after that, he came thus sad away?

CASCA Ay.

CASSIUS Did Cicero say anything?

CASCA Ay, he spoke Greek.   275

CASSIUS To what effect?

CASCA Nay, an I tell you that, I'll ne'er look you i'th' face
again. But those that understood him smiled at one another
and shook their heads; but, for mine own part, it was Greek
to me. I could tell you more news too. Marullus and Flavius, 280
for pulling scarves° off Caesar's images, are put to silence.°
Fare you well. There was more foolery yet, if I could
remember it.

CASSIUS Will you sup with me tonight, Casca?

CASCA No, I am promised forth.°   285

CASSIUS Will you dine with me tomorrow?

CASCA Ay, if I be alive, and your mind hold, and your dinner
worth the eating.

CASSIUS Good. I will expect you.

CASCA Do so. Farewell both.   *Exit*   290

BRUTUS What a blunt fellow is this grown to be!
He was quick mettle° when he went to school.

CASSIUS So is he now in execution
Of any bold or noble enterprise,
However° he puts on this tardy form.°   295
This rudeness° is a sauce to his good wit,°
Which gives men stomach° to digest his words
With better appetite.

BRUTUS And so it is. For this time I will leave you.
Tomorrow, if you please to speak with me,   300
I will come home to you; or, if you will,
Come home to me, and I will wait for you.

---

281 scarves decorations, festoons | **put to silence** dismissed from office (so reported
in Plutarch; Shakespeare's wording ominously suggests that they were executed)
285 promised forth engaged to dine out   **292 quick mettle** of a lively temperament
295 However however much | **tardy form** air of ennui and disengagement
296 rudeness rough manner | **wit** intellect   **297 stomach** appetite, inclination

CASSIUS I will do so. Till then, think of the world.°

Exit Brutus

Well, Brutus, thou art noble. Yet I see
Thy honorable mettle° may be wrought   305
From that it is disposed.° Therefore it is meet°
That noble minds keep ever with their likes;
For who so firm that cannot be seduced?
Caesar doth bear me hard,° but he loves Brutus.
If I were Brutus now, and he were Cassius,   310
He should not humor me.° I will this night
In several hands° in at his windows throw,
As if they came from several citizens,
Writings, all tending to the great opinion
That Rome holds of his name, wherein obscurely   315
Caesar's ambition shall be glancèd° at.
And after this let Caesar seat him sure,°
For we will shake him, or worse days endure.   *Exit*

ACT 1
SCENE 3
Location: A street.

Thunder and lightning. Enter, [meeting,]
Casca [with his sword drawn] and Cicero

CICERO Good even, Casca. Brought you Caesar home?
Why are you breathless? And why stare you so?
CASCA Are not you moved, when all the sway° of earth
Shakes like a thing unfirm? Oh, Cicero,

303 **the world** the state of the world 305 **mettle** (as often, the word combines the senses of *mettle*, "temperament," and *metal*, "substance;" the latter meaning continues here in the chemical metaphor of metal that is *wrought* or transmuted; as *honorable mettle* [or noble metal], gold cannot be transmuted into base substances, and yet Cassius proposes to do just that with Brutus; compare this with 1.1.61) 305–6 **wrought . . . disposed** turned away from its natural disposition 306 **meet** fitting 309 **doth . . . hard** bears me a grudge and keeps me on a short rein 311 **He . . . humor me** I wouldn't put up with being cajoled or humored (*he* could refer to Caesar or Brutus) 312 **several hands** different handwritings 316 **glancèd** hinted 317 **seat him sure** seat himself securely in power (watch out)
3 **sway** established order

I have seen tempests when the scolding winds   5
Have rived the knotty oaks, and I have seen
Th'ambitious ocean swell and rage and foam
To be exalted with° the threat'ning clouds;
But never till tonight, never till now,
Did I go through a tempest dropping fire.   10
Either there is a civil strife in heaven,
Or else the world, too saucy with the gods,
Incenses them to send destruction.
CICERO   Why, saw you anything more wonderful?°
CASCA   A common slave—you know him well by sight—   15
Held up his left hand, which did flame and burn
Like twenty torches joined, and yet his hand,
Not sensible° of fire, remained unscorched.
Besides—I ha' not since put up° my sword—
Against° the Capitol I met a lion,   20
Who glazed° upon me and went surly by
Without annoying° me. And there were drawn
Upon a heap° a hundred ghastly° women,
Transformèd with their fear, who swore they saw
Men all in fire walk up and down the streets.   25
And yesterday the bird of night° did sit
Even at noonday upon the marketplace,
Hooting and shrieking. When these prodigies°
Do so conjointly° meet, let not men say,
"These are their reasons, they are natural,"   30
For I believe they are portentous things
Unto the climate° that they point upon.
CICERO   Indeed, it is a strange-disposèd time.
But men may construe things after their fashion,°
Clean from the purpose° of the things themselves.   35
Comes Caesar to the Capitol tomorrow?

8 exalted with raised to the level of   **14 more wonderful** else that was wondrous
18 Not sensible of not feeling   **19 put up** sheathed   **20 Against** in front of,
opposite   **21 glazed** stared glassily   **22 annoying** harming   **22–3 drawn . . . heap**
huddled together   **23 ghastly** pallid   **26 bird of night** owl, a bird of evil omen
28 prodigies abnormalities, wonders; for Roman and Elizabethan theories of prodigies
as divine revelations of future events, see 130–46, below   **29 conjointly meet**
coincide   **32 climate** region; for the interpretation of "prodigies" and "portentous
things" in Shakespeare's England, see 130–46, below   **34 after their fashion** in their
own way   **35 Clean . . . purpose** contrary to the actual import or meaning

CASCA He doth; for he did bid Antonio
  Send word to you he would be there tomorrow.
CICERO Good night then, Casca. This disturbèd sky
  Is not to walk in.
CASCA   Farewell, Cicero.   *Exit Cicero*   40

                         Enter Cassius

CASSIUS Who's there?
CASCA   A Roman.
CASSIUS   Casca, by your voice.
CASCA Your ear is good. Cassius, what night° is this!
CASSIUS A very pleasing night to honest men.
CASCA Who ever knew the heavens menace so?
CASSIUS Those that have known the earth so full of faults.   45
  For my part, I have walked about the streets,
  Submitting me unto the perilous night,
  And thus unbracèd,° Casca, as you see,
  Have bared my bosom to the thunder-stone;°
  And when the cross° blue lightning seemed to open   50
  The breast of heaven, I did present myself
  Even in the aim and very flash of it.
CASCA But wherefore did you so much tempt the heavens?
  It is the part of men to fear and tremble
  When the most mighty gods by tokens send   55
  Such dreadful heralds to astonish us.
CASSIUS You are dull, Casca, and those sparks of life
  That should be in a Roman you do want,°
  Or else you use not. You look pale, and gaze,
  And put on° fear, and cast yourself in wonder,°   60
  To see the strange impatience of the heavens.
  But if you would consider the true cause
  Why all these fires, why all these gliding ghosts,
  Why birds and beasts from quality and kind,°
  Why old men, fools, and children calculate,°   65
  Why all these things change from their ordinance,°

---

42 what night what a night   **48 unbracèd** with doublet unfastened   **49 thunder-stone** thunderbolt   **50 cross** forked, jagged   **58 want** lack   **60 put on** adopt, show signs of | **in wonder** into a state of wonder   **64 from . . . kind** (behaving) contrary to their true nature   **65 calculate** reckon, prophesy   **66 ordinance** established nature

Their natures, and preformèd° faculties,
To monstrous° quality—why, you shall find
That heaven hath infused them with these spirits
To make them instruments of fear and warning   70
Unto some monstrous state.°
Now could I, Casca, name to thee a man
Most like this dreadful night,
That thunders, lightens, opens graves, and roars
As doth the lion in the Capitol—   75
A man no mightier than thyself or me
In personal action, yet prodigious° grown
And fearful,° as these strange eruptions are.

CASCA 'Tis Caesar that you mean, is it not, Cassius?

CASSIUS Let it be who it is. For Romans now   80
Have thews° and limbs like to their ancestors';
But, woe the while,° our fathers' minds are dead,
And we are governed with our mothers' spirits.
Our yoke and sufferance° show us womanish.

CASCA Indeed, they say the senators tomorrow   85
Mean to establish Caesar as a king,
And he shall wear his crown by sea and land
In every place save here in Italy.

CASSIUS I know where I will wear this dagger then;
Cassius from bondage° will deliver Cassius.   90
Therein,° ye gods, you make the weak most strong;
Therein, ye gods, you tyrants do defeat.
Nor° stony tower, nor walls of beaten brass,
Nor airless dungeon, nor strong links of iron,
Can be retentive to the strength of spirit;°   95
But life, being weary of these worldly bars,°
Never lacks power to dismiss itself.
If I know this, know all the world besides,°

---

67 **preformèd** innate, congenital 68 **monstrous** unnatural 71 **Unto . . . state**
pointing to some disorder in the commonwealth or state of affairs 77 **prodigious**
ominous 78 **fearful** inspiring fear 81 **thews** sinews, muscles 82 **woe the while**
alas for the age 84 **yoke and sufferance** patience under the yoke 90 **bondage** for
the resonance of bondage in Elizabethan political rhetoric, see 162–66, below
91 **Therein** in the ability to commit suicide 93 **Nor** neither 95 **Can . . . spirit** can
confine a resolute spirit 96 **bars** (1) prison bars (2) burdens (such as tyranny)
98 **know . . . besides** let the rest of the world know

That part of tyranny that I do bear
I can shake off at pleasure.   *Thunder still*°
CASCA   So can I.   100
So every bondman in his own hand bears
The power to cancel his captivity.
CASSIUS   And why should Caesar be a tyrant then?
Poor man, I know he would not be a wolf
But that he sees the Romans are but sheep;   105
He were no lion, were° not Romans hinds.°
Those that with haste will make a mighty fire
Begin it with weak straws. What trash is Rome,
What rubbish and what offal,° when it serves
For the base matter° to illuminate   110
So vile a thing as Caesar! But, O grief,
Where hast thou led me? I perhaps speak this
Before a willing bondman; then I know
My answer must be made.° But I am armed,°
And dangers are to me indifferent.°   115
CASCA   You speak to Casca, and to such a man
That is no fleering° telltale. Hold. My hand.°
Be factious° for redress of all these griefs,°
And I will set this foot of mine as far
As who° goes farthest.   [*They shake hands*]
CASSIUS   There's a bargain made.   120
Now know you, Casca, I have moved already
Some certain of the noblest-minded Romans
To undergo with me an enterprise
Of honorable dangerous consequence;
And I do know by this° they stay for me   125
In Pompey's porch.° For now, this fearful night,
There is no stir or walking in the streets,

---

100 s.d. *Thunder still* continuous thunder   **106 were** would be | **hinds** (1) female of the red deer (2) servants, menials   **109 offal** refuse, wood shavings   **110 matter** fuel   **114 My answer . . . made** I will have to answer (to Caesar) for what I have said | **armed** (1) provided with weapons (2) morally fortified   **115 indifferent** unimportant   **117 fleering** fawning; scornful | **Hold. My hand** enough; here is my hand   **118 factious** active as a partisan | **griefs** grievances   **120 who** whoever **125 by this** by this time   **126 Pompey's porch** the porticus (colonnade) of Pompey's great open theater, dedicated in 55 BCE; according to most ancient commentators, Caesar was assassinated in an assembly room within the porticus; Shakespeare shifts the scene to "the Senate House" and "the Capitol"

And the complexion of the element°
In favor 's° like the work we have in hand,
Most bloody, fiery, and most terrible.   130

Enter Cinna

CASCA   Stand close° awhile, for here comes one in haste.
CASSIUS   'Tis Cinna; I do know him by his gait.
He is a friend.—Cinna, where haste you so?
CINNA   To find out you. Who's that? Metellus Cimber?
CASSIUS   No, it is Casca, one incorporate°   135
To our attempts. Am I not stayed for, Cinna?
CINNA   I am glad on't.° What a fearful night is this!
There's two or three of us have seen strange sights.
CASSIUS   Am I not stayed for? Tell me.
CINNA   Yes, you are. Oh, Cassius, if you could   140
But win the noble Brutus to our party—
CASSIUS   Be you content. Good Cinna, take this paper,
                                             [*giving papers*]
And look you lay it in the praetor's chair,°
Where Brutus may but find it.° And throw this
In at his window. Set this up with wax   145
Upon old Brutus'° statue. All this done,
Repair° to Pompey's porch, where you shall find us.
Is Decius Brutus and Trebonius there?
CINNA   All but Metellus Cimber, and he's gone
To seek you at your house. Well, I will hie,°   150
And so bestow these papers as you bade me.
CASSIUS   That done, repair to Pompey's theater.   *Exit Cinna*
Come, Casca, you and I will yet ere day
See Brutus at his house. Three parts° of him
Is ours already, and the man entire   155
Upon the next encounter yields him ours.
CASCA   Oh, he sits high in all the people's hearts;
And that which would appear offense in us,

128 **element** sky   129 **favor 's** appearance is   131 **close** concealed, still   135 **incorporate** admitted as a member   137 **on't** of it   143 **praetor's chair** official seat of a praetor, Roman magistrate ranking next below the consul (Brutus was praetor, one of sixteen)   144 **Where . . . it** where Brutus cannot help finding it   146 **old Brutus** (Lucius Junius Brutus; Brutus was reputed to be his descendant)   147 **Repair** proceed (also in line 152)   150 **hie** go quickly   154 **parts** quarters

His countenance, like richest alchemy,
Will change to virtue and to worthiness.° 160
CASSIUS Him and his worth, and our great need of him,
You have right well conceited.° Let us go,
For it is after midnight, and ere day
We will awake him and be sure of him.   *Exeunt*

ACT 2
SCENE 1

Location: Rome. Brutus's orchard, or garden.

Enter Brutus in his orchard

BRUTUS What, Lucius, ho!—
I cannot by the progress of the stars
Give guess how near to day.—Lucius, I say!—
I would it were my fault to sleep so soundly.—
When,° Lucius, when? Awake, I say! What, Lucius!   5

Enter Lucius

LUCIUS Called you, my lord?
BRUTUS Get me a taper° in my study, Lucius.
When it is lighted, come and call me here.
LUCIUS I will, my lord.   *Exit*
BRUTUS It must be by his death. And for my part   10
I know no personal cause to spurn at him,
But for the general.° He would be crowned.
How that might change his nature, there's the question.
It is the bright day that brings forth the adder,
And that craves° wary walking. Crown him—that°—   15
And then I grant we put a sting in him
That at his will he may do danger with.

158–60 that which . . . worthiness his endorsement and honorable name will convert into virtue and worthiness those things in our conspiracy that would otherwise seem offensive, just as alchemy is supposed to transform base metals into richest gold   **162 conceited** (1) conceived, grasped (2) expressed in a figure

5 When (an exclamation of impatience)   **7 Get . . . taper** put a candle for me   **12 general** general cause, common good   **15 craves** requires **| that** that is the issue

Th'abuse of greatness is when it disjoins
Remorse° from power. And to speak truth of Caesar,
I have not known when his affections swayed°   20
More than his reason. But 'tis a common proof°
That lowliness° is young ambition's ladder,
Whereto the climber-upward turns his face;
But when he once attains the upmost round°
He then unto the ladder turns his back,   25
Looks in the clouds, scorning the base degrees°
By which he did ascend. So Caesar may.
Then, lest he may, prevent. And since the quarrel
Will bear no color for the thing he is,°
Fashion it° thus: that what he is, augmented,   30
Would run to these and these extremities;
And therefore think him as a serpent's egg
Which, hatched, would, as his kind,° grow mischievous;°
And kill him in the shell.

                                            Enter Lucius

LUCIUS   The taper burneth in your closet,° sir.   35
Searching the window for a flint, I found
This paper,° thus sealed up, and I am sure
It did not lie there when I went to bed.
                                   Gives him the letter
BRUTUS   Get you to bed again. It is not day.
Is not tomorrow, boy, the ides of March?   40
LUCIUS   I know not, sir.
BRUTUS   Look in the calendar and bring me word.
LUCIUS   I will, sir.   *Exit*
BRUTUS   The exhalations° whizzing in the air
Give so much light that I may read by them.   45
                             Opens the letter and reads
   "Brutus, thou sleep'st. Awake, and see thyself!

---

19 Remorse scruple, compassion   **20 affections swayed** passions ruled   **21 proof** experience   **22 lowliness** pretended humbleness   **24 round** rung   **26 base degrees** (1) lower rungs (2) persons of lower social station   **29 Will . . . is** can carry no appearance of justice so far as his conduct to date is concerned   **30 Fashion it** put the matter   **33 as his kind** according to its nature | **mischievous** harmful   **35 closet** private chamber, study   **37 This paper** presumably the letter that Cassius mentions at 1.3.144-45   **44 exhalations** meteors

Shall Rome, etc. Speak, strike, redress!"
"Brutus, thou sleep'st. Awake!"
Such instigations have been often dropped
Where I have took them up.   50
"Shall Rome, etc." Thus must I piece it out:°
Shall Rome stand under one man's awe? What, Rome?
My ancestors did from the streets of Rome
The Tarquin drive, when he was called a king.
"Speak, strike, redress!" Am I entreated   55
To speak and strike? O Rome, I make thee promise,
If the redress will follow,° thou receivest
Thy full petition at° the hand of Brutus.

                                        Enter Lucius

LUCIUS   Sir, March is wasted fifteen days.

                                        Knock within

BRUTUS   'Tis good. Go to the gate; somebody knocks.   60
                                        [*Exit Lucius*]
Since Cassius first did whet me against Caesar,
I have not slept.
Between the acting of a dreadful thing
And the first motion,° all the interim is
Like a phantasma° or a hideous dream.   65
The genius and the mortal instruments
Are then in council;° and the state of man,
Like to a little kingdom, suffers then
The nature of an° insurrection.

                                        Enter Lucius

LUCIUS   Sir, 'tis your brother° Cassius at the door,   70
    Who doth desire to see you.
BRUTUS   Is he alone?
LUCIUS
    No, sir. There are more with him.
BRUTUS   Do you know them?

51 **piece it out** complete, fill in   57 **If . . . follow** if striking Caesar will lead to the
reform of grievances   58 **at** from   64 **motion** proposal or impulse   65 **phantasma**
hallucination   66–7 **The genius . . . council** the tutelary god or attendant spirit
allotted to every person at birth is then intensely at debate with the person's physical
faculties and passionate nature   69 **The nature of an** a kind of   70 **brother**
brother-in-law (Cassius had married a sister of Brutus)

LUCIUS   No, sir. Their hats are plucked about their ears,
And half their faces buried in their cloaks,
That by no means I may discover them   75
By any mark of favor.°
BRUTUS   Let 'em enter.   [*Exit Lucius*]
They are the faction. O conspiracy,
Sham'st thou to show thy dangerous brow by night,
When evils are most free?° Oh, then, by day
Where wilt thou find a cavern dark enough   80
To mask thy monstrous visage? Seek none, conspiracy!
Hide it in smiles and affability;
For if thou put thy native semblance on,
Not Erebus° itself were dim enough
To hide thee from prevention.°   85

Enter the conspirators, Cassius, Casca, Decius,
Cinna, Metellus [Cimber], and Trebonius

CASSIUS   I think we are too bold upon° your rest.
Good morrow, Brutus. Do we trouble you?
BRUTUS   I have been up this hour, awake all night.
Know I these men that come along with you?
CASSIUS   Yes, every man of them, and no man here   90
But honors you; and every one doth wish
You had but that opinion of yourself
Which every noble Roman bears of you.
This is Trebonius.
BRUTUS   He is welcome hither.
CASSIUS   This, Decius Brutus.
BRUTUS   He is welcome too.   95
CASSIUS   This, Casca; this, Cinna; and this, Metellus Cimber.
BRUTUS   They are all welcome.
What watchful cares° do interpose themselves
Betwixt your eyes and night?
CASSIUS   Shall I entreat a word?   100
They [Brutus and Cassius] whisper

---

76 **favor** appearance   79 **free** free to roam at will   84 **Erebus** primeval Darkness
(sprung, according to Hesiod, from Chaos and his sister Night)   85 **prevention**
detection and being forestalled   86 **upon** in intruding upon   98 **watchful cares**
sleep-preventing worries

DECIUS Here° lies the east. Doth not the day break here?
CASCA No.
CINNA Oh, pardon, sir, it doth; and yon gray lines
That fret° the clouds are messengers of day.
CASCA You shall confess that you are both deceived.   105
Here, as I point my sword, the sun arises,
Which is a great way growing° on the south,
Weighing° the youthful season of the year.
Some two months hence, up higher toward the north
He first presents his fire; and the high° east   110
Stands, as the Capitol, directly here.
BRUTUS [*coming forward*]
Give me your hands all over,° one by one.
CASSIUS And let us swear our resolution.
BRUTUS No, not an oath. If not the face of men,
The sufferance of our souls, the time's abuse—   115
If these be motives weak, break off betimes,°
And every man hence to his idle° bed;
So let high-sighted° tyranny range on
Till each man drop by lottery.° But if these,°
As I am sure they do, bear fire enough   120
To kindle cowards° and to steel° with valor
The melting spirits of women, then, countrymen,
What need we any spur but our own cause
To prick° us to redress? What other bond
Than secret Romans that have spoke the word°   125
And will not palter?° And what other oath
Than honesty to honesty° engaged
That this shall be or we will fall for it?

101 **Here** (Decius points eastward) 104 **fret** mark with interlacing lines 107 **growing** encroaching 108 **Weighing** considering, in consequence of 110 **high** due 112 **all over** one and all 114–16 **If** . . . **betimes** if the gravely serious faces of Romans, the suffering we feel, the corruptions of the present day are insufficient to move us, we should break off at once 117 **idle** (1) unused (2) in which men are idle 118 **high-sighted** upward-gazing (compare with 2.1.26); or haughty, looking down from on high 119 **by lottery** as the capricious tyrant chances to pick on him I **these** these injustices just cited 121 **cowards** even cowards I **steel** harden 124 **prick** spur 125 **Than** . . . **word** than the word of Romans who, having given their word of honor, will remain secret 126 **palter** shift position evasively 127 **honesty** personal honor

Swear priests and cowards and men cautelous,
Old feeble carrions, and such suffering souls   130
That welcome wrongs; unto bad causes swear
Such creatures as men doubt.° But do not stain
The even° virtue of our enterprise,
Nor th'insuppressive° mettle of our spirits,
To think that or our cause or° our performance   135
Did need an oath, when every drop of blood
That every Roman bears—and nobly bears—
Is guilty of a several bastardy°
If he do break the smallest particle
Of any promise that hath passed from him.   140

CASSIUS But what of Cicero? Shall we sound him?
I think he will stand very strong with us.

CASCA Let us not leave him out.

CINNA   No, by no means.

METELLUS Oh, let us have him, for his silver hairs
Will purchase° us a good opinion   145
And buy men's voices to commend our deeds.
It shall be said his judgment ruled our hands;
Our youths and wildness shall no whit appear,
But all be buried in his gravity.

BRUTUS Oh, name him not. Let us not break with° him,   150
For he will never follow anything
That other men begin.

CASSIUS Then leave him out.

CASCA Indeed he is not fit.

DECIUS Shall no man else be touched but only Caesar?   155

CASSIUS Decius, well urged. I think it is not meet°
Mark Antony, so well beloved of Caesar,
Should outlive Caesar. We shall find of° him
A shrewd contriver; and you know his means,
If he improve° them, may well stretch so far   160

129–32 Swear . . . doubt let priests and cowards and shifty old men tottering on the
brink of the grave swear oaths, and long-suffering souls that submit supinely to
wrongs; it is contemptible, untrustworthy persons like these who swear oaths to bad
causes 133 even steadfast, consistent 134 insuppressive indomitable 135 or . . .
or either . . . or 138 a several bastardy an individual act unworthy of his parentage
145 purchase procure (playing on the financial sense of *silver,* line 144) 150 break
with confide in 156 meet fitting 158 of in 160 improve exploit, make good use of

As to annoy° us all. Which to prevent,
Let Antony and Caesar fall together.
BRUTUS Our course will seem too bloody, Caius Cassius,
To cut the head off and then hack the limbs,
Like wrath in death and envy° afterwards;   165
For Antony is but a limb of Caesar.
Let's be sacrificers, but not butchers, Caius.
We all stand up against the spirit of Caesar,
And in the spirit of men there is no blood.
Oh, that we then could come by Caesar's spirit   170
And not dismember Caesar! But, alas,
Caesar must bleed for it. And, gentle° friends,
Let's kill him boldly, but not wrathfully;
Let's carve him as a dish fit for the gods,
Not hew him as a carcass fit for hounds.   175
And let our hearts, as subtle masters do,
Stir up their servants° to an act of rage
And after seem to chide 'em. This shall make
Our purpose necessary, and not envious;°
Which so appearing to the common eyes,   180
We shall be called purgers,° not murderers.
And for° Mark Antony, think not of him;
For he can do no more than Caesar's arm
When Caesar's head is off.
CASSIUS   Yet I fear him,
For in the engrafted° love he bears to Caesar—   185
BRUTUS Alas, good Cassius, do not think of him.
If he love Caesar, all that he can do
Is to himself—take thought° and die for Caesar.
And that were much he should,° for he is given
To sports, to wildness, and much company.   190
TREBONIUS There is no fear° in him. Let him not die,
For he will live, and laugh at this hereafter.
                                        Clock strikes°

161 **annoy** injure   165 **envy** malice   172 **gentle** noble   177 **their servants** our
hands   179 **envious** malicious   181 **purgers** (1) those who heal by bleeding the
patient (2) those who purify by means of sacrifice   182 **for** as for   185 **engrafted**
firmly implanted   188 **take thought** give way to melancholy   189 **much he should**
more than is to be expected of him, hence unlikely; or, eminently desirable   191 **no
fear** nothing to fear   192.1 *Clock strikes* (an anachronism much commented upon;
the mechanical clock was not invented until c. 1300)

BRUTUS   Peace! Count the clock.

CASSIUS   The clock hath stricken three.

TREBONIUS   'Tis time to part.

CASSIUS   But it is doubtful yet
Whether Caesar will come forth today or no;   195
For he is superstitious grown of late,
Quite from the main opinion he held once
Of fantasy,° of dreams, and ceremonies.
It may be these apparent° prodigies,
The unaccustomed terror of this night,   200
And the persuasion of his augurers°
May hold him from the Capitol today.

DECIUS   Never fear that. If he be so resolved,
I can o'ersway him; for he loves to hear
That unicorns may be betrayed with trees,°   205
And bears with glasses,° elephants with holes,°
Lions with toils,° and men with flatterers;
But when I tell him he hates flatterers,
He says he does, being then most flattered.
Let me work;   210
For I can give his humor° the true bent,
And I will bring him to the Capitol.

CASSIUS   Nay, we will all of us be there to fetch him.

BRUTUS   By the eighth hour.° Is that the uttermost?°

CINNA   Be that the uttermost, and fail not then.   215

METELLUS   Caius Ligarius doth bear Caesar hard,°
Who rated° him for speaking well of Pompey.
I wonder none of you have thought of him.

BRUTUS   Now, good Metellus, go along by him.°
He loves me well, and I have given him reasons;   220
Send him but hither, and I'll fashion° him.

---

198 **fantasy** imaginings | **ceremonies** omens drawn from the performance of some
rite   199 **apparent** manifest, both visible and obvious   201 **augurers** augurs,
official interpreters of omens   205 **unicorns . . . trees** by having the unicorn
imprison itself by driving its horn into a tree as it charges at the hunter   206 **glasses**
mirrors (enabling the hunter to approach the bear while it dazzles itself in the
mirror) | **holes** pitfalls   207 **toils** nets, snares   211 **humor** disposition   214 **the
eighth hour** 8 A.M. (the Elizabethan way of reckoning time; by Roman reckoning,
the day began at 6 A.M., so that *the eighth hour* would be 2 P.M.) | **uttermost** latest
216 **bear Caesar hard** bear a grudge toward Caesar (see 1.2.309n)   217 **rated**
rebuked   219 **by him** by way of his house   221 **fashion** shape (to our purposes)

CASSIUS The morning comes upon 's. We'll leave you, Brutus.
And, friends, disperse yourselves; but all remember
What you have said, and show yourselves true Romans.
BRUTUS Good gentlemen, look fresh and merrily;   225
Let not our looks put on° our purposes,
But bear it as our Roman actors do,
With untired spirits and formal constancy.°
And so good morrow to you every one.
                                    Exeunt. Manet° Brutus
Boy! Lucius!°—Fast asleep? It is no matter.   230
Enjoy the honey-heavy dew of slumber.
Thou hast no figures° nor no fantasies
Which busy care draws in the brains of men;
Therefore thou sleep'st so sound.
                                    Enter Portia

PORTIA   Brutus, my lord!
BRUTUS Portia, what mean you? Wherefore rise you now?   235
It is not for your health thus to commit
Your weak condition to the raw cold morning.
PORTIA Nor for yours neither. You've ungently,° Brutus,
Stole from my bed. And yesternight, at supper,
You suddenly arose, and walked about   240
Musing and sighing, with your arms across,°
And when I asked you what the matter was,
You stared upon me with ungentle looks.
I urged you further; then you scratched your head
And too impatiently stamped with your foot.   245
Yet I insisted, yet° you answered not,
But with an angry wafture° of your hand
Gave sign for me to leave you. So I did,
Fearing to strengthen that impatience
Which seemed too much enkindled, and withal°   250

226 put on display, wear in open view   228 formal constancy steadfast appearance,
decorum   229.1 Manet he remains on stage   230 Lucius (Brutus calls to his
servant, who is evidently within, asleep, after having admitted the conspirators at
line 85; later, at line 310, he is still within when Brutus calls to him)   232 figures
imaginings   238 ungently discourteously, unkindly   241 across folded (a sign of
melancholy)   246 Yet . . . yet still . . . still   247 wafture waving   250 withal
moreover

Hoping it was but an effect of humor,°
Which sometime hath his° hour with every man.
It will not let you eat, nor talk, nor sleep,
And could it work so much upon your shape
As it hath much prevailed on your condition,°   255
I should not know you° Brutus. Dear my lord,
Make me acquainted with your cause of grief.
BRUTUS I am not well in health, and that is all.
PORTIA Brutus is wise, and were he not in health
He would embrace the means to come by it.   260
BRUTUS Why, so I do.° Good Portia, go to bed.
PORTIA Is Brutus sick? And is it physical°
To walk unbracèd° and suck up the humors°
Of the dank morning? What, is Brutus sick,
And will he steal out of his wholesome bed   265
To dare the vile contagion of the night,
And tempt the rheumy and unpurgèd° air
To add unto his sickness? No, my Brutus,
You have some sick offense within your mind,
Which by the right and virtue of my place   270
I ought to know of. [*She kneels*] And upon my knees
I charm° you, by my once-commended beauty,
By all your vows of love, and that great vow
Which did incorporate and make us one,
That you unfold to me, your self, your half,   275
Why you are heavy,° and what men tonight
Have had resort to you; for here have been
Some six or seven, who did hide their faces
Even from darkness.
BRUTUS   Kneel not, gentle Portia.
                              [*He raises her*]
PORTIA I should not need if you were gentle Brutus.   280
Within the bond of marriage, tell me, Brutus,

251 **humor** imbalance of temperament 252 **his** its 255 **condition** inner state of mind 256 **know you** recognize you as 261 **so I do** (said with a double meaning not perceived by Portia: I seek through Caesar's death the means to better the health of the state) 262 **physical** healthful 263 **unbracèd** with loosened clothing | **humors** damps, mists 267 **rheumy and unpurgèd** conducive to illness and not cleansed of its impurities (which night air was thought to contain) 272 **charm** conjure, entreat 276 **heavy** sad

Is it excepted° I should know no secrets
That appertain to you? Am I your self
But as it were in sort or limitation,°
To keep° with you at meals, comfort your bed,   285
And talk to you sometimes? Dwell I but in the suburbs°
Of your good pleasure? If it be no more,
Portia is Brutus' harlot, not his wife.
BRUTUS   You are my true and honorable wife,
As dear to me as are the ruddy drops   290
That visit my sad heart.
PORTIA   If this were true, then should I know this secret.
I grant I am a woman, but withal°
A woman that Lord Brutus took to wife.
I grant I am a woman, but withal   295
A woman well reputed, Cato's daughter.°
Think you I am no stronger than my sex,
Being so fathered and so husbanded?
Tell me your counsels, I will not disclose 'em.
I have made strong proof of my constancy,   300
Giving myself a voluntary wound
Here, in the thigh. Can I bear that with patience,
And not my husband's secrets?
BRUTUS   O ye gods,
Render me worthy of this noble wife!

                                               Knock [within]

Hark, hark, one knocks. Portia, go in awhile,   305
And by and by thy bosom shall partake
The secrets of my heart.
All my engagements I will construe° to thee,
All the charactery° of my sad brows.
Leave me with haste.   *Exit Portia*
   [*Calling*]   Lucius, who's that knocks?   310

      Enter Lucius and [Caius] Ligarius [wearing a kerchief]

---

282 **excepted** made an exception that   284 **in . . . limitation** only up to a point (a
legal phrase)   285 **keep** stay, be   286 **suburbs** periphery (in Elizabethan London,
prostitutes frequented the suburbs)   293 **withal** in addition   296 **Cato's daughter**
(Cato the Younger of Utica was famous for his integrity; he sided with Pompey
against Caesar in 48 B.C. and later killed himself rather than submit to Caesar's
tyranny; he was Brutus's uncle as well as his father-in-law)   308 **construe** explain
fully   309 **charactery** handwriting, what is figured there

LUCIUS   Here is a sick man° that would speak with you.
BRUTUS   Caius Ligarius, that Metellus spake of.
  Boy, stand aside.   [*Exit Lucius*]
              Caius Ligarius, how?°
LIGARIUS   Vouchsafe° good morrow from a feeble tongue.
BRUTUS   Oh, what a time have you chose out, brave° Caius,   315
  To wear a kerchief! Would you were not sick!
LIGARIUS   I am not sick, if Brutus have in hand
  Any exploit worthy the name of honor.
BRUTUS   Such an exploit have I in hand, Ligarius,
  Had you a healthful ear to hear of it.   320
LIGARIUS   By all the gods that Romans bow before,
  I here discard my sickness!   [*He throws off his kerchief*]
              Soul of Rome!
  Brave son, derived from honorable loins!
  Thou like an exorcist hast conjured up
  My mortifièd° spirit. Now bid me run,   325
  And I will strive with things impossible,
  Yea, get the better of them. What's to do?
BRUTUS   A piece of work that will make sick men whole.°
LIGARIUS   But are not some whole that we must make sick?
BRUTUS   That must we also. What it is, my Caius,   330
  I shall unfold to thee as we are going
  To whom° it must be done.
LIGARIUS   Set on your foot,
  And with a heart new-fired I follow you
  To do I know not what; but it sufficeth
  That Brutus leads me on.   *Thunder*
BRUTUS   Follow me, then.   *Exeunt* 335

❖

311 **sick man** (in Elizabethan medicine, a poultice was often applied to the forehead of a patient and wrapped in a handkerchief; hence the kerchief in line 316)   313 **how?** how are you?   314 **Vouchsafe** Deign (to accept)   315 **brave** noble   325 **mortifièd** deadened   328 **whole** healthy, free of the disease of tyranny   332 **To whom** to him to whom

ACT 2
SCENE 2

Location: Caesar's house.

Thunder and lightning. Enter Julius Caesar, in his nightgown°

CAESAR Nor° heaven nor earth have been at peace tonight.
Thrice hath Calpurnia in her sleep cried out,
"Help, ho, they murder Caesar!"—Who's within?

Enter a Servant

SERVANT My lord?
CAESAR Go bid the priests do present sacrifice°   5
And bring me their opinions of success.°
SERVANT I will, my lord.   *Exit*

Enter Calpurnia

CALPURNIA What mean you, Caesar? Think you to walk forth?
You shall not stir out of your house today.
CAESAR Caesar shall forth. The things that threatened me   10
Ne'er looked but on my back. When they shall see
The face of Caesar, they are vanishèd.
CALPURNIA Caesar, I never stood on ceremonies,°
Yet now they fright me. There is one within,
Besides the things that we have heard and seen,   15
Recounts most horrid sights seen by the watch.°
A lioness hath whelpèd° in the streets,
And graves have yawned° and yielded up their dead.
Fierce fiery warriors fight upon the clouds
In ranks and squadrons and right form° of war,   20
Which drizzled blood upon the Capitol.
The noise of battle hurtled° in the air;
Horses did neigh, and dying men did groan,
And ghosts did shriek and squeal about the streets.

0.2 **nightgown** housecoat 1 **Nor** Neither 5 **present sacrifice** immediate examination of the entrails of sacrificed animals for omens 6 **success** the result, what will follow 13 **stood on ceremonies** attached importance to omens 16 **watch** (an anachronism, since there was no *watch*, or "body of night watchmen," in Caesar's Rome) 17 **whelpèd** given birth 18 **yawned** gaped 20 **right form** regular formation 22 **hurtled** clashed

Oh, Caesar, these things are beyond all use,° 25
And I do fear them.
CAESAR What can be avoided
Whose end is purposed by the mighty gods?
Yet Caesar shall go forth; for these predictions
Are to the world in general as to Caesar.
CALPURNIA When beggars die there are no comets seen; 30
The heavens themselves blaze forth° the death of princes.
CAESAR Cowards die many times before their deaths;
The valiant never taste of death but once.
Of all the wonders that I yet have heard,
It seems to me most strange that men should fear, 35
Seeing that death, a necessary end,
Will come when it will come.

Enter a Servant

What say the augurers?°
SERVANT They would not have you to stir forth today.
Plucking the entrails of an offering forth,
They could not find a heart within the beast. 40
CAESAR The gods do this in shame of cowardice.
Caesar should be a beast without a heart
If he should stay at home today for fear.
No, Caesar shall not. Danger knows full well
That Caesar is more dangerous than he. 45
We are two lions littered in one day,
And I the elder and more terrible;
And Caesar shall go forth.
CALPURNIA Alas, my lord,
Your wisdom is consumed in confidence.°
Do not go forth today! Call it my fear 50
That keeps you in the house, and not your own.
We'll send Mark Antony to the Senate House,
And he shall say you are not well today.
Let me, upon my knee, prevail in this. [*She kneels*]

---

25 use normal experience   **31 blaze forth** proclaim (in a blaze of light)   **37 augurers** priests who revealed the will of the gods by interpreting thunder, lightning, and animal behavior; for Roman augury and its early modern counterparts, see 130–32, below   **49 consumed in confidence** destroyed by overconfidence

CAESAR   Mark Antony shall say I am not well,   55
And for thy humor° I will stay at home.

[He raises her]

Enter Decius

Here's Decius Brutus. He shall tell them so.
DECIUS   Caesar, all hail! Good morrow, worthy Caesar.
I come to fetch you to the Senate House.
CAESAR   And you are come in very happy° time   60
To bear my greeting to the senators
And tell them that I will not come today.
Cannot is false, and that I dare not, falser;
I will not come today. Tell them so, Decius.
CALPURNIA   Say he is sick.
CAESAR   Shall Caesar send a lie?   65
Have I in conquest stretched mine arm so far
To be afeard to tell graybeards the truth?
Decius, go tell them Caesar will not come.
DECIUS   Most mighty Caesar, let me know some cause,
Lest I be laughed at when I tell them so.   70
CAESAR   The cause is in my will: I will not come.
That is enough to satisfy the Senate.
But for your private satisfaction,
Because I love you, I will let you know.
Calpurnia here, my wife, stays me at home.   75
She dreamt tonight° she saw my statue,
Which like a fountain with an hundred spouts
Did run pure blood; and many lusty° Romans
Came smiling and did bathe their hands in it.
And these does she apply for° warnings and portents   80
Of evils imminent, and on her knee
Hath begged that I will stay at home today.
DECIUS   This dream is all amiss interpreted;°
It was a vision fair and fortunate.
Your statue spouting blood in many pipes,   85
In which so many smiling Romans bathed,

---

56 humor whim   **60 happy** opportune   **76 tonight** last night   **78 lusty** lively,
merry   **80 apply for** interpret as   **83 interpreted** for Elizabethan dream theory, see
152–59, below

Signifies that from you great Rome shall suck
Reviving blood, and that great men shall press°
For tinctures,° stains, relics, and cognizance.°
This by Calpurnia's dream is signified.   90
CAESAR   And this way have you well expounded it.
DECIUS   I have, when you have heard what I can say;
And know it now. The Senate have concluded
To give this day a crown to mighty Caesar.
If you shall send them word you will not come,   95
Their minds may change. Besides, it were a mock
Apt to be rendered° for someone to say
"Break up the Senate till another time
When Caesar's wife shall meet with better dreams."
If Caesar hide himself, shall they not whisper   100
"Lo, Caesar is afraid"?
Pardon me, Caesar, for my dear dear love
To your proceeding° bids me tell you this,
And reason to my love is liable.°
CAESAR   How foolish do your fears seem now, Calpurnia!   105
I am ashamèd I did yield to them.
Give me my robe, for I will go.

> *Enter Brutus, Ligarius, Metellus,*
> *Casca, Trebonius, Cinna, and Publius*

And look where Publius is come to fetch me.
PUBLIUS   Good morrow, Caesar.
CAESAR   Welcome, Publius.
What, Brutus, are you stirred so early too?   110
Good morrow, Casca. Caius Ligarius,
Caesar was ne'er so much your enemy
As that same ague° which hath made you lean.
What is't o'clock?
BRUTUS   Caesar, 'tis strucken eight.°

---

88 **press** crowd around   89 **tinctures** handkerchiefs dipped in the blood of martyrs, with healing powers; or colors in a coat of arms (*tinctures, stains,* and *relics* are all venerated properties, as though Caesar were a saint) | **cognizance** heraldic emblems worn by a nobleman's followers   96–7 **mock . . . rendered** sarcastic remark apt to be made   103 **proceeding** advantage   104 **reason . . . liable** my reasoning is swayed by my affection   113 **ague** fever   114 **eight** 8 A.M. (see 2.1.214n on Roman time)

CAESAR I thank you for your pains and courtesy.   115
                                              Enter Antony
    See, Antony, that revels long o' nights,
    Is notwithstanding up. Good morrow, Antony.
ANTONY So to most noble Caesar.
CAESAR [*to a Servant*] Bid them prepare within.°
                                              [*Exit Servant*]
    I am to blame to be thus waited for.   120
    Now, Cinna. Now, Metellus. What, Trebonius,
    I have an hour's talk in store for you;
    Remember that you call on me today.
    Be near me, that I may remember you.
TREBONIUS Caesar, I will. [*Aside*] And so near will I be   125
    That your best friends shall wish I had been further.
CAESAR Good friends, go in and taste some wine with me,
    And we, like friends, will straightway go together.
BRUTUS [*aside*] That every like is not the same,° O Caesar,
    The heart of Brutus earns° to think upon!   *Exeunt* 130

ACT 2
SCENE 3
Location: A street near the Capitol.

Enter Artemidorus [reading a paper]

ARTEMIDORUS "Caesar, beware of Brutus; take heed of Cassius;
    come not near Casca; have an eye to Cinna; trust not
    Trebonius; mark well Metellus Cimber; Decius Brutus loves
    thee not; thou hast wronged Caius Ligarius. There is but one
    mind in all these men, and it is bent against Caesar. If thou   5

---

119 prepare within set out wine in the other room and prepare to leave (perhaps
addressed to the servant who entered at line 37, or to Calpurnia); the ritual
drinking of wine is a pledge of friendship that should preclude violence; see lines
127–8 **129 That . . . same** that not all those who behave "like friends" (line 128)
are actually so (proverbial) **130 earns** grieves

be'st not immortal, look about you. Security gives° way to
conspiracy. The mighty gods defend thee! Thy lover,°
                          Artemidorus.''
Here will I stand till Caesar pass along,
And as a suitor will I give him this.   10
My heart laments that virtue cannot live
Out of the teeth of emulation.°
If thou read this, O Caesar, thou mayest live;
If not, the Fates with traitors do contrive.°   *Exit*

ACT 2
SCENE 4

Location: Before the house of Brutus.

                         Enter Portia and Lucius

PORTIA   I prithee, boy, run to the Senate House.
Stay not to answer me, but get thee gone.—
Why dost thou stay?
LUCIUS   To know my errand, madam.
PORTIA   I would have had thee there and here again
Ere I can tell thee what thou shouldst do there.   5
[*Aside*] O constancy,° be strong upon my side;
Set a huge mountain 'tween my heart and tongue!
I have a man's mind, but a woman's might.
How hard it is for women to keep counsel!°—
Art thou here yet?
LUCIUS   Madam, what should I do?   10
Run to the Capitol, and nothing else?
And so return to you, and nothing else?
PORTIA   Yes, bring me word, boy, if thy lord look well,
For he went sickly forth; and take good note
What Caesar doth, what suitors press to him.   15
Hark, boy, what noise is that?

6 **Security gives way** overconfidence opens a path   7 **lover** friend   12 **Out . . .
emulation** beyond the bite of grudging envy   14 **contrive** conspire
6 **constancy** resolution   9 **counsel** a secret

LUCIUS I hear none, madam.
PORTIA Prithee, listen well.
I heard a bustling rumor,° like a fray,°
And the wind brings it from the Capitol.   20
LUCIUS Sooth,° madam, I hear nothing.

Enter the Soothsayer

PORTIA Come hither, fellow. Which way hast thou been?
SOOTHSAYER At mine own house, good lady.
PORTIA What is't o'clock?
SOOTHSAYER   About the ninth hour,° lady.
PORTIA Is Caesar yet gone to the Capitol?   25
SOOTHSAYER Madam, not yet. I go to take my stand,
To see him pass on to the Capitol.
PORTIA Thou hast some suit to Caesar, hast thou not?
SOOTHSAYER That I have, lady, if it will please Caesar
To be so good to Caesar as to hear me: 30
I shall beseech him to befriend himself.
PORTIA Why, know'st thou any harm 's intended towards him?
SOOTHSAYER
None that I know will be, much that I fear may chance.
Good morrow to you. Here the street is narrow.
The throng that follows Caesar at the heels,   35
Of senators, of praetors,° common suitors,
Will crowd a feeble man almost to death.
I'll get me to a place more void,° and there
Speak to great Caesar as he comes along.   *Exit*
PORTIA I must go in. Ay me, how weak a thing   40
The heart of woman is! O Brutus,
The heavens speed thee in thine enterprise!—
Sure, the boy heard me.—Brutus hath a suit
That Caesar will not grant.—Oh, I grow faint.—
Run, Lucius, and commend me to my lord;   45
Say I am merry.° Come to me again
And bring me word what he doth say to thee.
                          Exeunt [separately]

---

19 bustling rumor confused sound | **fray** fight   **21 Sooth** truly   **24 the ninth hour**
9 A.M. (in Roman reckoning, the ninth hour would be 3 P.M.)   **36 praetors** judges
38 void empty, uncrowded   **46 merry** cheerful (not "mirthful")

❖

ACT 3
SCENE 1

*Location: Before the Capitol, and,
following line 12, within the Capitol.*

*Flourish. Enter Caesar, Brutus, Cassius, Casca,
Decius, Metellus [Cimber], Trebonius, Cinna, Antony,
Lepidus, Artemidorus, Publius, [Popilius Lena], and
the Soothsayer; [others following°]*

CAESAR [*to the Soothsayer*]   The ides of March are come.

SOOTHSAYER   Ay, Caesar, but not gone.

ARTEMIDORUS   Hail, Caesar! Read this schedule.°

DECIUS   Trebonius doth desire you to o'erread,
At your best leisure, this his humble suit.   5

ARTEMIDORUS   O Caesar, read mine first, for mine's a suit
That touches Caesar nearer. Read it, great Caesar.

CAESAR   What touches us ourself shall be last served.°

ARTEMIDORUS   Delay not, Caesar, read it instantly.

CAESAR   What, is the fellow mad?

PUBLIUS   Sirrah,° give place.°   10

CASSIUS
What, urge you your petitions in the street?
Come to the Capitol.

                    [*Caesar goes to the Capitol and
                    takes his place, the rest following*]

POPILIUS [*to Cassius*]   I wish your enterprise today may thrive.

CASSIUS   What enterprise, Popilius?

POPILIUS [*to Cassius*]   Fare you well.   15

                              [*He advances to Caesar*]

BRUTUS   What said Popilius Lena?

CASSIUS   He wished today our enterprise might thrive.
I fear our purpose is discoverèd.

0.4 others following (citizens may be present, though not certainly so; see lines 83
and 93–4)   **3 schedule** document   **8 What … served** in Plutarch, Caesar is anxious
to read the letter precisely because it "touches" his interests; see 108–9, below
10 Sirrah fellow (a form of address to a social inferior) | **place** way

BRUTUS Look how he makes to Caesar. Mark him.

[*Popilius speaks apart to Caesar*]

CASSIUS Casca, be sudden, for we fear prevention.   20
Brutus, what shall be done? If this be known,
Cassius or Caesar never shall turn back,
For I will slay myself.°

BRUTUS   Cassius, be constant.°
Popilius Lena speaks not of our purposes;
For look, he smiles, and Caesar doth not change.°   25

CASSIUS Trebonius knows his time, for look you, Brutus,
He draws Mark Antony out of the way.

[*Exit Trebonius with Antony*]

DECIUS Where is Metellus Cimber? Let him go
And presently prefer° his suit to Caesar.

BRUTUS He is addressed.° Press near and second him.   30

CINNA Casca, you are the first that rears your hand.

[*They press near Caesar*]

CAESAR Are we all ready? What is now amiss
That Caesar and his Senate must redress?

METELLUS [*kneeling*]
Most high, most mighty, and most puissant° Caesar,
Metellus Cimber throws before thy seat   35
An humble heart—

CAESAR   I must prevent thee, Cimber.
These couchings and these lowly courtesies°
Might fire the blood of ordinary men,
And turn preordinance and first decree
Into the law of children.° Be not fond°   40
To think that Caesar bears such rebel° blood
That will be thawed from the true quality°
With that which melteth fools—I mean, sweet words,
Low-crookèd curtsies, and base spaniel fawning.

22–3 Cassius . . . myself either Cassius or Caesar will never return from the Capitol alive, for I will commit suicide if this attempt fails   **23 be constant** hold steady   **25 change** change expression   **29 presently prefer** immediately urge   **30 addressed** ready   **34 puissant** powerful   **37 couchings . . . courtesies** kneelings and submissive bows   **39–40 And turn . . . children** and turn preordained law into the kinds of childish and flexible rules that children use in their games   **40 fond** so foolish as   **41 rebel** rebellious against reason   **42 true quality** proper firmness and stability (the metaphor is from alchemy)

Thy brother by decree is banishèd.   45
If thou dost bend° and pray and fawn for him,
I spurn thee like a cur out of my way.
Know, Caesar doth not wrong, nor without cause
Will he be satisfied.
METELLUS   Is there no voice more worthy than my own   50
   To sound more sweetly in great Caesar's ear
   For the repealing° of my banished brother?
BRUTUS [*kneeling*]   I kiss thy hand, but not in flattery, Caesar,
   Desiring thee that Publius Cimber may
   Have an immediate freedom of repeal.°   55
CAESAR   What, Brutus?
CASSIUS [*kneeling*]   Pardon, Caesar! Caesar, pardon!
   As low as to thy foot doth Cassius fall,
   To beg enfranchisement° for Publius Cimber.
CAESAR   I could be well moved, if I were as you;
   If I could pray to move,° prayers would move me.   60
   But I am constant as the northern star,°
   Of whose true-fixed and resting° quality
   There is no fellow° in the firmament.
   The skies are painted with unnumbered sparks;
   They are all fire and every one doth shine;   65
   But there's but one in all doth hold his place.
   So in the world: 'tis furnished well with men,
   And men are flesh and blood, and apprehensive;°
   Yet in the number I do know but one
   That unassailable holds on his rank,°   70
   Unshaked of motion.° And that I am he,
   Let me a little show it even in this:
   That I was constant Cimber should be banished,
   And constant do remain to keep him so.
CINNA [*kneeling*]
   O Caesar—
CAESAR   Hence! Wilt thou lift up Olympus?°   75

---

46 bend bow   **52 repealing** recall   **55 freedom of repeal** permission to return
58 enfranchisement restoration of citizenship   **60 pray to move** make petition (as
you do)   **61 northern star** polestar   **62 resting** remaining stationary   **63 fellow**
equal   **68 apprehensive** capable of perception   **70 rank** place in line or file,
position   **71 Unshaked of motion** (1) unswayed by petitions (2) with perfect
steadiness   **75 Olympus** mountain dwelling of the Greek gods

DECIUS *[kneeling]*
  Great Caesar—
CAESAR   Doth not Brutus bootless° kneel?
CASCA   Speak hands for me!
      They stab Caesar, [Casca first, Brutus last]
CAESAR   *Et tu, Brutè?*° Then fall, Caesar!   *Dies*
CINNA   Liberty! Freedom! Tyranny is dead!
  Run hence, proclaim, cry it about the streets.   80
CASSIUS   Some to the common pulpits,° and cry out
  "Liberty, freedom, and enfranchisement!"°
BRUTUS   People and senators, be not affrighted.
  Fly not; stand still. Ambition's debt° is paid.
CASCA   Go to the pulpit, Brutus.
DECIUS   And Cassius too.   85
BRUTUS   Where's Publius?°
CINNA   Here, quite confounded with this mutiny.°
METELLUS   Stand fast together, lest some friend of Caesar's
  Should chance—
BRUTUS   Talk not of standing.° Publius, good cheer.   90
  There is no harm intended to your person,
  Nor to no Roman else. So tell them, Publius.
CASSIUS   And leave us, Publius, lest that the people,
  Rushing on us, should do your age some mischief.
BRUTUS   Do so, and let no man abide° this deed   95
  But we the doers.   *[Exeunt all but the conspirators]*

                      Enter Trebonius

CASSIUS   Where is Antony?
TREBONIUS   Fled to his house amazed.
  Men, wives, and children stare, cry out, and run
  As° it were doomsday.
BRUTUS   Fates, we will know your pleasures.
  That we shall die, we know; 'tis but the time,   100
  And drawing days out, that men stand upon.°

76 bootless in vain   **78 Et tu, Brutè?** You too, Brutus? (literally, "Even thou")
81 common pulpits public platforms or rostra   **82 enfranchisement** restoration of
civil rights (cf. line 58 above)   **84 Ambition's debt** what Caesar's ambition deserved
86 Publius (an old senator, too confused to flee)   **87 mutiny** uprising, discord
90 standing making a stand   **95 abide** (1) suffer the consequences of (2) remain
here with   **99 As** as if   **100–1 'tis . . . upon** it is only the time of our deaths, and
how long we have to live, that we are uncertain about, make a question of

CASCA   Why, he that cuts off twenty years of life
Cuts off so many years of fearing death.
BRUTUS   Grant that, and then is death a benefit.
So are we Caesar's friends, that have abridged   105
His time of fearing death. Stoop, Romans, stoop,
And let us bathe our hands in Caesar's blood
Up to the elbows and besmear our swords.
Then walk we forth even to the marketplace,°
And, waving our red weapons o'er our heads,   110
Let's all cry "Peace, freedom, and liberty!"
CASSIUS
Stoop, then, and wash. [*They bathe their hands and weapons*]
How many ages hence
Shall this our lofty scene be acted over
In states unborn and accents° yet unknown!
BRUTUS   How many times shall Caesar bleed in sport,°   115
That now on Pompey's basis lies along°
No worthier than the dust!
CASSIUS   So oft as that shall be,
So often shall the knot° of us be called
The men that gave their country liberty.   120
DECIUS   What, shall we forth?
CASSIUS   Ay, every man away.
Brutus shall lead, and we will grace his heels
With the most boldest and best hearts of Rome.

                              Enter a Servant

BRUTUS   Soft, who comes here? A friend of Antony's.
SERVANT [*kneeling*]   Thus, Brutus, did my master bid me kneel;   125
Thus did Mark Antony bid me fall down,
And, being prostrate, thus he bade me say:
"Brutus is noble, wise, valiant, and honest;
Caesar was mighty, bold, royal, and loving.
Say I love Brutus and I honor him;   130
Say I feared Caesar, honored him, and loved him.
If Brutus will vouchsafe that Antony

---

109 the marketplace the Forum   **114 accents** languages   **115 in sport** for
entertainment   **116 on Pompey's . . . along** lies prostrate on the pedestal of
Pompey's statue   **119 knot** group

May safely come to him and be resolved°
How Caesar hath deserved to lie in death,
Mark Antony shall not love Caesar dead   135
So well as Brutus living, but will follow
The fortunes and affairs of noble Brutus
Thorough° the hazards of this untrod state°
With all true faith." So says my master Antony.
BRUTUS Thy master is a wise and valiant Roman;   140
I never thought him worse.
Tell him, so° please him come unto this place,
He shall be satisfied and, by my honor,
Depart untouched.
SERVANT   I'll fetch him presently.°
                                        Exit Servant
BRUTUS I know that we shall have him well to friend.°   145
CASSIUS I wish we may. But yet have I a mind
That fears° him much, and my misgiving still
Falls shrewdly to the purpose.°

                                        Enter Antony

BRUTUS But here comes Antony.—Welcome, Mark Antony.
ANTONY O mighty Caesar! Dost thou lie so low?   150
Are all thy conquests, glories, triumphs, spoils,
Shrunk to this little measure? Fare thee well.—
I know not, gentlemen, what you intend,
Who else must be let blood,° who else is rank;°
If I myself, there is no hour so fit   155
As Caesar's death's hour, nor no instrument
Of half that worth as those your swords, made rich
With the most noble blood of all this world.
I do beseech ye, if you bear me hard,°
Now, whilst your purpled° hands do reek° and smoke,   160
Fulfill your pleasure. Live° a thousand years,
I shall not find myself so apt° to die;

---

133 **be resolved** receive an explanation 138 **Thorough** through | **untrod state** still unexplored state of affairs 142 **so** if it should 144 **presently** immediately 145 **to friend** for a friend 147 **fears** distrusts 148 **Falls . . . purpose** is intensely to the point 154 **let blood** bled (a medical term), killed | **rank** swollen, diseased (and hence in need of bleeding) 159 **bear me hard** bear ill will to me 160 **purpled** bloody | **reek** steam 161 **Live** if I should live 162 **apt** ready

No place will please me so, no mean of death,
As here by Caesar, and by you cut off,
The choice and master spirits of this age.   165
BRUTUS   Oh, Antony, beg not your death of us.
Though now we must appear bloody and cruel,
As by our hands and this our present act
You see we do, yet see you but our hands
And this the bleeding business they have done.   170
Our hearts you see not. They are pitiful;°
And pity to the general wrong of Rome—
As fire drives out fire, so pity pity°—
Hath done this deed on Caesar. For your part,
To you our swords have leaden° points, Mark Antony.   175
Our arms in strength of malice, and our hearts
Of brothers' temper,° do receive you in
With all kind love, good thoughts, and reverence.
CASSIUS   Your voice shall be as strong as any man's
In the disposing of new dignities.°   180
BRUTUS   Only be patient till we have appeased
The multitude, beside themselves with fear,
And then we will deliver you the cause
Why I, that did love Caesar when I struck him,
Have thus proceeded.
ANTONY   I doubt not of your wisdom.   185
Let each man render me his bloody hand.
                    [*He shakes hands with the conspirators*]
First, Marcus Brutus, will I shake with you;
Next, Caius Cassius, do I take your hand;
Now, Decius Brutus, yours; now yours, Metellus;
Yours, Cinna; and, my valiant Casca, yours;   190
Though last, not least in love, yours, good Trebonius.
Gentlemen all—alas, what shall I say?
My credit° now stands on such slippery ground
That one of two bad ways you must conceit° me,
Either a coward or a flatterer.   195

---

171 pitiful full of pity   **173 pity pity** pity for the general wrong of Rome has driven
out pity for Caesar   **175 leaden** blunt   **176–7 Our . . . temper** both our arms, though
seeming strong in enmity, and our hearts, full of brotherly feeling   **180 dignities**
offices of state   **193 credit** credibility   **194 conceit** think, judge

That I did love thee, Caesar, oh, 'tis true!
If then thy spirit look upon us now,
Shall it not grieve thee dearer° than thy death
To see thy Antony making his peace,
Shaking the bloody fingers of thy foes—   200
Most noble—in the presence of thy corpse?
Had I as many eyes as thou hast wounds,
Weeping as fast as they stream forth thy blood,
It would become me better than to close°
In terms of friendship with thine enemies.   205
Pardon me, Julius! Here wast thou bayed,° brave hart,°
Here didst thou fall, and here thy hunters stand,
Signed in thy spoil° and crimsoned in thy lethe.°
O world, thou wast the forest to this hart,
And this indeed, O world, the heart of thee!   210
How like a deer, strucken by many princes,
Dost thou here lie!
CASSIUS   Mark Antony—
ANTONY   Pardon me, Caius Cassius.
The enemies° of Caesar shall say this;
Then in a friend it is cold modesty.°   215
CASSIUS   I blame you not for praising Caesar so,
But what compact mean you to have with us?
Will you be pricked° in number of our friends,
Or shall we on and not depend on you?
ANTONY   Therefore I took your hands, but was indeed   220
Swayed from the point by looking down on Caesar.
Friends am I with you all, and love you all,
Upon this hope, that you shall give me reasons
Why and wherein Caesar was dangerous.
BRUTUS   Or else were this° a savage spectacle.   225
Our reasons are so full of good regard°

---

198 **dearer** more deeply   204 **close** come to an agreement   206 **bayed** brought to
bay | **hart** stag (with pun on *heart*)   208 **Signed . . . spoil** marked with the tokens
of your slaughter (the *spoil* in hunting is the cutting up of the quarry and
distribution of reward to the hounds) | **lethe** river of oblivion in the underworld,
here associated with death and blood (perhaps fused with Cocytus, river of blood in
the underworld)   214 **The enemies** even the enemies   215 **cold modesty** sober
moderation   218 **pricked** marked down   225 **else were this** otherwise this would be
226 **regard** account, consideration

That were you, Antony, the son of Caesar,
You should be satisfied.

ANTONY　　　　　　　　　That's all I seek,
And am moreover suitor that I may
Produce° his body to the marketplace,°　　　　　　　　230
And in the pulpit,° as becomes a friend,
Speak in the order° of his funeral.

BRUTUS　You shall, Mark Antony.

CASSIUS　　　　　　　　　Brutus, a word with you.
[*Aside to Brutus*] You know not what you do. Do not
　consent
That Antony speak in his funeral.　　　　　　　　235
Know you how much the people may be moved
By that which he will utter?

BRUTUS [*aside to Cassius*]　　　　By your pardon:
I will myself into the pulpit first
And show the reason of our Caesar's death.
What Antony shall speak, I will protest°　　　　　　　240
He speaks by leave and by permission,
And that we are contented Caesar shall
Have all true rites and lawful ceremonies.
It shall advantage more than do us wrong.

CASSIUS [*aside to Brutus*]
I know not what may fall.° I like it not.　　　　　　　245

BRUTUS　Mark Antony, here, take you Caesar's body.
You shall not in your funeral speech blame us,
But speak all good you can devise of Caesar,
And say you do't by our permission.
Else shall you not have any hand at all　　　　　　　250
About his funeral. And you shall speak
In the same pulpit whereto I am going,
After my speech is ended.

ANTONY　　　　　　　　　Be it so.
I do desire no more.

BRUTUS　Prepare the body then, and follow us.　　　　　　　255

　　　　　　　　　　　　Exeunt. Manet° Antony

---

230 Produce bring forth | **marketplace** forum　**231 pulpit** public platform　**232 order** ceremony　**240 protest** announce, insist　**245 fall** befall, happen　**255.1 Manet** he remains onstage

ANTONY Oh, pardon me, thou bleeding piece of earth,
That I am meek and gentle with these butchers!°
Thou art the ruins of the noblest man
That ever livèd in the tide of times.°
Woe to the hand that shed this costly° blood!   260
Over thy wounds now do I prophesy—
Which, like dumb mouths, do ope their ruby lips
To beg the voice and utterance of my tongue—
A curse shall light upon the limbs of men;
Domestic fury and fierce civil strife   265
Shall cumber° all the parts of Italy;
Blood and destruction shall be so in use
And dreadful objects° so familiar
That mothers shall but smile when they behold
Their infants quartered° with the hands of war,   270
All pity choked with custom of fell deeds;°
And Caesar's spirit, ranging° for revenge,
With Ate° by his side come hot from hell,
Shall in these confines° with a monarch's° voice
Cry havoc° and let slip° the dogs of war,   275
That this foul deed shall smell above the earth
With carrion men, groaning for burial.

      Enter Octavius's Servant

You serve Octavius Caesar, do you not?
SERVANT I do, Mark Antony.
ANTONY Caesar did write for him to come to Rome.   280
SERVANT He did receive his letters,° and is coming,
And bid me say to you by word of mouth—
O Caesar!—   *[Seeing the body]*
ANTONY Thy heart is big. Get thee apart and weep.
Passion,° I see, is catching, for mine eyes,   285

---

257 butchers precisely the reaction that Brutus had hoped to avoid (2.1.167) **259 tide of times** course of all history **260 costly** (1) valuable (2) fraught with dire consequences **266 cumber** overwhelm; entangle, burden **268 objects** sights **270 quartered** cut to pieces **271 custom . . . deeds** the familiarity of cruel deeds **272 ranging** roaming up and down in search of prey **273 Ate** goddess of discord and moral chaos **274 confines** regions | **monarch's** authoritative **275 Cry havoc** give the signal for sack, pillage, and slaughter, taking no prisoners | **let slip** unleash **281 letters** (not necessarily plural; the Latin word for letter, *litterae*, has a plural form) **285 Passion** sorrow

Seeing those beads of sorrow stand in thine,
Began to water. Is thy master coming?
SERVANT   He lies° tonight within seven leagues° of Rome.
ANTONY   Post° back with speed and tell him what hath chanced.°
Here is a mourning Rome,° a dangerous Rome,   290
No Rome° of safety for Octavius yet;
Hie hence and tell him so. Yet stay awhile;
Thou shalt not back till I have borne this corpse
Into the marketplace. There shall I try,°
In my oration, how the people take   295
The cruel issue° of these bloody men,
According to the which° thou shalt discourse
To young Octavius° of the state of things.
Lend me your hand.   *Exeunt [with Caesar's body]*

ACT 3
SCENE 2

Location: The Forum.

*Enter Brutus and [presently] goes into the
pulpit, and Cassius, with the Plebeians*

PLEBEIANS   We will be satisfied! Let us be satisfied!°
BRUTUS   Then follow me, and give me audience, friends.—
Cassius, go you into the other street
And part° the numbers.
Those that will hear me speak, let 'em stay here;   5
Those that will follow Cassius, go with him;
And public reasons shall be renderèd
Of Caesar's death.
FIRST PLEBEIAN   I will hear Brutus speak.
SECOND PLEBEIAN   I will hear Cassius, and compare their reasons
When severally° we hear them renderèd.   10
            [Exit Cassius, with some of the Plebeians]

288 **lies** lodges | **seven leagues** about twenty miles   289 **Post** ride | **chanced**
happened   291 **Rome** (with pun on "room," as at 1.2.156)   294 **try** test   296 **cruel
issue** outcome of the cruelty   297 **the which** the outcome of which   298 **young
Octavius** (he was eighteen in March of 44 B.C.)

1 **be satisfied** have an explanation   4 **part** divide   10 **severally** separately

THIRD PLEBEIAN   The noble Brutus is ascended. Silence!

BRUTUS   Be patient till the last.
Romans, countrymen, and lovers,° hear me for my cause,
and be silent that you may hear. Believe me for mine honor,
and have respect to mine honor, that you may believe.   15
Censure° me in your wisdom, and awake your senses,° that
you may the better judge. If there be any in this assembly,
any dear friend of Caesar's, to him I say that Brutus' love to
Caesar was no less than his. If then that friend demand why
Brutus rose against Caesar, this is my answer: not that I   20
loved Caesar less, but that I loved Rome more. Had you
rather Caesar were living and die all slaves, than that Caesar
were dead, to live all free men?° As Caesar loved me, I weep
for him; as he was fortunate, I rejoice at it; as he was valiant,
I honor him; but, as he was ambitious, I slew him. There is   25
tears for his love; joy for his fortune; honor for his valor;
and death for his ambition. Who is here so base that would
be a bondman? If any, speak, for him have I offended. Who
is here so rude° that would not be a Roman? If any, speak,
for him have I offended. Who is here so vile that will not   30
love his country? If any, speak, for him have I offended. I
pause for a reply.

ALL   None, Brutus, none!

BRUTUS   Then none have I offended. I have done no more to
Caesar than you shall do to Brutus.° The question of his   35
death is enrolled° in the Capitol, his glory not extenuated°
wherein he was worthy, nor his offenses enforced° for which
he suffered death.

Enter Mark Antony [and others] with Caesar's body

Here comes his body, mourned by Mark Antony, who,
though he had no hand in his death, shall receive the benefit   40
of his dying, a place in the commonwealth, as which of you

13 **lovers** friends (this speech by Brutus is in what Plutarch calls the Lacedemonian
or Spartan style, brief and sententious; its content is original with Shakespeare)
16 **Censure** judge | **senses** intellectual powers   21–23 **Had . . . men?** for a reading
of this complex question, see p. xxx of the Introduction   29 **rude** barbarous   35 **than
. . . Brutus** (in lines 43–44 below, Brutus offers to die for Rome if his country should
ask)   35–36 **The question . . . enrolled** the considerations that necessitated his death
are recorded   36 **extenuated** minimized   37 **enforced** exaggerated, insisted upon

shall not? With this I depart, that, as I slew my best lover°
for the good of Rome, I have the same dagger for myself
when it shall please my country to need my death.°

ALL   Live, Brutus, live, live!   *[Brutus comes down]*   45

FIRST PLEBEIAN   Bring him with triumph home unto his house.

SECOND PLEBEIAN°   Give him a statue with his ancestors.

THIRD PLEBEIAN   Let him be Caesar.

FOURTH PLEBEIAN   Caesar's better parts
Shall be crowned in Brutus.

FIRST PLEBEIAN
We'll bring him to his house with shouts and clamors.   50

BRUTUS   My countrymen—

SECOND PLEBEIAN   Peace, silence! Brutus speaks.

FIRST PLEBEIAN   Peace, ho!

BRUTUS   Good countrymen, let me depart alone,
And, for my sake, stay here with Antony.
Do grace° to Caesar's corpse, and grace his° speech   55
Tending to° Caesar's glories, which Mark Antony,
By our permission, is allowed to make.
I do entreat you, not a man depart,
Save I alone, till Antony have spoke.   *Exit*

FIRST PLEBEIAN   Stay, ho, and let us hear Mark Antony.   60

THIRD PLEBEIAN   Let him go up into the public chair.
We'll hear him. Noble Antony, go up.

ANTONY   For Brutus' sake I am beholding° to you.
                              [He goes into the pulpit]

FOURTH PLEBEIAN   What does he say of Brutus?

THIRD PLEBEIAN   He says, for Brutus' sake   65
He finds himself beholding to us all.

FOURTH PLEBEIAN   'Twere best he speak no harm of Brutus here.

FIRST PLEBEIAN
This Caesar was a tyrant.

THIRD PLEBEIAN   Nay, that's certain.
We are blest that Rome is rid of him.

---

42 lover friend   **43–44 I . . . death** compare Caesar offering his throat to the people
(1.2.263–66)   **47 SECOND PLEBEIAN** (not the same person who exited at line 10; the
numbering here refers to those who stay to hear Brutus)   **55 Do grace** show respect
| **grace his speech** listen courteously to Antony's speech   **56 Tending to** relating to,
dealing with   **63 beholding** beholden

SECOND PLEBEIAN   Peace! Let us hear what Antony can say.   70
ANTONY   You gentle Romans—
ALL   Peace, ho! Let us hear him.
ANTONY   Friends,° Romans, countrymen, lend me your ears.
I come to bury Caesar, not to praise him.
The evil that men do lives after them;
The good is oft interrèd with their bones.   75
So let it be with Caesar. The noble Brutus
Hath told you Caesar was ambitious.
If it were so, it was a grievous fault,
And grievously hath Caesar answered° it.
Here, under leave° of Brutus and the rest—   80
For Brutus is an honorable man,
So are they all, all honorable men—
Come I to speak in Caesar's funeral.
He was my friend, faithful and just to me;
But Brutus says he was ambitious,   85
And Brutus is an honorable man.
He hath brought many captives home to Rome,
Whose ransoms did the general coffers fill.
Did this in Caesar seem ambitious?
When that the poor have cried, Caesar hath wept;   90
Ambition should be made of sterner stuff.
Yet Brutus says he was ambitious,
And Brutus is an honorable man.
You all did see that on the Lupercal°
I thrice presented him a kingly crown,   95
Which he did thrice refuse. Was this ambition?
Yet Brutus says he was ambitious,
And sure he is an honorable man.
I speak not to disprove what Brutus spoke,
But here I am to speak what I do know.   100
You all did love him once, not without cause.
What cause withholds you then to mourn for him?

---

72 Friends (this speech by Antony is thought to illustrate the Asiatic or "florid" style of speaking; in it Shakespeare gathers various hints from Plutarch ("Marcus Antonius" and "Dion") and Appian, but the speech is Shakespeare's invention) **79 answered** paid the penalty for   **80 under leave** by permission   **94 Lupercal** (see 1.1.66 and note)

O judgment! Thou art fled to brutish beasts,
And men have lost their reason. Bear with me;
My heart is in the coffin there with Caesar,   105
And I must pause till it come back to me.
FIRST PLEBEIAN Methinks there is much reason in his sayings.
SECOND PLEBEIAN If thou consider rightly of the matter,
Caesar has had great wrong.
THIRD PLEBEIAN   Has he, masters?°
I fear there will a worse come in his place.   110
FOURTH PLEBEIAN
Marked ye his words? He would not take the crown,
Therefore 'tis certain he was not ambitious.
FIRST PLEBEIAN If it be found so, some will dear abide it.°
SECOND PLEBEIAN
Poor soul, his eyes are red as fire with weeping.
THIRD PLEBEIAN
There's not a nobler man in Rome than Antony.   115
FOURTH PLEBEIAN Now mark him. He begins again to speak.
ANTONY But yesterday the word of Caesar might
Have stood against the world. Now lies he there,
And none so poor to do him reverence.°
Oh, masters, if I were disposed to stir   120
Your hearts and minds to mutiny° and rage,
I should do Brutus wrong, and Cassius wrong,
Who, you all know, are honorable men.
I will not do them wrong; I rather choose
To wrong the dead, to wrong myself and you,   125
Than I will wrong such honorable men.
But here's a parchment with the seal of Caesar.
I found it in his closet;° 'tis his will.
                            [*He shows the will*]
Let but the commons° hear this testament—
Which, pardon me, I do not mean to read—   130
And they would go and kiss dead Caesar's wounds
And dip their napkins° in his sacred blood,

109 **masters** good sirs 113 **dear abide it** pay a heavy penalty for it 119 **And none**
... **reverence** and yet no one is below him in fortune now, no one of even the lowest
social station to look up to and revere him 121 **mutiny** riot, tumult 128 **closet**
private chamber, study 129 **commons** common people 132 **napkins** handkerchiefs
(compare 2.2.75–90)

Yea, beg a hair of him for memory,
And dying, mention it within their wills,
Bequeathing it as a rich legacy   135
Unto their issue.
FOURTH PLEBEIAN   We'll hear the will! Read it, Mark Antony.
ALL   The will, the will! We will hear Caesar's will.
ANTONY   Have patience, gentle friends: I must not read it.
It is not meet° you know how Caesar loved you.   140
You are not wood, you are not stones, but men;
And being men, hearing the will of Caesar,
It will inflame you, it will make you mad.
'Tis good you know not that you are his heirs,
For if you should, oh, what would come of it?   145
FOURTH PLEBEIAN   Read the will! We'll hear it, Antony.
You shall read us the will, Caesar's will.
ANTONY   Will you be patient? Will you stay awhile?
I have o'ershot myself° to tell you of it.
I fear I wrong the honorable men   150
Whose daggers have stabbed Caesar; I do fear it.
FOURTH PLEBEIAN   They were traitors. "Honorable men"!
ALL   The will! The testament!
SECOND PLEBEIAN
They were villains, murderers. The will! Read the will!
ANTONY   You will compel me then to read the will?   155
Then make a ring about the corpse of Caesar
And let me show you him that made the will.
Shall I descend? And will you give me leave?
ALL   Come down.
SECOND PLEBEIAN   Descend.   160
THIRD PLEBEIAN   You shall have leave.
        [*Antony comes down. They gather around Caesar*]
FOURTH PLEBEIAN   A ring; stand round.
FIRST PLEBEIAN   Stand from the hearse.° Stand from the body.
SECOND PLEBEIAN   Room for Antony, most noble Antony!
ANTONY   Nay, press not so upon me. Stand farre° off.   165
ALL   Stand back! Room! Bear back!

---

140 meet fitting that   **149 o'ershot myself** gone further than I should   **163 hearse**
bier   **165 farre** farther

ANTONY   If you have tears, prepare to shed them now.
You all do know this mantle.° I remember
The first time ever Caesar put it on;
'Twas on a summer's evening in his tent,   170
That day he overcame the Nervii.°
Look, in this place ran Cassius' dagger through.
See what a rent the envious° Casca made.
Through this the well-belovèd Brutus stabbed,
And as he plucked his cursèd steel away,   175
Mark how the blood of Caesar followed it,
As rushing out of doors to be resolved°
If Brutus so unkindly° knocked or no;
For Brutus, as you know, was Caesar's angel.°
Judge, O you gods, how dearly Caesar loved him!   180
This was the most unkindest° cut of all;
For when the noble Caesar saw him stab,
Ingratitude, more strong than traitors' arms,
Quite vanquished him. Then burst his mighty heart,
And in his mantle muffling up his face,   185
Even at the base of Pompey's statue,
Which all the while ran blood, great Caesar fell.
Oh, what a fall was there, my countrymen!
Then I, and you, and all of us fell down,
Whilst bloody treason flourished over us.   190
Oh, now you weep, and I perceive you feel
The dint° of pity. These are gracious° drops.
Kind souls, what° weep you when you but behold
Our Caesar's vesture° wounded? Look you here,
Here is himself, marred as you see with traitors.   195
                              [*He lifts Caesar's mantle*]
FIRST PLEBEIAN   Oh, piteous spectacle!
SECOND PLEBEIAN   O noble Caesar!
THIRD PLEBEIAN   Oh, woeful day!

---

168 mantle cloak, toga   **171 the Nervii** the Belgian tribe whose defeat in 57 B.C.
is described in Caesar's *Gallic Wars,* 2.15–28   **173 envious** malicious, spiteful
177 be resolved learn for certain   **178 unkindly** cruelly and unnaturally   **179 angel**
(1) daimon or genius, guardian angel (2) best beloved   **181 unkindest** (1) most cruel
(2) most unnatural (the double superlative was grammatically acceptable in
Shakespeare's day)   **192 dint** impression | **gracious** (1) kindly (2) pious (3) regenerate
193 what why, or how much   **194 vesture** clothing

FOURTH PLEBEIAN Oh, traitors, villains!

FIRST PLEBEIAN Oh, most bloody sight!   200

SECOND PLEBEIAN We will be revenged.

ALL Revenge! About!° Seek! Burn! Fire! Kill! Slay! Let not a
traitor live!

ANTONY Stay, countrymen.

FIRST PLEBEIAN Peace there! Hear the noble Antony.   205

SECOND PLEBEIAN We'll hear him, we'll follow him, we'll die
with him!

ANTONY Good friends, sweet friends, let me not stir you up
To such a sudden flood of mutiny.
They that have done this deed are honorable.   210
What private griefs° they have, alas, I know not,
That made them do it. They are wise and honorable,
And will no doubt with reasons answer you.
I come not, friends, to steal away your hearts.
I am no orator, as Brutus is,   215
But, as you know me all, a plain blunt man
That love my friend, and that they know full well
That gave me public leave° to speak of him.
For I have neither wit, nor words, nor worth,
Action, nor utterance, nor the power of speech°   220
To stir men's blood. I only speak right on.
I tell you that which you yourselves do know,
Show you sweet Caesar's wounds, poor poor dumb mouths,
And bid them speak for me. But were I Brutus,
And Brutus Antony, there were an Antony   225
Would ruffle up° your spirits and put a tongue
In every wound of Caesar that should move
The stones of Rome to rise and mutiny.

ALL We'll mutiny!

FIRST PLEBEIAN We'll burn the house of Brutus!

THIRD PLEBEIAN Away, then! Come, seek the conspirators.   230

ANTONY Yet hear me, countrymen. Yet hear me speak.

ALL Peace, ho! Hear Antony, most noble Antony!

---

202 About! to work! **211 griefs** grievances **218 public leave** permission to speak
publicly **219–20 neither . . . speech** neither intelligence, vocabulary, moral
authority, gesture, rhetorical skill, nor polished delivery **226 ruffle up** stir to anger

ANTONY Why, friends, you go to do you know not what.
Wherein hath Caesar thus deserved your loves?
Alas, you know not. I must tell you then: 235
You have forgot the will I told you of.
ALL Most true. The will! Let's stay and hear the will.
ANTONY Here is the will, and under Caesar's seal.
To every Roman citizen he gives,
To every several° man, seventy-five drachmas.°   240
SECOND PLEBEIAN Most noble Caesar! We'll revenge his death.
THIRD PLEBEIAN O royal Caesar!
ANTONY Hear me with patience.
ALL Peace, ho!
ANTONY Moreover, he hath left you all his walks,   245
His private arbors, and new-planted orchards,
On this side Tiber; he hath left them you,
And to your heirs forever—common pleasures,°
To walk abroad and recreate yourselves.
Here was a Caesar! When comes such another?   250
FIRST PLEBEIAN Never, never! Come, away, away!
We'll burn his body in the holy place
And with the brands fire the traitors' houses.
Take up the body.
SECOND PLEBEIAN   Go fetch fire!
THIRD PLEBEIAN Pluck down benches!   255
FOURTH PLEBEIAN Pluck down forms, windows,° anything!
                  Exeunt Plebeians [with the body]
ANTONY Now let it work. Mischief, thou art afoot.
Take thou what course thou wilt.

                  Enter [Octavius's] Servant
                  How now, fellow?
SERVANT Sir, Octavius is already come to Rome.
ANTONY Where is he?   260
SERVANT He and Lepidus are at Caesar's house.

---

240 **several** individual | **drachmas** coins (this is a substantial bequest) 248 **common
pleasures** public pleasure gardens (in which) 256 **forms, windows** benches,
window frames and shutters

ANTONY   And thither will I straight to visit him.
  He comes upon a wish.° Fortune is merry,°
  And in this mood will give us anything.
SERVANT   I heard him say Brutus and Cassius   265
  Are rid° like madmen through the gates of Rome.
ANTONY   Belike° they had some notice of° the people,
  How I had moved them. Bring me to Octavius.

                                                Exeunt

ACT 3
SCENE 3

Location: A street.

Enter Cinna the poet, and after him the Plebeians

CINNA   I dreamt tonight° that I did feast with Caesar,
  And things unluckily charge my fantasy.°
  I have no will to wander forth of doors,
  Yet something leads me forth.
FIRST PLEBEIAN   What is your name?   5
SECOND PLEBEIAN   Whither are you going?
THIRD PLEBEIAN   Where do you dwell?
FOURTH PLEBEIAN   Are you a married man or a bachelor?
SECOND PLEBEIAN   Answer every man directly.
FIRST PLEBEIAN   Ay, and briefly.   10
FOURTH PLEBEIAN   Ay, and wisely.
THIRD PLEBEIAN   Ay, and truly, you were best.°
CINNA   What is my name? Whither am I going? Where do I
  dwell? Am I a married man or a bachelor? Then to answer
  every man directly and briefly, wisely and truly: wisely I say, 15
  I am a bachelor.
SECOND PLEBEIAN   That's as much as to say they are fools that
  marry. You'll bear me a bang° for that, I fear. Proceed
  directly.°

263 **upon a wish** just when wanted | **merry** favorably disposed   266 **Are rid** have
ridden   267 **Belike** likely enough | **of** about; or, from

1 **tonight** last night   2 **unluckily . . . fantasy** oppress my imagination with foreboding
12 **you were best** you'd better   18 **bear . . . bang** get a beating from me   19 **directly**
without evasion

CINNA   Directly,° I am going to Caesar's funeral.   20
FIRST PLEBEIAN   As a friend or an enemy?
CINNA   As a friend.
SECOND PLEBEIAN   That matter is answered directly.
FOURTH PLEBEIAN   For your dwelling—briefly.
CINNA   Briefly, I dwell by the Capitol.   25
THIRD PLEBEIAN   Your name, sir, truly.
CINNA   Truly, my name is Cinna.
FIRST PLEBEIAN   Tear him to pieces! He's a conspirator!
CINNA   I am Cinna the poet, I am Cinna the poet!
FOURTH PLEBEIAN   Tear him for his bad verses, tear him for his   30
    bad verses!
CINNA   I am not Cinna the conspirator.
FOURTH PLEBEIAN   It is no matter, his name's Cinna. Pluck but
    his name out of his heart, and turn him going.°
THIRD PLEBEIAN   Tear him, tear him! Come, brands, ho,   35
    firebrands! To Brutus', to Cassius'; burn all! Some to
    Decius' house, and some to Casca's; some to Ligarius'.
    Away, go!
                Exeunt all the Plebeians, [dragging off Cinna]

ACT 4
SCENE 1

Location: Rome. A table is perhaps set out.

Enter Antony [with a list], Octavius, and Lepidus

ANTONY   These many, then, shall die. Their names are pricked.°
OCTAVIUS   Your brother too must die. Consent you, Lepidus?
LEPIDUS   I do consent—
OCTAVIUS   Prick him down, Antony.
LEPIDUS   Upon condition Publius shall not live,
    Who is your sister's son, Mark Antony.   5

---

20 Directly (1) straight there (2) at once   **34 turn him going** send him packing
1 pricked marked down on a list (with a stylus making an impression on a wax
tablet, or piercing a sheet of paper)

ANTONY   He shall not live. Look, with a spot° I damn° him.
But Lepidus, go you to Caesar's house.
Fetch the will hither, and we shall determine
How to cut off some charge in legacies.°
LEPIDUS   What, shall I find you here?   10
OCTAVIUS   Or° here or at the Capitol.   *Exit Lepidus*
ANTONY   This is a slight, unmeritable° man,
Meet to be sent on errands. Is it fit,
The threefold° world divided, he should stand
One of the three to share it?
OCTAVIUS   So you thought him,   15
And took his voice° who should be pricked to die
In our black sentence° and proscription.°
ANTONY
Octavius, I have seen more days than you;
And though we lay these honors on this man
To ease ourselves of divers sland'rous° loads,   20
He shall but bear them as the ass bears gold,
To groan and sweat under the business,
Either led or driven as we point the way;
And having brought our treasure where we will,
Then take we down his load, and turn him off,   25
Like to the empty° ass, to shake his ears
And graze in commons.°
OCTAVIUS   You may do your will;
But he's a tried and valiant soldier.
ANTONY   So is my horse, Octavius, and for that
I do appoint him store of provender.°   30
It is a creature that I teach to fight,
To wind,° to stop, to run directly on,°

---

6 spot mark (on the list) | **damn** condemn   **8–9 determine** . . . **legacies** find a way to reduce the outlay of Caesar's estate, by altering the will   **11 Or** either   **12 slight, unmeritable** insignificant and undeserving   **14 threefold** consisting of Europe, Africa, and Asia; the Roman world was divided among the triumvirate, with most of Gaul on both sides of the Alps to Antony, Spain and Old Gaul to Lepidus, and Africa, Sardinia, and Sicily to Octavius   **16 took his voice** acceded to his opinion (about Publius)   **17 black sentence** death sentence | **proscription** (proscription branded a man as an outlaw, confiscated his property, offered a reward for his murder, and prohibited his sons and grandsons from holding public office)   **20 sland'rous** giving cause for slander   **26 empty** unloaded   **27 commons** public pasture   **30 provender** fodder   **32 wind** turn (horse trainer's term) | **directly on** straight ahead

His corporal° motion governed by my spirit.
And in some taste° is Lepidus but so.
He must be taught, and trained, and bid go forth—   35
A barren-spirited fellow, one that feeds
On objects, arts, and imitations,°
Which, out of use and staled° by other men,
Begin his fashion.° Do not talk of him
But as a property.° And now, Octavius,   40
Listen° great things. Brutus and Cassius
Are levying powers.° We must straight make head.°
Therefore let our alliance be combined,°
Our best friends made,° our means stretched;°
And let us presently go sit in council   45
How covert matters may be best disclosed°
And open perils surest answerèd.°
OCTAVIUS   Let us do so, for we are at the stake°
And bayed about° with many enemies;
And some that smile have in their hearts, I fear,   50
Millions of mischiefs.   *Exeunt*

ACT 4
SCENE 2
Location: Camp near Sardis, in Asia Minor.
Before Brutus's tent.

Drum. Enter Brutus, Lucilius, [Lucius,]
and the army. Titinius and Pindarus meet them

BRUTUS   Stand, ho!
LUCILIUS   Give the word, ho, and stand!°

33 **corporal** bodily   34 **taste** degree, sense   37 **On** . . . **imitations** on curiosities, artificial things, and the following of fashion—copied things merely, taken up secondhand   38 **staled** made common or cheap   39 **Begin his fashion** are for him the ultimate in fashion   40 **property** tool   41 **Listen** hear   42 **powers** armies I **straight make head** immediately raise an army   43 **let** . . . **combined** let us work as one   44 **made** mustered, made certain I **stretched** used to fullest advantage, extended to the utmost   46 **How** . . . **disclosed** (to determine) how hidden dangers may best be discovered   47 **surest answerèd** most safely met   48 **at the stake** like a bear in the sport of bearbaiting   49 **bayed about** surrounded as by baying dogs
1–2 **Stand** . . . **stand!** Halt! Pass the word!

BRUTUS What now, Lucilius, is Cassius near?
LUCILIUS He is at hand, and Pindarus is come
To do you salutation from his master.   5
BRUTUS He greets me well.° Your master, Pindarus,
In his own change, or by ill officers,°
Hath given me some worthy° cause to wish
Things done, undone; but if he be at hand
I shall be satisfied.°
PINDARUS   I do not doubt   10
But that my noble master will appear
Such as he is, full of regard and honor.°
BRUTUS He is not doubted.—A word, Lucilius.
                    [*Brutus and Lucilius speak apart*]
How he received you let me be resolved.°
LUCILIUS With courtesy and with respect enough,   15
But not with such familiar instances°
Nor with such free and friendly conference°
As he hath used of old.
BRUTUS   Thou hast described
A hot friend cooling. Ever note, Lucilius:
When love begins to sicken and decay   20
It useth an enforcèd° ceremony.
There are no tricks in plain and simple faith.
But hollow° men, like horses hot at hand,°
Make gallant show and promise of their mettle;°
                                    Low march within
But when they should endure the bloody spur,   25
They fall their crests° and like deceitful jades
Sink° in the trial. Comes his army on?

6 He . . . well his greetings are welcome 7 In . . . officers whether from an
alteration in his feelings toward me or through the acts of unworthy subordinates
8 worthy justifiable 10 be satisfied have things explained to my satisfaction
12 full . . . honor deserving all respect and honor 14 resolved informed, put out
of doubt 16 familiar instances proofs of intimate friendship 17 conference
conversation 21 enforcèd constrained 23 hollow insincere | hot at hand
restless and full of spirit when held in, at the start 24 mettle spirit 26 fall their
crests lower their necks (literally, the ridge or mane of the neck), hang their heads
| jades worthless horses 27 Sink give way, fail

LUCILIUS   They mean this night in Sardis° to be quartered.
The greater part, the horse in general,°
Are come with Cassius.

Enter Cassius and his powers

BRUTUS   Hark, he is arrived.   30
March gently° on to meet him.
CASSIUS   Stand, ho!
BRUTUS   Stand, ho! Speak the word along.
FIRST SOLDIER   Stand!
SECOND SOLDIER   Stand!   35
THIRD SOLDIER   Stand!
CASSIUS   Most noble brother, you have done me wrong.
BRUTUS   Judge me, you gods! Wrong I mine enemies?
And if not so, how should I wrong a brother?
CASSIUS   Brutus, this sober form° of yours hides wrongs;   40
And when you do them—
BRUTUS   Cassius, be content;°
Speak your griefs softly. I do know you well.
Before the eyes of both our armies here,
Which should perceive nothing but love from us,
Let us not wrangle. Bid them move away.   45
Then in my tent, Cassius, enlarge° your griefs,
And I will give you audience.
CASSIUS   Pindarus,
Bid our commanders lead their charges° off
A little from this ground.
BRUTUS   Lucius, do you the like, and let no man   50
Come to our tent till we have done our conference.
Let Lucilius° and Titinius guard our door.

Exeunt. Manent Brutus and Cassius
[*Lucilius and Titinius stand guard at the door*]

❖

28 **Sardis** (the capital city of Lydia in Asia Minor)   29 **the horse in general** all the cavalry   31 **gently** mildly, not hostilely   40 **sober form** dignified manner, appearance   41 **be content** keep calm   46 **enlarge** speak freely   48 **charges** troops   52 **Lucilius** (the Folio reads *Lucius* here and *Lucillius* in line 50, but, when Shakespeare interpolated a passage in the next scene at lines 124–66, he evidently intended to have Lucilius guarding the door)

ACT 4
SCENE 3

Location: The scene is continuous. Brutus and Cassius remain onstage, which now represents the interior of Brutus's tent.

CASSIUS That you have wronged me doth appear in this:
You have condemned and noted° Lucius Pella°
For taking bribes here of the Sardians,
Wherein my letters,° praying° on his side,
Because I knew the man, was slighted off.°   5
BRUTUS You wronged yourself to write in such a case.
CASSIUS In such a time as this it is not meet°
That every nice° offense should bear his comment.°
BRUTUS Let me tell you, Cassius, you yourself
Are much condemned to have° an itching palm,   10
To sell and mart° your offices for gold
To undeservers.
CASSIUS   I an itching palm?
You know that you are Brutus that speaks this,
Or, by the gods, this speech were else your last.
BRUTUS The name of Cassius honors° this corruption,   15
And chastisement doth therefore hide his head.°
CASSIUS Chastisement?
BRUTUS Remember March, the ides of March remember.
Did not great Julius bleed for justice' sake?
What villain touched his body that did stab   20
And not for justice?° What, shall one of us,
That struck the foremost man of all this world
But° for supporting robbers,° shall we now
Contaminate our fingers with base bribes,

---

2 noted publicly disgraced | **Lucius Pella** a Roman praetor in Sardis   **4 letters** letter (see 3.1.281n) | **praying** entreating   **5 slighted off** slightingly dismissed   **7 meet** fitting   **8 nice** trivial | **bear his comment** be taken note of (*his* means "its")   **10 condemned to have** accused of having   **11 mart** traffic in   **15 honors** lends the appearance of honor to, countenances   **16 And . . . head** and for that reason those who might rebuke such corruption are reluctant to speak out   **20–1 What . . . justice?** which of us was villain enough to stab for any cause other than justice?   **23 But** only | **robbers** (according to Plutarch, Caesar "was a favorer and suborner of all of them that did rob and spoil by his countenance and authority")

And sell the mighty space of our large honors° 25
For so much trash° as may be graspèd thus?
I had rather be a dog and bay the moon
Than such a Roman.
CASSIUS   Brutus, bait° not me.
I'll not endure it. You forget yourself
To hedge me in.° I am a soldier, I, 30
Older in practice, abler than yourself
To make conditions.°
BRUTUS   Go to! You are not, Cassius.
CASSIUS   I am.
BRUTUS   I say you are not. 35
CASSIUS   Urge° me no more; I shall forget myself.
Have mind upon your health. Tempt° me no farther.
BRUTUS   Away, slight° man!
CASSIUS   Is't possible?
BRUTUS   Hear me, for I will speak.
Must I give way and room° to your rash choler?° 40
Shall I be frighted when a madman stares?°
CASSIUS   O ye gods, ye gods! Must I endure all this?
BRUTUS   All this? Ay, more. Fret till your proud heart break.
Go show your slaves how choleric you are,
And make your bondmen° tremble. Must I budge?° 45
Must I observe° you? Must I stand and crouch°
Under your testy humor?° By the gods,
You shall digest° the venom of your spleen°
Though it do split you; for, from this day forth,
I'll use you for my mirth, yea, for my laughter, 50
When you are waspish.°
CASSIUS   Is it come to this?
BRUTUS   You say you are a better soldier.
Let it appear so; make your vaunting° true,

25 the mighty . . . honors the greatness of our honorable reputations and the high offices we have power to confer   26 trash money (despised in Brutus's stoic philosophy)   28 bait harass   30 hedge me in crowd me, limit my authority   32 make conditions manage affairs, make decisions about Lucius Pella and other officers   36 Urge provoke   37 Tempt provoke   38 slight insignificant   40 way and room free course and scope | choler wrathful temperament   41 stares looks wildly at me   45 bondmen (probably not distinguished from "slaves" in line 44) | budge flinch   46 observe defer to | crouch cringe   47 humor temperament   48 digest swallow | spleen irascibility   51 waspish hotheaded   53 vaunting boasting

And it shall please me well. For mine own part,
I shall be glad to learn of noble men.°   55
CASSIUS   You wrong me every way! You wrong me, Brutus.
I said an elder soldier, not a better.
Did I say "better"?
BRUTUS   If you did, I care not.
CASSIUS   When Caesar lived he durst not thus have moved° me.
BRUTUS   Peace, peace! You durst not so have tempted him.   60
CASSIUS   I durst not?
BRUTUS   No.
CASSIUS   What, durst not tempt him?
BRUTUS   For your life you durst not.
CASSIUS   Do not presume too much upon my love.
I may do that I shall be sorry for.   65
BRUTUS   You have done that you should be sorry for.
There is no terror, Cassius, in your threats,
For I am armed so strong in honesty
That they pass by me as the idle wind,
Which I respect not.° I did send to you   70
For certain sums of gold, which you denied me;
For I can raise no money° by vile means.
By heaven, I had rather coin my heart
And drop my blood for drachmas than to wring
From the hard hands of peasants their vile trash   75
By any indirection.° I did send
To you for gold to pay my legions,
Which you denied me. Was that done like Cassius?
Should I have answered Caius Cassius so?
When Marcus Brutus grows so covetous   80
To lock such rascal counters° from his friends,
Be ready, gods, with all your thunderbolts,
Dash him to pieces!
CASSIUS   I denied you not.

---

55 I shall . . . men (said sarcastically: "wouldn't it be a nice surprise to learn that
some men can be noble after all?", or, "I am glad to be corrected by such a noble
person as yourself")   59 moved angered   70 respect not pay no attention to   72 can
raise no money refuse to raise money   76 indirection devious or unjust means
81 rascal counters paltry sums (*counters* were uncurrent coins or disks used by
shopkeepers as tokens in making reckonings)

BRUTUS You did.
CASSIUS   I did not. He was but a fool
That brought my answer back. Brutus hath rived° my heart.   85
A friend should bear his friend's infirmities,
But Brutus makes mine greater than they are.
BRUTUS I do not, till you practice them on me.
CASSIUS You love me not.
BRUTUS   I do not like your faults.
CASSIUS A friendly eye could never see such faults.   90
BRUTUS A flatterer's would not, though they do appear
As huge as high Olympus.
CASSIUS Come, Antony, and young Octavius, come,
Revenge yourselves alone on Cassius;
For Cassius is aweary of the world,   95
Hated by one he loves, braved° by his brother,
Checked° like a bondman, all his faults observed,
Set in a notebook, learned and conned by rote°
To cast into my teeth. Oh, I could weep
My spirit from mine eyes! There is my dagger,   100
[*offering his unsheathed dagger*]
And here my naked breast; within, a heart
Dearer° than Pluto's° mine, richer than gold.
If that thou be'st a Roman, take it forth.
I, that denied° thee gold, will give my heart.
Strike, as thou didst at Caesar; for I know,   105
When thou didst hate him worst, thou loved'st him better
Than ever thou loved'st Cassius.
BRUTUS   Sheathe your dagger.
Be angry when you will, it shall have scope;°
Do what you will, dishonor shall be humor.°
Oh, Cassius, you are yokèd with° a lamb   110
That carries anger as the flint bears fire,
Who, much enforcèd,° shows a hasty spark

And straight° is cold again.

CASSIUS   Hath Cassius lived
To be but mirth and laughter to his Brutus
When grief and blood ill-tempered° vexeth him?   115

BRUTUS When I spoke that, I was ill-tempered too.

CASSIUS Do you confess so much? Give me your hand.

BRUTUS And my heart too.   [*They embrace*]

CASSIUS   Oh, Brutus!

BRUTUS   What's the matter?

CASSIUS Have not you love enough to bear with me,
When that rash humor° which my mother gave me   120
Makes me forgetful?

BRUTUS   Yes, Cassius, and from henceforth,
When you are overearnest with your Brutus,
He'll think your mother chides, and leave you so.°

> *Enter a Poet [followed by Lucilius and Titinius,*
> *who have been standing guard at the door]*

POET Let me go in to see the generals!
There is some grudge between 'em; 'tis not meet   125
They be alone.

LUCILIUS   You shall not come to them.

POET Nothing but death shall stay me.

CASSIUS How now? What's the matter?

POET For shame, you generals! What do you mean?
Love and be friends, as two such men should be;   130
For I have seen more years, I'm sure, than ye.

CASSIUS Ha, ha, how vilely doth this cynic° rhyme!

BRUTUS Get you hence, sirrah. Saucy fellow, hence!

CASSIUS Bear with him, Brutus. 'Tis his fashion.

BRUTUS I'll know his humor when he knows his time.°   135
What should the wars do with these jigging° fools?
Companion,° hence!

CASSIUS   Away, away, begone!   *Exit Poet*

---

113 straight at once   **115 blood ill-tempered** disposition imbalanced by the humors
of the body   **120 that rash humor** choler, anger   **123 leave you so** let it go at that
132 cynic rude fellow; also one claiming to be a Cynic philosopher, hence outspoken
135 I'll . . . time I'll indulge his eccentric behavior when he knows the proper time for
it   **136 jigging** rhyming in jerky doggerel   **137 Companion** fellow

BRUTUS Lucilius and Titinius, bid the commanders
Prepare to lodge their companies tonight.
CASSIUS And come yourselves, and bring Messala with you
Immediately to us.   [*Exeunt Lucilius and Titinius*]   140
BRUTUS [*to Lucius within*] Lucius, a bowl of wine.
CASSIUS I did not think you could have been so angry.
BRUTUS Oh, Cassius, I am sick of many griefs.
CASSIUS Of your philosophy you make no use
If you give place° to accidental evils.°   145
BRUTUS No man bears sorrow better. Portia is dead.
CASSIUS Ha? Portia?
BRUTUS She is dead.
CASSIUS How scaped I killing° when I crossed you so?
Oh, insupportable and touching loss!   150
Upon what sickness?
BRUTUS   Impatient of my absence,
And grief that young Octavius with Mark Antony
Have made themselves so strong—for with her death°
That tidings came—with this she fell distract
And, her attendants absent, swallowed fire.°   155
CASSIUS And died so?
BRUTUS   Even so.
CASSIUS   O ye immortal gods!

Enter Boy [Lucius] with wine and tapers

BRUTUS Speak no more of her.—Give me a bowl of wine.—
In this I bury all unkindness, Cassius.   *Drinks*
CASSIUS My heart is thirsty for that noble pledge.
Fill, Lucius, till the wine o'erswell the cup;   160
I cannot drink too much of Brutus' love.

[*He drinks. Exit Lucius*]

Enter Titinius° and Messala

---

145 place way | accidental evils misfortunes caused by chance (which should be a matter of indifference to a philosopher like Brutus) 149 scaped I killing did I escape being killed 153 her death news of her death 155 swallowed fire (according to Plutarch, as translated by Thomas North, Portia "took hot burning coals and cast them in her mouth, and kept her mouth so close that she choked herself") 161.2 Titinius (Lucilius does not return with Titinius, as he was ordered to do at lines 139–40, probably because he was not in Shakespeare's original version of this scene)

BRUTUS Come in, Titinius. Welcome, good Messala.
Now sit we close about this taper here
And call in question° our necessities.   [*They sit*]
CASSIUS Portia, art thou gone?
BRUTUS   No more, I pray you.   165
Messala, I have here receivèd letters°
That young Octavius and Mark Antony
Come down upon us with a mighty power,°
Bending° their expedition° toward Philippi.
                                         [*He shows a letter*]
MESSALA Myself have letters of the selfsame tenor.   170
BRUTUS With what addition?
MESSALA That by proscription° and bills of outlawry
Octavius, Antony, and Lepidus
Have put to death an hundred senators.
BRUTUS Therein our letters do not well agree;   175
Mine speak of seventy senators that died
By their proscriptions, Cicero being one.
CASSIUS Cicero one?
MESSALA   Cicero is dead,
And by that order of proscription.
Had you your letters from your wife, my lord?   180
BRUTUS No, Messala.
MESSALA Nor nothing in your letters writ of her?°
BRUTUS Nothing, Messala.
MESSALA   That, methinks, is strange.
BRUTUS Why ask you? Hear you aught of her in yours?
MESSALA No, my lord.   185
BRUTUS Now, as you are a Roman, tell me true.
MESSALA Then like a Roman bear the truth I tell,
For certain she is dead, and by strange manner.

164 call in question consider, discuss 166 letters (probably a single letter. See 3.1.281n and 4.3.4n) 168 power army 169 Bending directing | expedition rapid march; warlike enterprise 172 proscription (see the note at 4.1.17) 180–94 Had ... so (this passage is sometimes regarded as contradictory to lines 142–65 and redundant; perhaps it is the original account of Portia's death, and lines 142–65 are part of a later interpolation, but it is also possible that both are intended, the first being Brutus's intimate revelation of the news to his friend and the second being Brutus's recovery of his stoic reserve now on display for Messala and Titinius) 182 nothing ... her nothing written about her in the letter or letters you've received

BRUTUS Why, farewell, Portia. We must die, Messala.
With meditating that she must die once,°   190
I have the patience to endure it now.
MESSALA Even so° great men great losses should endure.
CASSIUS I have as much of this in art° as you,
But yet my nature could not bear it so.°
BRUTUS Well, to our work alive.° What do you think   195
Of marching to Philippi presently?
CASSIUS I do not think it good.
BRUTUS   Your reason?
CASSIUS   This it is:
'Tis better that the enemy seek us.
So shall he waste his means, weary his soldiers,
Doing himself offense,° whilst we, lying still,   200
Are full of rest, defense, and nimbleness.
BRUTUS Good reasons must of force° give place to better.
The people twixt Philippi and this ground
Do stand but in a forced affection,
For they have grudged us contribution.   205
The enemy, marching along by them,
By them shall make a fuller number up,
Come on refreshed, new-added, and encouraged;
From which advantage shall we cut him off
If at Philippi we do face him there,   210
These people at our back.°
CASSIUS   Hear me, good brother—
BRUTUS Under your pardon.° You must note beside
That we have tried the utmost of our friends;
Our legions are brim full, our cause is ripe.
The enemy increaseth every day;   215
We, at the height, are ready to decline.
There is a tide in the affairs of men
Which, taken at the flood, leads on to fortune;
Omitted, all the voyage of their life

190 **once** at some time 192 **Even so** in just such a way 193 **art** the acquired theoretical wisdom of stoical fortitude (as contrasted with the gifts of *nature* in line 194) 195 **alive** concerning us who are alive and dealing with present and future realities 200 **offense** harm 202 **of force** necessarily 211 **These . . . back** with the people our enemy would otherwise recruit being instead in territory we control 212 **Under your pardon** excuse me, let me continue

Is bound in° shallows and in miseries.   220
On such a full sea are we now afloat,
And we must take the current when it serves
Or lose our ventures.°
CASSIUS   Then, with your will,° go on.
We'll along ourselves and meet them at Philippi.
BRUTUS The deep of night is crept upon our talk,   225
And nature must obey necessity,
Which we will niggard° with a little rest.
There is no more to say.
CASSIUS   No more. Good night.
Early tomorrow will we rise and hence.°
BRUTUS   Lucius!

                                        Enter Lucius
                My gown.°   [*Exit Lucius*]
                        Farewell, good Messala.   230
Good night, Titinius. Noble, noble Cassius,
Good night and good repose.
CASSIUS   Oh, my dear brother!
This was an ill beginning of the night.
Never come such division 'tween our souls!
Let it not, Brutus.   235
                Enter Lucius with the gown
BRUTUS   Everything is well.
CASSIUS   Good night, my lord.
BRUTUS   Good night, good brother.
TITINIUS, MESSALA   Good night, Lord Brutus.
BRUTUS   Farewell, everyone.   240
                Exeunt [all but Brutus and Lucius]
Give me the gown. Where is thy instrument?°
LUCIUS   Here in the tent.
BRUTUS   What, thou speak'st drowsily!
Poor knave,° I blame thee not; thou art o'erwatched.°

---

220 **bound in** confined to   223 **ventures** investments (of enterprise at sea) | **with
your will** as you wish   227 **niggard** stint (by sleeping only briefly)   229 **hence**
depart   230 **gown** housecoat   241 **instrument** perhaps a lute or cittern   243 **knave**
boy | **o'erwatched** tired from lack of sleep

Call Claudius and some other of my men;
I'll have them sleep on cushions in my tent.   245
LUCIUS [*calling*]   Varro and Claudius!

Enter Varro and Claudius

VARRO   Calls my lord?
BRUTUS   I pray you, sirs, lie in my tent and sleep.
It may be I shall raise° you by and by
On business to my brother Cassius.   250
VARRO   So please you, we will stand and watch your pleasure.°
BRUTUS   I will not have it so. Lie down, good sirs.
It may be I shall otherwise bethink me.°
                                    [*Varro and Claudius lie down*]
Look, Lucius, here's the book I sought for so;
I put it in the pocket of my gown.   255
LUCIUS   I was sure Your Lordship did not give it me.
BRUTUS   Bear with me, good boy, I am much forgetful.
Canst thou hold up thy heavy eyes awhile
And touch° thy instrument a strain° or two?
LUCIUS   Ay, my lord, an't° please you.
BRUTUS   It does, my boy.   260
I trouble thee too much, but thou art willing.
LUCIUS   It is my duty, sir.
BRUTUS   I should not urge thy duty past thy might;
I know young bloods° look for a time of rest.
LUCIUS   I have slept, my lord, already.   265
BRUTUS   It was well done, and thou shalt sleep again;
I will not hold thee long. If I do live,
I will be good to thee.
                        Music, and a song [*Lucius falls asleep*]
This is a sleepy tune. O murd'rous° slumber,
Layest thou thy leaden mace° upon my boy,   270
That plays thee music? Gentle knave, good night;
I will not do thee so much wrong to wake thee.
If thou dost nod, thou break'st thy instrument;

---

249 raise rouse   **251 watch your pleasure** wakefully await your commands
253 otherwise bethink me change my mind   **259 touch** play on | **strain** tune, musical
phrase   **260 an't** if it   **264 young bloods** youthful constitutions   **269 murd'rous**
producing the likeness of death   **270 leaden mace** heavy staff of office (used by a
sheriff to touch the shoulder of one being placed under arrest)

I'll take it from thee. And, good boy, good night.

[*He removes Lucius's instrument, and begins to read*]
Let me see, let me see; is not the leaf turned down   275
Where I left reading? Here it is, I think.

Enter the Ghost of Caesar°

How ill this taper burns!° Ha! Who comes here?
I think it is the weakness of mine eyes
That shapes this monstrous apparition.
It comes upon° me.—Art thou any thing?   280
Art thou some god, some angel, or some devil,
That mak'st my blood cold and my hair to stare?°
Speak to me what thou art.
GHOST   Thy evil spirit, Brutus.
BRUTUS   Why com'st thou?
GHOST   To tell thee thou shalt see me at Philippi.   285
BRUTUS   Well; then I shall see thee again?
GHOST   Ay, at Philippi.
BRUTUS   Why, I will see thee at Philippi, then.   [*Exit Ghost*]
Now I have taken heart, thou vanishest.
Ill spirit, I would hold more talk with thee.—   290
Boy, Lucius! Varro! Claudius! Sirs, awake!
Claudius!
LUCIUS   The strings, my lord, are false.°
BRUTUS   He thinks he still is at his instrument.—
Lucius, awake!
LUCIUS   My lord?   295
BRUTUS   Didst thou dream, Lucius, that thou so cried'st out?
LUCIUS   My lord, I do not know that I did cry.
BRUTUS   Yes, that thou didst. Didst thou see anything?
LUCIUS   Nothing, my lord.
BRUTUS   Sleep again, Lucius. Sirrah Claudius!   300
[*To Varro*] Fellow thou, awake!
VARRO   My lord?
CLAUDIUS   My lord?
[*They get up*]

---

277 How . . . burns! (ghostly apparitions were thought to be accompanied by such effects as lights burning low and blue) **277.1 Enter the Ghost of Caesar** for Elizabethan accounts of ghosts, see pp. 146–51, below **280 upon** toward **282 stare** stand on end **292 false** out of tune

BRUTUS   Why did you so cry out, sirs, in your sleep?

VARRO, CLAUDIUS   Did we, my lord?

BRUTUS   Ay. Saw you anything?

VARRO   No, my lord, I saw nothing.

CLAUDIUS   Nor I, my lord.

BRUTUS   Go and commend me° to my brother Cassius.   305
   Bid him set on his powers betimes before,°
   And we will follow.

VARRO, CLAUDIUS   It shall be done, my lord.

Exeunt

ACT 5
SCENE 1

Location: The plains of Philippi, in Macedonia.

Enter Octavius, Antony, and their army

OCTAVIUS   Now, Antony, our hopes are answerèd.
   You said the enemy would not come down,
   But keep° the hills and upper regions.
   It proves not so. Their battles° are at hand;
   They mean to warn° us at Philippi here,   5
   Answering before we do demand of them.

ANTONY   Tut, I am in their bosoms,° and I know
   Wherefore they do it. They could be content
   To visit other places,° and come down
   With fearful bravery,° thinking by this face°   10
   To fasten in our thoughts that they have courage;
   But 'tis not so.°

Enter a Messenger

---

305 commend me deliver my greetings   **306 set . . . before** march away with his troops early in the morning, before me

3 keep remain in   **4 battles** armies   **5 warn** challenge   **7 bosoms** secret councils   **9 visit other places** be elsewhere   **10 fearful bravery** (1) awesome ostentation (2) a show of bravery to conceal their fear | **face** pretense (of courage)   **12 'tis not so** (1) their plan cannot deceive us (2) they have no courage

MESSENGER Prepare you, generals.
The enemy comes on in gallant show.
Their bloody sign° of battle is hung out,
And something to be° done immediately.   15
ANTONY Octavius, lead your battle softly° on
Upon the left hand of the even field.
OCTAVIUS Upon the right hand, I. Keep thou the left.
ANTONY Why do you cross° me in this exigent?°
OCTAVIUS I do not cross you,° but I will do so.°   *March* 20

Drum. Enter Brutus, Cassius, and their army;
[Lucilius, Titinius, Messala, and others]

BRUTUS They stand and would have parley.
CASSIUS Stand fast, Titinius. We must out° and talk.
OCTAVIUS Mark Antony, shall we give sign of battle?
ANTONY No, Caesar, we will answer on their charge.°
Make forth.° The generals would have some words.   25
OCTAVIUS [*to his officers*] Stir not until the signal.
[The two sides advance toward one another]
BRUTUS Words before blows. Is it so, countrymen?
OCTAVIUS Not that we love words better, as you do.
BRUTUS Good words are better than bad strokes, Octavius.
ANTONY In your bad strokes, Brutus, you give good words.°   30
Witness the hole you made in Caesar's heart,
Crying "Long live! Hail, Caesar!"
CASSIUS   Antony,
The posture of your blows are° yet unknown;
But for° your words, they rob the Hybla° bees,
And leave them honeyless.   35
ANTONY Not stingless too?
BRUTUS Oh, yes, and soundless too.
For you have stol'n their buzzing, Antony,
And very wisely° threat° before you sting.

14 **bloody sign** red flag or crimson coat of arms as battle signal   15 **to be** is to be
16 **softly** warily, with restraint   19 **cross** contradict I **exigent** critical moment
20 **cross you** contradict you perversely I **do so** do as I said   22 **out** go out   24 **answer**
on their charge respond when they attack   25 **Make forth** march forward   30 **In . . .**
words as you deliver cruel blows, Brutus, you use deceiving flattery   33 **The**
posture . . . are how you will strike your blows is   34 **for** as for I **Hybla** a mountain
and a town in ancient Sicily, famous for honey   39 **very wisely** (said ironically;
Brutus suggests that Antony is all bluster and no action) I **threat** threaten

ANTONY   Villains! You did not so° when your vile daggers   40
Hacked one another in the sides of Caesar.
You showed your teeth° like apes, and fawned like hounds,
And bowed like bondmen, kissing Caesar's feet,
Whilst damnèd Casca, like a cur, behind,
Struck Caesar on the neck. Oh, you flatterers!   45
CASSIUS   Flatterers? Now, Brutus, thank yourself!
This tongue had not offended so today
If Cassius might have ruled.°
OCTAVIUS   Come, come, the cause.° If arguing make us sweat,
The proof° of it will turn to redder drops.   50
Look,   [*He draws*]
I draw a sword against conspirators.
When think you that the sword goes up° again?
Never, till Caesar's three-and-thirty° wounds
Be well avenged, or till another Caesar°   55
Have added slaughter to° the sword of traitors.
BRUTUS   Caesar, thou canst not die by traitors' hands,
Unless thou bring'st them with thee.°
OCTAVIUS   So I hope.
I was not born to die on Brutus' sword.°
BRUTUS   Oh, if° thou wert the noblest of thy strain,°   60
Young man, thou couldst not die more honorable.
CASSIUS   A peevish° schoolboy,° worthless° of such honor,
Joined with a masker and a reveler!°
ANTONY   Old Cassius still.°
OCTAVIUS   Come, Antony, away!—
Defiance, traitors, hurl we in your teeth.   65
If you dare fight today, come to the field;
If not, when you have stomachs.
                    Exeunt Octavius, Antony, and army

40 **so** give warning   42 **showed your teeth** in smiles   48 **ruled** prevailed (in urging
that Antony be killed [see 2.1.156–62])   49 **the cause** to our business   50 **proof**
trial   53 **up** in its sheath   54 **three-and-thirty** (Plutarch has it three-and-twenty)
55 **another Caesar** myself, Octavius   56 **Have . . . to** has also been slaughtered by
57–8 **thou . . . thee** the only traitors here are in your own army   58–9 **So . . . sword**
(sardonically), I'm glad to hear that, since you are the traitor I mean, and since you
are not in my army, I cannot, according to your assertion, die at your hands   60 **if**
even if | **strain** lineage   62 **peevish** silly, childish | **schoolboy** (Octavius was
eighteen at the time of Caesar's assassination) | **worthless** unworthy   63 **a masker
. . . reveler** Antony, noted for his dissipation   64 **Old . . . still** Cassius, as envious
and ill-willed as ever (said sardonically)

CASSIUS   Why, now, blow wind, swell billow,° and swim bark!°
The storm is up, and all is on the hazard.°
BRUTUS   Ho, Lucilius! Hark, a word with you.   70
LUCILIUS (*stands forth*)   My lord?
                    [*Brutus and Lucilius converse apart*]
CASSIUS   Messala!
MESSALA (*stands forth*)   What says my general?
CASSIUS   Messala,
This is my birthday, as° this very day   75
Was Cassius born. Give me thy hand, Messala.
Be thou my witness that against my will,
As Pompey° was, am I compelled to set°
Upon one battle all our liberties.
You know that I held Epicurus° strong   80
And his opinion. Now I change my mind
And partly credit things that do presage.°
Coming from Sardis, on our former ensign°
Two mighty eagles fell,° and there they perched,
Gorging and feeding from our soldiers' hands,   85
Who to Philippi here consorted° us.
This morning are they fled away and gone,
And in their steads do ravens, crows, and kites°
Fly o'er our heads and downward look on us
As° we were sickly prey. Their shadows seem   90
A canopy most fatal,° under which
Our army lies, ready to give up the ghost.
MESSALA   Believe not so.
CASSIUS   I but° believe it partly,
For I am fresh of spirit and resolved
To meet all perils very constantly.°   95

---

68 **billow** wave I **swim bark** let the sailing vessel swim for its life   **69 on the
hazard** at stake   75 **as** inasmuch as   78 **Pompey** (the reference is to the battle of
Pharsalus, where Pompey was persuaded to fight Caesar against his own judgment)
I **set** stake   80 **Epicurus** Greek philosopher (341–270 B.C.) who, because he held
the gods to be indifferent to human affairs, spurned belief in omens or superstitions
82 **presage** foretell events   83 **former ensign** foremost standard, the legion's
aquila, a tall standard surmounted by the image of an eagle   84 **fell** swooped
down   86 **consorted** accompanied   88 **kites** scavenger birds (also raptors)   90 **As**
as if   91 **fatal** presaging death   93 **but** only   95 **constantly** resolutely

BRUTUS Even so, Lucilius.°   [*He rejoins Cassius*]
CASSIUS   Now, most noble Brutus,
The gods° today stand friendly, that we may,
Lovers° in peace, lead on our days to age!°
But since the affairs of men rest still° incertain,
Let's reason° with the worst that may befall.   100
If we do lose this battle, then is this
The very last time we shall speak together.
What are you then determinèd to do?
BRUTUS Even by the rule of that philosophy
By which I did blame Cato° for the death   105
Which he did give himself—I know not how,
But I do find it cowardly and vile,
For fear of what might fall,° so to prevent°
The time° of life—arming myself with patience
To stay° the providence of some high powers   110
That govern us below.
CASSIUS   Then, if we lose this battle,
You are contented to be led in triumph
Thorough° the streets of Rome?
BRUTUS No, Cassius, no. Think not, thou noble Roman,
That ever Brutus will go bound to Rome;   115
He bears too great a mind. But this same day
Must end that work the ides of March begun.
And whether we shall meet again I know not;
Therefore our everlasting farewell take.
Forever and forever farewell, Cassius!   120
If we do meet again, why, we shall smile;
If not, why then this parting was well made.

96 **Even so, Lucilius** (this phrase marks the end of Brutus's private conversation apart with Lucilius) 97 **The gods** may the gods 98 **Lovers** friends ǀ **age** old age 99 **still** always 100 **reason** reckon 105 **Cato** Marcus Porcius Cato, Brutus's father-in-law, who killed himself to avoid submission to Caesar in 46 B.C. (see 2.1.296 and note); Brutus's condemnation of Cato's suicide out of fear of failure can perhaps be reconciled with lines 114–17 below and with Brutus's own later suicide (5.5.50), since on that occasion Brutus is responding to certain defeat and disgrace; the seeming contradiction may also be owing to an ambiguity in North's Plutarch 108 **fall** befall ǀ **prevent** anticipate the end, cut short 109 **time** term, extent 110 **stay** await 113 **Thorough** through

CASSIUS Forever and forever farewell, Brutus!
If we do meet again, we'll smile indeed;
If not, 'tis true this parting was well made.   125
BRUTUS Why, then, lead on. Oh, that a man might know
The end of this day's business ere° it come!
But it sufficeth that the day will end,
And then the end is known.—Come, ho, away!

Exeunt

ACT 5
SCENE 2

Location: The plains of Philippi. The field of battle.

Alarum.° Enter Brutus and Messala

BRUTUS Ride, ride, Messala, ride, and give these bills°
Unto the legions on the other side.°
        [*He hands him written orders*] *Loud alarum*
Let them set on° at once; for I perceive
But cold demeanor° in Octavio's wing,
And sudden push gives them the overthrow.   5
Ride, ride, Messala! Let them all come down.°

Exeunt [*separately*]

ACT 5
SCENE 3

Location: The field of battle still.

Alarums. Enter Cassius [*carrying a standard*], *and Titinius*

CASSIUS Oh, look, Titinius, look, the villains° fly!
Myself have to mine own° turned enemy.

127 ere before

0.1 Alarum (this is seemingly an anticipatory stage direction; the battle actually begins with the *Loud alarum* at line 2; an *alarum* is off stage sounds, signifying a battle) **1 bills** orders **2 side** wing (i.e., Cassius's wing) **3 set on** attack **4 cold demeanor** faintheartedness **6 come down** from the hills, where the Republican army has been awaiting the signal to attack (see 5.1.2–3)

1 the villains my own troops **2 mine own** my own men

This ensign° here of mine was turning back;
I slew the coward and did take it° from him.
TITINIUS Oh, Cassius, Brutus gave the word too early,   5
Who, having some advantage on Octavius,
Took it too eagerly. His soldiers fell to spoil,°
Whilst we by Antony are all enclosed.

Enter Pindarus

PINDARUS Fly further off, my lord, fly further off!
Mark Antony is in your tents, my lord.   10
Fly therefore, noble Cassius, fly far off.
CASSIUS This hill is far enough. Look, look, Titinius:
Are those my tents where I perceive the fire?
TITINIUS They are, my lord.
CASSIUS   Titinius, if thou lovest me,
Mount thou my horse, and hide thy spurs in him   15
Till he have brought thee up to yonder troops
And here again, that I may rest assured
Whether yond troops are friend or enemy.
TITINIUS I will be here again even with a thought.°   *Exit*
CASSIUS Go, Pindarus, get higher on that hill.   20
My sight was ever thick.° Regard° Titinius,
And tell me what thou not'st about the field.

[*Pindarus° goes up*]

This day I breathèd first.° Time is come round,
And where I did begin, there shall I end.
My life is run his compass.°—Sirrah, what news?   25
PINDARUS (*above*) Oh, my lord!
CASSIUS What news?
PINDARUS [*above*]
Titinius is enclosèd round about
With horsemen, that make to him on the spur,°
Yet he spurs on. Now they are almost on him.   30

---

3 **ensign** bearer of the standard (a legion's *aquila,* or "eagle standard," had great
significance and needed to be guarded)   4 **it** the standard   7 **spoil** looting   19 **even
. . . thought** as quick as thought   21 **thick** imperfect, dim | **Regard** observe
22.1 *Pindarus goes up* (Pindarus may climb to the gallery, or may exit and ascend
behind the scenes; see line 35.1 and note)   23 **I breathèd first** it is my birthday   25 **his
compass** its circuit, circle (as drawn by a geometer's compass)   29 **make . . . spur**
approach him riding rapidly

Now, Titinius! Now some light.° Oh, he
Lights too. He's ta'en. (*Shout*) And hark! They shout for joy.
CASSIUS   Come down, behold no more.
Oh, coward that I am, to live so long
To see my best friend ta'en before my face!   35

            Enter° *Pindarus* [*from above*]

Come hither, sirrah.
In Parthia° did I take thee prisoner,
And then I swore thee, saving of° thy life,
That whatsoever I did bid thee do
Thou shouldst attempt it. Come now, keep thine oath;   40
Now be a freeman, and with this good sword,
That ran through Caesar's bowels, search this bosom.
Stand° not to answer. Here, take thou the hilts,°
And when my face is covered, as 'tis now,
Guide thou the sword. [*Pindarus does so*] Caesar, thou art
   revenged,   45
Even with the sword that killed thee.   [*He dies*]
PINDARUS   So, I am free, yet would not so° have been,
Durst I have done my will.° Oh, Cassius!
Far from this country Pindarus shall run,
Where never Roman shall take note of him.   [*Exit*]   50

   Enter Titinius [*wearing a garland of laurel*] *and Messala*

MESSALA   It is but change,° Titinius; for Octavius
Is overthrown by noble Brutus' power,
As Cassius' legions are by Antony.
TITINIUS   These tidings will well comfort Cassius.
MESSALA   Where did you leave him?
TITINIUS   All disconsolate,   55
With Pindarus his bondman, on this hill.
MESSALA   Is not that he that lies upon the ground?
TITINIUS   He lies not like the living. Oh, my heart!

---

31 light alight, dismount   **35.1** *Enter* (Pindarus may descend in full view of the
audience; see note at 22.1)   **37 Parthia** (what is now northern Iran)   **38 swore . . .
of** made you swear, when I spared   **43 Stand** delay | **hilts** sword hilt   **47 so** in this
manner   **48 Durst . . . will** if I had dared do what I wished   **51 change** exchange of
advantage, quid pro quo

MESSALA   Is not that he?

TITINIUS   No, this was he, Messala,
But Cassius is no more. O setting sun,   60
As in thy red rays thou dost sink to night,
So in his red blood Cassius' day is set.
The sun° of Rome is set. Our day is gone;
Clouds, dews, and dangers come; our deeds are done.
Mistrust° of my success hath done this deed.   65

MESSALA   Mistrust of good success hath done this deed.
O hateful Error, Melancholy's child,°
Why dost thou show to the apt° thoughts of men
The things that are not? O Error, soon conceived,
Thou never com'st unto a happy birth,   70
But kill'st the mother° that engendered thee.

TITINIUS   What, Pindarus! Where art thou, Pindarus?

MESSALA   Seek him, Titinius, whilst I go to meet
The noble Brutus, thrusting this report
Into his ears. I may say "thrusting" it,   75
For piercing steel and darts envenomèd
Shall be as welcome to the ears of Brutus
As tidings of this sight.

TITINIUS   Hie you, Messala,
And I will seek for Pindarus the while.

                      [*Exit Messala*]
Why didst thou send me forth, brave Cassius?   80
Did I not meet thy friends? And did not they
Put on my brows this wreath of victory
And bid me give it thee? Didst thou not hear their shouts?
Alas, thou hast misconstrued everything.
But, hold thee,° take this garland on thy brow.   85

        [*He places the garland on Cassius's brow*]
Thy Brutus bid me give it thee, and I
Will do his bidding. Brutus, come apace°
And see how I regarded Caius Cassius.

---

63 **sun** (with pun on *son*)   65 **Mistrust** Cassius's doubt   67 **Melancholy's child**
bred of pessimism   68 **apt** impressionable   71 **the mother** the melancholy person
who too readily believes the worst   85 **hold thee** wait   87 **apace** quickly

By your leave, gods! This is a Roman's part.
Come, Cassius' sword, and find Titinius' heart.   90
                [*He stabs himself and*] *dies*

    Alarum. Enter Brutus, Messala, young Cato, Strato,
      Volumnius, and Lucilius, [Labeo, and Flavius]

BRUTUS Where, where, Messala, doth his body lie?
MESSALA Lo, yonder, and Titinius mourning it.
BRUTUS Titinius' face is upward.
CATO   He is slain.
BRUTUS O Julius Caesar, thou art mighty yet!
Thy spirit walks abroad and turns our swords   95
In our own proper° entrails.   *Low alarums°*
CATO   Brave Titinius!
Look whe'er° he have not crowned dead Cassius.
BRUTUS Are yet two Romans living such as these?
The last of all the Romans, fare thee well!
It is impossible that ever Rome   100
Should breed thy fellow. Friends, I owe more tears
To this dead man than you shall see me pay.—
I shall find time, Cassius, I shall find time.—
Come, therefore, and to Thasos° send his body.
His funerals° shall not be in our camp,   105
Lest it discomfort us. Lucilius, come,
And come, young Cato, let us to the field.
Labeo and Flavius, set our battles° on.
'Tis three o'clock, and, Romans, yet ere night°
We shall try fortune in a second fight.   110
              Exeunt [with the bodies]

---

96 own proper very own   **96 s.d.** *Low alarums* offstage sound effects suggesting the activity of distant battle   **97 whe'er** whether   **104 Thasos** an island off the coast of Thrace, near Philippi   **105 funerals** funeral obsequies   **108 battles** armies   **109 yet ere night** (the historical battles fought at Philippi were actually weeks apart)

ACT 5
SCENE 4

Location: Scene continues at the field of battle.

Alarum. Enter Brutus, Messala,
[young] Cato, Lucilius, and Flavius

BRUTUS Yet, countrymen, oh, yet hold up your heads!
                    [Exit, followed by Messala and Flavius]
CATO What bastard doth not?° Who will go with me?
  I will proclaim my name about the field:
  I am the son of Marcus Cato, ho!
  A foe to tyrants, and my country's friend.   5
  I am the son of Marcus Cato, ho!

                    Enter soldiers, and fight

LUCILIUS And I am Brutus, Marcus Brutus I!
  Brutus, my country's friend! Know me for Brutus!
                    [Young Cato is slain by Antony's men]
  O young and noble Cato, art thou down?
  Why, now thou diest as bravely as Titinius,   10
  And mayst be honored, being Cato's son.
FIRST SOLDIER *[capturing Lucilius]*
  Yield, or thou diest.
LUCILIUS *[offering money]* Only I yield to die.°
  There is so much that thou wilt kill me straight;°
  Kill Brutus, and be honored in his death.
FIRST SOLDIER We must not. A noble prisoner!   15
SECOND SOLDIER Room, ho! Tell Antony, Brutus is ta'en.

                    Enter Antony

FIRST SOLDIER I'll tell the news. Here comes the General.—
  Brutus is ta'en, Brutus is ta'en, my lord.
ANTONY Where is he?
LUCILIUS Safe, Antony, Brutus is safe enough.   20
  I dare assure thee that no enemy

---

2 What . . . not? who is so base that he would not do so? **12 Only . . . die**
I surrender only on condition that I die at your hands **13 There . . . straight** here is
money if you will kill me at once

Shall ever take alive the noble Brutus.
The gods defend him from so great a shame!
When you do find him, or alive° or dead,
He will be found like Brutus, like himself.   25
ANTONY [*to First Soldier*]
   This is not Brutus, friend, but, I assure you,
   A prize no less in worth. Keep this man safe;
   Give him all kindness. I had rather have
   Such men my friends than enemies.—Go on,
   And see whe'er° Brutus be alive or dead;   30
   And bring us word unto Octavius' tent
   How everything is chanced.°
                    Exeunt [separately, some bearing Cato's body]

ACT 5
SCENE 5

Location: The field of battle still.

Enter Brutus, Dardanius, Clitus, Strato, and Volumnius

BRUTUS   Come, poor remains of friends, rest on this rock.
                                        [*He sits*]
CLITUS   Statilius showed the torchlight, but, my lord,
   He came not back. He is or ta'en° or slain.°
BRUTUS   Sit thee down, Clitus. Slaying is the word.
   It is a deed in fashion. Hark thee, Clitus.   5
                                   [*He whispers*]
CLITUS   What, I, my lord? No, not for all the world.
BRUTUS   Peace then. No words.
CLITUS   I'll rather kill myself.
BRUTUS   Hark thee, Dardanius.   [*He whispers*]
DARDANIUS   Shall I do such a deed?
             [*Dardanius and Clitus move away from Brutus*]

---

24 or alive either alive   **30 whe'er** whether   **32 is chanced** has fallen out
2–3 Statilius . . . slain (according to Plutarch, a scout named Statilius has gone through
the enemy lines to reconnoitre and to hold up a torch if all is well at Cassius's camp;
he signals back but is then captured and slain)   **3 or ta'en** either taken

CLITUS   Oh, Dardanius!

DARDANIUS   Oh, Clitus!   10

CLITUS   What ill request did Brutus make to thee?

DARDANIUS   To kill him, Clitus. Look, he meditates.

CLITUS   Now is that noble vessel full of grief,
  That it runs over even at his eyes.

BRUTUS   Come hither, good Volumnius. List° a word.   15

VOLUMNIUS   What says my lord?

BRUTUS   Why, this, Volumnius:
  The ghost of Caesar hath appeared to me
  Two several° times by night—at Sardis once,
  And this last night here in Philippi fields.
  I know my hour is come.

VOLUMNIUS   Not so, my lord.   20

BRUTUS   Nay, I am sure it is, Volumnius.
  Thou see'st the world, Volumnius, how it goes;
  Our enemies have beat° us to the pit.°   *Low alarums*
  It is more worthy to leap in ourselves
  Than tarry till they push us. Good Volumnius,   25
  Thou know'st that we two went to school together.
  Even for that our love° of old, I prithee,
  Hold thou my sword hilts° whilst I run on it.

VOLUMNIUS   That's not an office for a friend, my lord.
                                                    Alarum still

CLITUS   Fly, fly, my lord! There is no tarrying here.   30

BRUTUS   Farewell to you, and you, and you, Volumnius.
  Strato, thou hast been all this while asleep;
  Farewell to thee too, Strato. Countrymen,
  My heart doth joy that yet in all my life
  I found no man but he was true to me.   35
  I shall have glory by this losing day
  More than Octavius and Mark Antony
  By this vile conquest shall attain unto.
  So fare you well at once,° for Brutus' tongue
  Hath almost ended his life's history.   40

---

15 List listen to   **18 several** separate   **23 beat** driven | **pit** trap for wild animals; also, a grave   **27 that our love** that friendship of ours   **28 hilts** hilt   **39 at once** all together, or without further ado

Night hangs upon mine eyes; my bones would rest,
That have but labored to attain this hour.°
                    Alarum. Cry within, "Fly, fly, fly!"
CLITUS Fly, my lord, fly!
BRUTUS   Hence, I will follow.
        [*Exeunt Clitus, Dardanius, and Volumnius*]
I prithee, Strato, stay thou by thy lord.
Thou art a fellow of a good respect;°   45
Thy life hath had some smatch° of honor in it.
Hold then my sword, and turn away thy face,
While I do run upon it. Wilt thou, Strato?°
STRATO Give me your hand first. Fare you well, my lord.
BRUTUS Farewell, good Strato. [*He runs on his sword*] Caesar,
    now be still.   50
I killed not thee with half so good a will.   *Dies*

            Alarum. Retreat.° *Enter Antony, Octavius;*
            Messala, Lucilius [*as prisoners*]; *and the army*

OCTAVIUS What man is that?
MESSALA My master's man. Strato, where is thy master?
STRATO Free from the bondage you are in, Messala.
The conquerors can but make a fire of him,   55
For Brutus only overcame himself,°
And no man else hath honor by his death.
LUCILIUS So Brutus should be found. I thank thee, Brutus,
That thou hast proved Lucilius' saying° true.
OCTAVIUS All that served Brutus, I will entertain° them.   60
Fellow, wilt thou bestow thy time with me?
STRATO Ay, if Messala will prefer° me to you.
OCTAVIUS Do so, good Messala.
MESSALA How died my master, Strato?
STRATO I held the sword, and he did run on it.   65
MESSALA Octavius, then take him to follow° thee,
That did the latest° service to my master.

---

42 That . . . hour that have striven all life long only to achieve this moment of death
45 respect reputation   **46 some smatch** some flavor, a touch   **47–8 Hold . . .
Strato?** this is one of two versions of Brutus's death recounted by Plutarch; in the
other, Brutus runs himself through; see 127, below   **51.1 *Retreat*** signal to retire
56 Brutus . . . himself only Brutus conquered Brutus   **59 saying** (see 5.4.21–5)
60 entertain take into service   **62 prefer** recommend   **66 follow** serve   **67 latest** last

ANTONY   This was the noblest Roman of them all.
All the conspirators save only he
Did that they did in envy of great Caesar;   70
He only in a general° honest thought
And common good to all made one of them.
His life was gentle,° and the elements
So mixed in him that Nature might stand up
And say to all the world, "This was a man!"   75
OCTAVIUS   According to his virtue let us use him,
With all respect and rites of burial.
Within my tent his bones tonight shall lie,
Most like a soldier, ordered° honorably.
So call the field° to rest, and let's away   80
To part° the glories of this happy° day.
                    Exeunt omnes° [*with Brutus's body*]

71 **general** selfless (cf. 2.1.12n)   73 **gentle** noble | **elements** (humankind as a microcosm is made up of earth, air, fire, and water, formed into the four humors of phlegm, blood, yellow bile [or choler], and black bile [or melancholy], whose qualities were mingled in Brutus in due proportions)   79 **ordered** treated, arranged for; accorded solemn rites (cf. 1.2.25n)   80 **field** army in the field   81 **part** share | **happy** fortunate   81.1 *omnes* all

CONTEXTS

Sources

In 1579, Sir Thomas North translated into English Jacques Amyot's 1559 French translation of Plutarch's *Lives of the Greeks and Romans*. North's Plutarch was Shakespeare's principal source for *Timon of Athens*, *Coriolanus*, *Antony and Cleopatra*, and *Julius Caesar*. Scholars have detected in *Caesar* faint echoes of Thomas Kyd's *Cornelia* (a 1594 translation of Jacques Garnier's *Cornélie* [1574]) and small details from Appian's *Chronicle of the Romans' Wars* (translated into English in 1578), but in North's lives of Caesar, Brutus, and Antony, Shakespeare found his plot, character studies of his protagonists, and some inspiration for his conception of Roman oratory; he even helped himself to a few of North's choicer turns of phrase.

What can we learn from comparing Shakespeare's play to its source? Many scholars see in source study an opportunity to reveal Shakespeare's dramatic craft: to study the transformation of hundreds of pages of prose narrative and two tumultuous years of Roman history into a few hours of drama is to discover Shakespeare's approach to plotting, characterization, scene structure, and so on. A more elusive goal of source study is the recovery of authorial intention. If we attend closely to the movement from source to play, we may see evidence of the author's aims; some details of a literary work may seem merely arbitrary, but a sharp disjunction between text and source may strike us as a fossil record of an author's decision. *Caesar* is exceptionally tantalizing because, on the one hand, Shakespeare relied so heavily on a single source and because, on the other, he departed from that source in such striking ways. In North's Plutarch, the people are deeply offended by the triumph that Caesar celebrates to commemorate his triumph over Pompey's sons; the people idolize their tribunes for stripping crowns from statues of Caesar; Caesar is very eager to read Artemidorus's petition because it concerns his own interests; and the people hate Caesar at the time of his assassination. In Shakespeare's *Caesar*, by contrast, the people encourage Caesar's triumph; there is considerable enmity between the people and their tribunes; Caesar rebuffs Artemidorus precisely because the petition he urges "touches" Caesar ("What touches us ourself shall be last served" [3.1.8]); and Caesar retains a firm hold on the people's affection. Putting Shakespeare's source to one side, we might ask all sorts of critical questions about these scenes that would not seek to recover authorial intention: how, for example, might a theatrical audience's experience of the tribunes' harsh scolding of the people in the play's first scene shape their reaction to the news that "Marullus and Flavius, for pulling scarves off Caesar's images, are put to silence" (1.2.280–81)? However, when we juxtapose Shakespeare's tribunes and Plutarch's tribunes, the questions that emerge turn on intention and assume a correlation between meaning and authorial intention: why, for example, did Shakespeare transform Plutarch's popular heroes into the people's sour antagonists? Making extremely precise claims about an author's intentions is a tricky business, but attending to the changes and choices Shakespeare made as he fashioned his play out of Plutarch's biographies opens up a range of interpretive questions that might well transform our sense of the fundamental meaning of the play. Some such questions spring from massive reimaginings of Plutarchan history: why, for example, did Shakespeare wholly omit Plutarch's account of the people's growing antipathy toward Caesar, and how does Shakespeare's popular Caesar affect our interpretation of Brutus's and Cassius's actions? Other questions turn on small details: Plutarch offers two versions of Brutus's death—in the first, he runs himself through; in the second, he impales himself on a sword held for him by Strato. Why did Shakespeare prefer the second version?

Plutarch (c. 46–120 ce) and Sir Thomas North (1535–c. 1603)

Plutarch (Lucius [?] Mestrius Plutarchus) may not strike the same sparks for modern readers that fly from the names Homer, Plato, Aristotle, and Sophocles, but, during the Renaissance, his Parallel Lives—

juxtaposed biographies of great Greeks and Romans—and Moral
Essays *were among the most influential Greek texts. Born near Delphi
sometime before 50 CE, Plutarch was an educator, philosopher, and
biographer of considerable importance and influence in both Greece
and Rome. He died sometime after 120 CE.*[1]

  *Sir Thomas North, a son of Edward North, the first Baron North,
was admitted to Lincoln's Inn in 1556. Thomas, however, was more
interested in letters than law: in 1557, the first of his many translations
from Italian and French authors was published; his translation of
Plutarch (by way of Amyot) made his name. Edward North had been a
counselor to Mary I, and Thomas dedicated his first work to the
Catholic queen, but the family flourished under Elizabeth I. Thomas's
older brother Rodger served Elizabeth in several important positions,
and Thomas accompanied him on an embassy to the French court in
1573. Thomas himself enjoyed the support of important courtiers,
occasionally served the queen in various military capacities, and was
rewarded with a pension and a knighthood for helping to put down the
Essex Rebellion in 1601.*[2]

  The following selections from North's Plutarch *are taken from the
1579 edition; Shakespeare may well have read both the 1579 and the 1595
editions of North's translations. North included many marginal notes in
his editions of Plutarch, and I have reproduced some of them in footnotes.*

  Plutarch begins his Life of Julius Caesar *in medias res: Caesar,
already a prominent man, joins the Marian faction in the great struggle
between Marius and Sulla—"Sylla" in North's translation—for political supremacy. Caesar flees Rome to escape Sulla's murderous enmity;
after Sulla's power wanes, Caesar returns to Rome and resumes his
public career and his courtship of the people.*

Plutarch, from *Life of Julius Caesar*,
trans. Sir Thomas North (1579)

[Caesar's popularity]

It is reported that *Caesar* had an excellent natural gift to speak well
before the people, & besides that rare gift, he was excellently well
studied, so that doubtless he was counted the second man for elo-

[1]For biographical information about Plutarch and other classical authors, I have
consulted *The Oxford Companion to Classical Civilization*, ed. Simon Hornblower
and Antony Spawforth (Oxford: Oxford University Press, 1998).

[2]For biographical information about North and other Elizabethans and Jacobeans, I
have drawn on many sources, but *The Oxford Dictionary of National Biography*
(Oxford: Oxford University Press, 2004) has been especially valuable.

quence in his time,[3] and gave place to the first, because he would be the first and chiefest man of war and authority, being not yet come to the degree of perfection to speak well, which his nature could have performed in him, because he was given rather to follow wars and to manage great matters, which in the end brought him to be Lord of all ROME. . . .

. . . Now *Caesar* immediately won many men's good wills at ROME, through his eloquence, in pleading of their causes: and the people loved him marvelously also, because of the courteous manner he had to speak to every man, and to use them gently, being more ceremonious therein, than was looked for in one of his years. Furthermore, he ever kept a good board, and fared well at his table, and was very liberal besides: the which indeed did advance him forward, and brought him in estimation with the people. His enemies, judging that this favor of the common people[4] would soon quail when he could no longer hold out that charge and expense, suffered him to run on, till by little and little he was grown to be of great strength & power. But in fine, when they had thus given him the bridal to grow to this greatness, and that they could not then pull him back, though indeed in sight it would turn one day to the destruction of the whole state and common wealth of ROME: too late they found, that there is not so little a beginning of any thing, but continuance of time will soon make it strong, when through contempt there is no impediment to hinder the greatness. Thereupon, *Cicero*, like a wise shipmaster that feareth the calmness of the sea, was the first man, that mistrusting his manner of dealing in the common wealth, found out his craft & malice, which he cunningly cloaked under the habit of outward courtesy and familiarity. "And yet," said he, "when I consider how finely he combeth his faire bush of hair, and how smooth it lieth, and that I see him scratch his head with one finger only, my mind gives me then, that such a kind of man should not have so wicked a thought in his head as to overthrow the state of the common wealth." But this was long time after that. The first show and proof of the love and good will which the people did bear unto *Caesar* was when he sued to be Tribune of the soldiers (to wit, Colonel of a thousand footmen) standing against

[3]The first man for eloquence was Cicero.
[4]North's marginal note: "*Caesar a follower of the people.*"

Caius Pompilius, at what time he was preferred and chosen before him. But the second & more manifest proof than the first was at the death of his aunt *Julia*, the wife of *Marius* the elder. For being her nephew, he made a solemn oration in the market place in commendation of her, and at her burial did boldly venture to show forth the images of *Marius*: the which was the first time that they were seen after *Sylla's* victory, because that *Marius* and all his confederates had been proclaimed traitors and enemies to the common wealth. For when there were some that cried out upon *Caesar* for doing of it, the people on the other side kept a stir, and rejoiced at it, clapping of their hands, and thanked him, for that he had brought as it were out of hell, the remembrance of *Marius* honor again into ROME, which had so long time been obscured & buried. And where it had been an ancient custom of long time, that the ROMANS used to make funeral orations in praise of old Ladies and matrons when they dyed, but not of young women: *Caesar* was the first that praised his own wife with funeral oration when she was dead, the which also did increase the peoples good wills the more, seeing him of so kind & gentle nature.

[Caesar's victories in Spain, first consulship, and populist politics]

. . . marching forward against the CALLAECIANS and LUSITANI-ANS, he conquered all, & went as far as the great sea Oceanum, subduing all the people which before knew not the ROMANS for their Lords. There he took order for pacifying of the war, and did as wisely take order for the establishing of peace. For he did reconcile the cities together, and made them friends one with an other, but specially he pacified all suits of law, & strife, betwixt the debtors and creditors, which grew by reason of usury. For he ordained that the creditors should take yearly two parts of the revenue of their debtors, until such time as they had paid themselves: and that the debtors should have the third part to themselves to live withal. He having won great estimation by this good order taken, returned from his government very riche, and his soldiers also full of rich spoils, who called him Imperator, to say sovereign Captain. Now the ROMANS having a custom, that such as demanded honor of triumph, should remain a while without the city, and that they on the other side which sued for the Consulship, should of necessity be there in person: *Caesar* coming unhappily at that very time when the Consuls were chosen, he sent to pray the Senate to do him that favor, that being absent, he might by his friends sue for the Consulship. *Cato* at the first did vehemently inveigh against it, vouching an express law forbidding the contrary. But afterwards, perceiving that notwithstanding the reasons he alleged, many of the Senators (being won by *Caesar*) favored his request: yet he cunningly sought all he could to prevent them, prolonging time, dilating his oration until night. *Caesar* thereupon determined rather to give over the suit of his triumph, and to make suit for the Consulship: and so came into the city, and had such a device with him, as went beyond them all, but *Cato* only. His device was this, *Pompey* and *Crassus*, two of the greatest personages of the city of ROME, being at jar together, *Caesar* made them friends, and by that means got unto himself the power of them both: for, by color of that gentle act and friendship of his, he subtly (unawares to them all) did greatly alter and change the state of the common wealth. For it was not the private discord between *Pompey* and *Caesar*, as many men thought, that caused the civil war: but rather it was their agreement together, who joined all their powers first to overthrow the state of the Senate and nobility, and afterwards they fell at jar one with an other. But *Cato*, that then foresaw and prophesied many times what would follow, was taken but for a vain man: but afterwards they found him a wiser man, then happy in his counsel. Thus *Caesar* being brought unto the assembly of the election, in the midst of these two noble persons, whom he had before reconciled together: he was there chosen Consul, with *Calphurnius Bibulus*, without gainsaying or contradiction of any man. Now when he was entered into his office, he began to put forth laws meeter for a seditious Tribune of the people, than for a Consul: because by them he preferred the division of lands, and distributing of corn to every citizen, Gratis, to please them withal. But when the noble men of the Senate were against his device, he desiring no better occasion, began to cry out, and to protest, that by the overhardness and austerity of the Senate, they drove him against his will to lean unto the people: and thereupon having *Crassus* on the one side of him, and *Pompey* on the other, he asked them openly in the assembly, if they did give their consent unto the laws which he had put forth. They both answered, they did. Then he prayed them to stand by him against those that threatened him with force of sword to let[5] him. *Crassus* gave him his word, he would. *Pompey* also did the like, and added thereunto, that he would come with his sword and target both, against them that would withstand him with their swords. These words offended much the Senate, being far unmeet for his gravity, and indecent for the majesty and honor he carried, and most of all uncomely for the presence of the Senate whom he should have reverenced: and were speeches fitter for a rash light headed youth, than for his person. Howbeit the common people on the other side, they rejoiced.

[Caesar's popularity with the army]

Now *Caesar's* self did breed this noble courage and life in [his soldiers]. First, for that he gave them bountifully, & did honor them also, showing thereby, that he did not heap up riches in the wars to maintain his life afterwards in wantonness and pleasure, but that he did keep it in store, honorably to reward their valiant service: and that by so much he thought himself rich, by how much he was liberal in rewarding of them that had deserved it. Furthermore, they did not wonder so much at his valiantness in putting himself at every instant in such manifest danger, and in taking so extreme pains as he did, knowing that it was his greedy desire of honor that set him a fire, and pricked him forward to do it: but that he always continued all labor and hardness, more than his body could bear, that filled them all with admiration. For, concerning the constitution of his body, he was lean, white, and soft skinned, and often subject to headache, and other while to the falling sickness:[6] (the which took him the first time, as it is reported, in CORDUBA, a city of SPAIN) but yet therefore yielded not to the disease of his body, to make it a cloak to cherish him withal, but contrarily, took the pains of war, as a medicine to cure his sick body fighting always with his disease, traveling continually, living soberly, and commonly lying abroad in the field. For the most nights he slept in his coach or litter, and thereby bestowed his rest, to make him always able to do some thing: and in the day time, he would travel up and down the country to see towns, castles, and strong places. He had always a secre-

[5]Hinder.
[6]Epilepsy.

tary with him in his coach, who did still write as he went by the way, and a soldier behind him that carried his sword.

[After winning great victories in Gaul, Caesar plots against Pompey]

Now *Caesar* had of long time determined to destroy *Pompey*, and *Pompey* him also. For *Crassus*[7] being killed amongst the PARTHI- ANS, who only did see, that one of them two must needs fall: noth- ing kept *Caesar* from being the greatest person, but because he destroyed not *Pompey*, that was the greater: neither did any thing let *Pompey* to withstand that it should not come to pass, but because he did not first overcome *Caesar*, whom only he feared. For till then, *Pompey* had not long feared him, but always before set light by him, thinking it an easy matter for him to put him down when he would, sith he had brought him to that greatness he was come unto. But *Caesar* contrarily, having had that drift in his head from the beginning, like a wrestler that studieth for tricks to over- throw his adversary: he went far from ROME, to exercise himself in the wars of GAUL, where he did train his army, and presently by his valiant deeds did increase his fame and honor. By these means became *Caesar* as famous as *Pompey* in his doings, and lacked no more to put his enterprise in execution, but some occasions of color,[8] which *Pompey* partly gave him, and partly also the time delivered him, but chiefly, the hard fortune and ill government at that time of the common wealth at ROME. For they that made sure for honor and offices, bought the voices of the people with ready money, which they gave out openly to usury, without shame or fear. Thereupon, the common people that had sold their voices for money, came to the market place at the day of election, to fight for him that had hired them: not with their voices, but with their bows, slings, and swords. So that the assembly seldom time brake up, but that the pulpit for orations was defiled and sprinkled with the blood of them that were slain in the market place, the city remaining all that time without government of Magistrate, like a ship left without a Pilot. Insomuch, as men of deep judgment & discretion seeing such fury & madness of the people, thought

[7]The triumvirate of Crassus, Pompey, and Caesar had long dominated Roman politics.
[8]Pretexts.

themselves happy if the common wealth were no worse troubled than with the absolute state of a Monarchy & sovereign Lord to govern them. Furthermore, there were many that were not afraid to speak it openly, that there was no other help to remedy the troubles of the common wealth, but by the authority of one man only, that should command them all: & that this medicine must be ministered by the hands of him, that was the gentlest Physician, meaning covertly *Pompey.*

[Having defeated Pompey's forces, Caesar surveys the enemy camp and spares Brutus[9]]

As for them that were taken prisoners, *Caesar* did put many of them amongst his legions, and did pardon also many men of estimation, among whom *Brutus* was one, that afterwards slew *Caesar* himself: and it is reported, that *Caesar* was very sorry for him, when he could not immediately be found after the battle, and that he rejoiced again, when he knew he was alive, and that he came to yield himself unto him.

[Caesar defeats Pompey's sons, celebrates a triumph, becomes "perpetual dictator"]

This was the last war that *Caesar* made. But the triumph he made into ROME for the same, did as much offend the ROMANS, and more, then any thing that ever he had done before: because he had not overcome Captains that were strangers, nor barbarous kings, but had destroyed the sons of the noblest man in ROME, whom fortune had overthrown. . . . This notwithstanding, the ROMANS inclining to *Caesar's* prosperity, and taking the bit in the mouth, supposing that to be ruled by one man alone, it would be a good mean for them to take breath a little, after so many troubles and miseries as they had abided in these civil wars: they chose him per-petual Dictator. This was a plain tyranny: for to this absolute power of Dictator, they added this, never to be afraid to be deposed. *Cicero* propounded before the Senate, that they should give him such honors as were meet for a man: howbeit others afterwards

---

[9]The civil war waged between Caesar and Pompey, in which Cato, Cicero, and most of the Senate sided with Pompey, ended in 48 BCE with the Battle of Pharsalus.

added to, honors beyond all reason. For, men striving who should most honor him, they made him hateful and troublesome to themselves that most favor him, by reason of the unmeasurable greatness and honors which they gave him. Thereupon it is reported, that even they that most hated him, were no less favorers and furtherers of his honors, than they that most flattered him: because they might have greater occasions to rise and that it might appear they had just cause and colour to attempt that they did against him. And now for himself, after he had ended his civil wars, he did so honorably behave himself, that there was no fault to be found in him: and therefore me thinks, amongst other honors they gave him, he rightly deserved this, that they should build him a temple of clemency, to thank him for his courtesy he had used unto them in his victory. For he pardoned many of them that had borne arms against him, and furthermore, did prefer some of them to honor and office in the common wealth: as amongst others, *Cassius* and *Brutus*, both the which were made Praetors. And where *Pompey's* images had been thrown down, he caused them to be set up again: whereupon *Cicero* said then, that *Caesar* setting up *Pompey's* images again, he made his own to stand the surer. And when some of his friends did counsel him to have a guard for the safety of his person, and some also did offer themselves to serve him: he would never consent to it, but said, it was better to die once, than always to be afraid of death. But to win himself the love and good will of the people, as the honorablest guard and best safety he could have: he made common feasts again, & general distributions of corn.

[Caesar's monarchic ambitions and the decline of his popularity]

. . . the chiefest cause that made him mortally hated,[10] was the covetous desire he had to be called king: which first gave the people just cause, and next his secret enemies, honest colour to bear him ill will. This notwithstanding, they that procured him this honor & dignity, gave it out among the people, that it was written in the Sybilline prophecies, how the ROMANS might overcome the PARTHIANS, if they made war with them, and were led by a king, but otherwise that they were unconquerable. And furthermore they

---

[10]North's marginal note: "*Why Caesar was hated.*"

were so bold besides, that *Caesar* returning to ROME from the city
of ALBA, when they came to salute him, they called him king. But
the people being offended, and *Caesar* also angry, he said he was
not called king, but *Caesar*. Then every man keeping silence, he
went his way heavy and sorrowful. When they had decreed divers
honors for him in the Senate, the Consuls and Praetors accompanied with the whole assembly of the Senate, went unto him in the
market place, where he was set by the pulpit for orations, to tell him
what honors they had decreed for him in his absence. But he sitting
still in his majesty, disdaining to rise up unto them when they came
in, as if they had been private men, answered them: that his honors
had more need to be cut off than enlarged. This did not only offend
the Senate, but the common people also, to see that he should so
lightly esteem of the Magistrates of the common wealth: insomuch
as every man that might lawfully go his way, departed thence very
sorrowfully. Thereupon also *Caesar* rising, departed home to his
house, and tearing open his doublet collar, making his neck bare, he
cried out aloud to his friends, that his throat was ready to offer to
any man that would come and cut it. Notwithstanding, it is
reported, that afterwards to excuse this folly, he imputed it to his
disease, saying, that their wits are not perfect which have his disease
of the falling evil, when standing of their feet they speak to the common people, but are soon troubled with a trembling of their body,
and a sudden dimness and giddiness. But that was not true. For he
would have risen up to the Senate, but *Cornelius Balbus* one of his
friends (but rather a flatterer) would not let him, saying: what, do
you not remember that you are *Caesar*, and will you not let them
reverence you, and do their duties? Besides these occasions and
offences, there followed also his shame and reproach, abusing the
Tribunes of the people in this sort. At that time, the feast Lupercalia
was celebrated, the which in old time men say was the feast of shep-
herds or herd men, and is much like unto the feast of the LYCÆNS
in ARCADIA. But howsoever it is, that day there are diverse noble
men sons, young men, (and some of them Magistrates themselves
that govern them) which run naked through the city, striking in
sport them they meet in their way, with leather thongs, hair and all
on, to make them give place. And many noble women, and gentle
women also, go of purpose to stand in their way, and do put forth
their hands to be stricken, as scholars hold them out to their school-

master, to be stricken with the ferula:[11] persuading themselves that
being with child, they shall have good delivery, and also being barren, that it will make them to conceive with child. *Caesar* sat to
behold that sport upon the pulpit for orations, in a chair of gold,
appareled in triumphing manner. *Antonius*, who was Consul at that
time, was one of them that ran this holy course. So when he came
into the market place, the people made a lane for him to run at liberty, and he came to *Caesar*, and presented him a Diadem wreathed
about with laurel. Whereupon there rose a certain cry of rejoicing,
not very great, done only by a few, appointed for the purpose. But
when *Caesar* refused the Diadem, then all the people together made
an outcry of joy. Then *Antonius* offering it him again, there was a
second shout of joy, but yet of a few. But when *Caesar* refused it
again the second time, then all the whole people shouted. *Caesar*
having made this proof, found that the people did not like of it, and
thereupon rose out of his chair, and commanded the crown to be
carried unto *Jupiter* in the Capitol.[12] After that, there were set up
images of *Caesar* in the city with Diadems upon their heads, like
kings: Those, the two Tribunes, *Flavius* and *Marullus*, went and
pulled down: and furthermore, meeting with them that first saluted
Caesar as king, they committed them to prison. The people followed them rejoicing at it, and called them *Brutes*: because of *Brutus*, who had in old time driven the kings out of ROME, & that
brought the kingdom of one person, unto the government of the
Senate and people. *Caesar* was so offended withal, that he deprived
Marullus and *Flavius* of their Tribuneships, and accusing them, he
spake also against the people, and called them *Bruti*, and *Cumani*,
to wit, beasts, and fools. Hereupon the people went straight unto
Marcus Brutus, who from his father came of the first *Brutus*, and by
his mother, of the house of the *Servilians*, a noble house as any was
in ROME, and was also nephew and son in law of *Marcus Cato*.

[Calpurnia's dream and other harbingers of Caesar's death]

Certainly, destiny may easier be foreseen, then avoided: considering
the strange & wonderful signs that were said to be seen before *Caesar's* death. For touching the fires in the element, and spirits running

---

[11]A rod used to punish students.

[12]For another version of these events, see pp. 125–26.

up and down in the night, and also these solitary birds to be seen at noon days sitting in the great market place: are not all these signs perhaps worth the noting, in such a wonderful chance as happened. But *Strabo* the Philosopher writeth, that diverse men were seen going up and down in fire: and furthermore, that there was a slave of the soldiers, that did cast a marvelous burning flame out of his hand, insomuch as they that saw it, thought he had been burnt, but when the fire was out, it was found he had no hurt. *Caesar* self[13] also doing sacrifice unto the gods, found that one of the beasts which was sacrificed had no heart: and that was a strange thing in nature, how a beast could live without a heart. Furthermore, there was a certain Soothsayer that had given *Caesar* warning long time afore, to take heed of the day of the Ides of March, (which is the fifteenth of the month), for on that day he should be in great danger. That day being come, *Caesar* going unto the Senate house, and speaking merrily to the Soothsayer, told him, "the Ides of March be come"; "so be they," softly answered the Soothsayer, "but yet are they not past." And the very day before, *Caesar* supping with *Marcus Lepidus*, sealed certain letters as he was wont to do at the board: so talk falling out amongst them, reasoning what death was best: he preventing their opinions, cried out aloud, "death unlooked for." Then going to bed the same night as his manner was, and lying with his wife *Calpurnia*, all the windows and doors of his chamber flying open, the noise awoke him, and made him afraid when he saw such lights but more, when he heard his wife *Calpurnia*, being fast a sleep, weep and sigh, and put forth many fumbling lamentable speeches. For she dreamed that *Caesar* was slain, and that she had him in her arms. Others also do deny that she had any such dream, as amongst other, *Titus Livius* writeth, that it was in this sort: the Senate having set upon the top of *Caesar's* house, for an ornament and setting forth of the same, a certain pinnacle, *Calpurnia* dreamed that she saw it broken down, and that she thought she lamented and wept for it. Insomuch that *Caesar* rising in the morning, she prayed him if it were possible, not to go out of the doors that day, but to adjourn the session of the Senate, until an other day. And if that he made no reckoning of her dream, yet that he would search further of the Soothsayers by their sacrifices, to know what

[13]Caesar himself.

should happen [to] him that day. Thereby it seemed that *Caesar* likewise did fear and suspect somewhat, because his wife *Calpurnia* until that time was never given to any fear or superstition: and then, for that he saw her so troubled in mind with this dream she had. But much more afterwards, when the Soothsayers having sacrificed many beasts one after an other, told him that none did like them: then he determined to send *Antonius* to adjourn the session of the Senate. But in the mean time came *Decius Brutus*, surnamed *Albinus*, in whom *Caesar* put such confidence, that in his last will and testament be had appointed him to be his next heir, and yet was of the conspiracy with *Cassius* and *Brutus*: he fearing that if *Caesar* did adjourn the session that day, the conspiracy would out, laughed the Soothsayers to scorn, and reproved *Caesar*, saying that he gave the Senate occasion to mislike with him, and that they might think he mocked them, considering that by his commandment they were assembled, and that they were ready willingly to grant him all things, and to proclaim him king of all the provinces of the Empire of ROME out of ITALY, and that he should wear his Diadem in all other places, both by sea and land. And furthermore, that if any man should tell them from him, they should depart for that present time, and return again when *Calpurnia* should have better dreams: what would his enemies and ill willers say, and how could they like of his friends' words? And who could persuade them otherwise, but that they would think his dominion a slavery unto them, and tyrannical in himself? "And yet if it be so," said he, "that you utterly mislike of this day, it is better that you go yourself in person, and saluting the Senate, to dismiss them till an other time." Therewithal he took *Caesar* by the hand, and brought him out of his house.

[Artemidorus tries to warn Caesar of the conspiracy; Caesar's death]

And one *Artemidorus* also borne in the Isle of GNIDOS, a Doctor of Rhetoric in the Greek tongue, who by means of his profession was very familiar with certain of *Brutus'* confederates, and therefore knew the most part of all their practices against *Caesar*: came & brought him a little bill written with his own hand, of all that he meant to tell him. He marking how *Caesar* received all the supplications that were offered him, and that he gave them straight to his men that were about him, pressed nearer to him, and said: "*Caesar*, read this memorial to yourself, and that quickly, for they be matters of great weight and touch you nearly." *Caesar* took it of him, but could never read it, though he many times attempted it, for the number of people that did salute him: but holding it still in his hand, keeping it to himself, went on withal into the Senate house. . . . For these things, they may seem to come by chance, but the place where the murder was prepared, and where the Senate were assembled, and where also there stood up an image of *Pompey* dedicated by himself amongst other ornaments which he gave unto the Theater: all these were manifest proofs that it was the ordinance of some god, that made this treason to be executed, specially in that very place. It is also reported, that *Cassius* (though otherwise he did favor the doctrine of *Epicurus*) beholding the image of *Pompey*, before they entered into the action of their traitorous enterprise: he did softly call upon it, to aide him. But the instant danger of the present time, taking away his former reason, did suddenly put him into a furious passion, and made him like a man half besides himself. Now *Antonius*, that was a faithful friend to *Caesar*, and a valiant man besides of his hands, him *Decius Brutus Albinus* entertained out of the Senate house, having begun a long tale of set purpose. So *Caesar* coming into the house, all the Senate stood up on their feet to do him honor. Then part of *Brutus* company and confederates stood round about *Caesar's* chair, and part of them also came towards him, as though they made suit with *Metellus Cimber*, to call home his brother again from banishment: and thus prosecuting still their suit, they followed *Caesar*, till he was set in his chair. Who, denying their petitions, and being offended with them one after an other, because the more they were denied, the more they pressed upon him, and were the earnester with him: *Metellus* at length, taking his gown with both his hands, pulled it over his neck, which was the sign given the confederates to set upon him. Then *Casca* behind him struck him in the neck with his sword, howbeit the wound was not great nor mortal, because it seemed, the fear of such a devilish attempt did amaze him, and take his strength from him, that he killed him not at the first blow. But *Caesar* turning straight unto him, caught hold of his sword, and held it hard: and they both cried out, *Caesar* in Latin: "O vile traitor *Casca*, what doest thou?" And *Casca* in Greek to his brother, "brother, help me." At the beginning of this stir, they that were present, not knowing of the conspiracy were so amazed with the horrible sight they saw that they had no power to fly, neither to help him, not so much, as once to make any outcry. They on the other side that had conspired his death, compassed him in on every side with their swords drawn in their hands, that *Caesar* turned him no where, but he was stricken at by some, and still had naked swords in his face, and was hacked and mangled among them, as a wild beast taken of hunters. For it was agreed among them, that every man should give him a wound, because all their parts should be in this murder: and then *Brutus* himself gave him one wound about his privities. Men report also that *Caesar* did still defend himself against the rest, running every way with his body: but when he saw *Brutus* with his sword drawn in his hand, then he pulled his gown over his head, and made no more resistance, and was driven either casually, or purposely, by the counsel of the conspirators, against the base whereupon *Pompey's* image stood, which ran all of a gore blood, till he was slain. Thus it seemed, that the image took just revenge of *Pompey's* enemy, being thrown down on the ground at his feet, and yielding up his ghost there, for the number of wounds he had upon him. For it is reported, that he had three and twenty wounds upon his body: and diverse of the conspirators did hurt themselves, striking one body with so many blows.

[Brutus appeals to the people; Brutus and Antony speak to the people]

Brutus and his confederates on the other side, being yet hot with this murder they had committed, having their swords drawn in their hands, came all in a troupe together out of the Senate, and went into the market place, not as men that made countenance to fly, but otherwise boldly holding up their heads like men of courage, and called to the people to defend their liberty, and stayed to speak with every great personage whom they met in their way. Of them, some followed this troupe, and went amongst them, as if they had been of the conspiracy, and falsely challenged part of the honor with them: among them was *Caius Octavius*, and *Lentulus Spinther*. But both of them were afterwards put to death, for their vain covetousness of honor, by *Antonius*, and *Octavius Caesar* the younger: and yet had no part of that honor for the which they were put to death, neither did any man believe that they were any of the confederates, or of counsel with them. For they that did put them to death, took revenge rather of the will they had to offend, then of any fact they had committed. The next morning, *Brutus* and his confederates came into the market place to speak unto the people, who gave them such audience, that it seemed they neither greatly reproved, nor allowed the fact: for by their great silence they showed, that they were sorry for *Caesar's* death, and also that they did reverence *Brutus*. Now the Senate granted general pardon for all that was past, and to pacify every man, ordained besides, that *Caesar's* funerals should be honored as a god, and established all things that he had done: and gave certain provinces also, and convenient honors unto *Brutus* and his confederates, whereby every man thought all things were brought to good peace & quietness again. But when they had opened *Caesar's* testament, and found a liberal legacy of money, bequeathed unto every citizen of ROME, and that they saw his body (which was brought into the market place) all bemangled with gashes of swords: then there was no order to keep the multitude and common people quiet, but they plucked up forms, tables, and stools, and laid them all about the body, & setting them a fire, burnt the corpse. Then when the fire was well kindled, they took the firebrands, and went unto their houses that had slain *Caesar*, to set them a fire. Others also ran up and down the city to see if they could meet with any of them, to cut them in pieces: howbeit they could meet with never a man of them, because they had locked themselves up safely in their houses.

**Plutarch, from *Life of Marcus Brutus*,
trans. Sir Thomas North (1579)**

[Brutus's famous ancestors were the foes of kings and would-be kings]

Marcus Brutus came of that *Junius Brutus*, for whom the ancient ROMANS made his statue of brass to be set up in the Capitol, with the images of the kings, holding a naked sword in his hand: because he had valiantly put down the TARQUINS from their kingdom of ROME. But that *Junius Brutus* being of a sour stern nature, not

Michelangelo Buonarotti, bust of Brutus (1540).

softened by reason, being like unto sword blades of too hard a temper: was so subject to his choler and malice he bare unto the tyrants, that for their sakes he caused his own sons to be executed. But this *Marcus Brutus* in contrary manner, whose life we presently write, having framed his manners of life by the rules of virtue and study of Philosophy, and having employed his wit, which was gentle and constant, in attempting of great things: me thinks he was rightly made and framed unto virtue. So that his very enemies which wish him most hurt, because of his conspiracy against *Julius Caesar*: if there were any noble attempt done in all this conspiracy, they refer it wholly unto *Brutus*, and all the cruel and violent acts unto *Cassius*, who was *Brutus'* familiar friend, but not so well given, and conditioned as he. His mother *Servilia*, it is thought came of the blood of *Servilius Hala*, who, when *Spurius Melius* went about to make himself king, and to bring it to pass had enticed the common people to rebel: took a dagger and hid it close under his arm, and went into the market place. When he was come thither, he made as though he had somewhat to say unto him, and pressed as near him as he could: wherefore *Melius* stooping down with his head, to hear what he would say, *Brutus* stabbed him in with his dagger, and slew him. . . . *Marcus Cato* the Philosopher was brother unto *Servilia M. Brutus'* mother: whom *Brutus* studied most to follow of all the other ROMANS, because he was his Uncle, and afterwards he married his daughter [Portia].

[Brutus takes Pompey's side in his struggle with Caesar; Caesar believed that he was Brutus's father]

Afterwards when the Empire of ROME was divided into factions, and that *Caesar* and *Pompey* both were in arms one against the other, and that all the Empire of ROME was in garboyle and uproar: it was thought then that *Brutus* would take part with *Caesar*, because *Pompey* not long before had put his father unto death. But *Brutus* preferring the respect of his country and common wealth, before private affection, and persuading himself that *Pompey* had juster cause to enter into arms then *Caesar*: he then took part with *Pompey*, though oftentimes meeting him before, he thought scorn to speak to him, thinking it a great sin and offence in him, to speak to the murderer of his father. But then submitting himself unto *Pompey*, as unto the head of the common wealth: he sailed into SICILIA, Lieutenant under *Sestius* that was Governor of that province. But when he saw that there was no way to rise, nor to do any noble exploits, and that *Caesar* & *Pompey* were both camped together, and fought for victory: he went of himself unsent for into MACEDON, to be partaker of the danger. It is reported that *Pompey* being glad, and wondering at his coming when he saw him come to him: he rose out of his chair, and went and embraced him before them all, and used him as honorably, as he could have done the noblest man that took his part. *Brutus* being in *Pompey's* camp, did nothing but study all day long, except he were with *Pompey*, & not only the days before, but the self same day also before the great battle was fought in the fields of PHARSALIA, where *Pompey* was overthrown. It was in the middest of summer, and the sun was very hot, besides that the camp was lodged near unto marshes, and they that carried his tent, tarried long before they came: whereupon, being very weary with travel, scant any meat came into his mouth at dinner time. Furthermore, when others slept, or thought what would happen the morrow after: he fell to his book, and wrote all day long till night, writing a breviary of *Polybius*. It is reported that *Caesar* did not forget him, and that he gave his Captains charge before the battle, that they should beware they killed not *Brutus* in fight, and if he yielded willingly unto them, that then they should bring him unto him: but if he resisted, and would not be taken, then that they should let him go, and do him no hurt. Some say he did this for *Servilia's* sake, *Brutus* mother. For when he was a young man, he had been acquainted with *Servilia*, who was extremely in love with him. And because *Brutus* was borne in that time when their love was hottest, he persuaded himself that he begat him. . . . So, after *Pompey's* overthrow at the battle of PHARSALIA, and that he fled to the sea: when *Caesar* came to besiege his camp, *Brutus* went out of the camp gates unseen of any man, and leapt into a marsh full of water and reeds. Then when night was come, he crept out, and went unto the city of LARISSA: from whence he wrote unto *Caesar*, who was very glad that he had scaped, and sent for him to come unto him. When *Brutus* was come, he did not only pardon him, but also kept him always about him, and did as much honor and esteem him, any man he had in his company.

[Brutus's great prominence; Cassius's hatred of tyranny; Cassius's attempts to win Brutus over to the conspiracy]

And surely, in my opinion, I am persuaded that *Brutus* might indeed have come to have been the chiefest man of ROME, if he could have contented himself for a time to have been next unto *Caesar*, & to have suffered his glory and authority, which he had gotten by his great victories, to consume with time. But *Cassius* being a choleric man, and hating *Caesar* privately, more than he did the tyranny openly: he incensed *Brutus* against him. It is also reported, that *Brutus* could evil away with[14] the tyranny, and that *Cassius* hated the tyranny: making many complaints for the injuries he had done him, and amongst others, for that he had taken away his Lions from him. *Cassius* had provided them for his sports, when he should be Aedile, and they were found in the city of MEGARA, when it was won by *Calenus*, and *Caesar* kept them. The rumor went, that these Lions did marvelous great hurt to the MAGARIANS. For when the city was taken, they brake their cages where they were tied up, and turned them loose, thinking they would have done great mischief to the enemies, and have kept them from setting upon them: but the Lions contrary to expectation, turned upon themselves that fled unarmed, & did so cruelly tore some in pieces, that it pitied their enemies to see them. And this was the cause, as some do report, that made *Cassius* conspire against *Caesar*. But this holdeth no water. For *Cassius* even from his cradle could not abide any manner of tyrant, as it appeared when he was but a boy, & went unto the same school that *Faustus*, the son of *Sylla* did. And *Faustus* bragging among other boys, highly boasted of his father's kingdom: *Cassius* rose up on his feet, and gave him two good wirts[15] on the ear. *Faustus'* governors would have put this matter in suit against *Cassius:* But *Pompey* would not suffer them, but caused the two boys to be brought before him, and asked them how the matter came to pass. Then *Cassius*, as it is written of him, said unto the other: "go to *Faustus*, speak again and thou darest, before this noble man here, the same words that made me angry with thee, that my fists may walk once again about thine ears." Such was *Cassius'* hot stirring nature. But of *Brutus*, his friends and

[14]Tolerate.
[15]Cuffs.

country men, both by divers procurements, and sundry rumors of the city, and by many bills also, did openly call and procure him to do that he did. For, under the image of his ancestor *Junius Brutus*, that drove the kings out of ROME, they wrote: O, that it pleased the gods thou wert now alive, *Brutus:* and again, that thou wert here among us now. His tribunal (or chair) where he gave audience during the time he was Praetor, was full of such bills: *Brutus*, thou art asleep, and art not *Brutus* indeed. And of all this, *Caesar's* flatterers were the cause: who beside many other exceeding and unspeakable honors they daily devised for him, in the night time they did put Diadems upon the heads of his images, supposing thereby to allure the common people to call him king, instead of Dictator. Howbeit it turned to the contrary, as we have written more at large in *Julius Caesars* life.

[Brutus joins the conspiracy]

Cassius asked [Brutus] if he were determined to be in the Senate house, the first day of the month of March, because he heard say that *Caesar's* friends should move the counsel that day, that *Caesar* should he called king by the Senate. *Brutus* answered him, he would not be there. "But if we be sent for," said *Cassius*, "how then?" "For myself," then said *Brutus*, "I mean not to hold my peace, but to withstand it, and rather die then lose my liberty." *Cassius* being bold, and taking hold of this word: "why," quod he, "what ROMAN is he alive that will suffer thee to die for thy liberty? What, knowest thou not that thou art *Brutus*? Thinkest thou that they be cobblers, tapsters, or such like base mechanical people, that write these bills and scrolls which are found daily in thy Praetor's chair, and not the noblest men and best citizens that do it? No, be thou well assured, that of other Praetors they look for gifts, common distributions amongst the people, and for common plays, and to see fencers fight at the sharp, to show the people pastime: but at thy hands, they specially require (as a due debt unto them) the taking away of the tyranny, being fully bent to suffer any extremity for thy sake, so that thou wilt show thyself to be the man thou art taken for, and that they hope thou art." Thereupon he kissed *Brutus*, and embraced him: and so each taking leave of other, they went both to speak with their friends about it.

[To gain her husband's trust, Portia wounds herself in the thigh]

His wife *Porcia* [Portia] (as we have told you before) was the daughter of *Cato*, whom *Brutus* married being his cousin, not a maiden, but a young widow after the death of her first husband *Bibulus*, by whom she had also a young son called *Bibulus*, who afterwards wrote a book of the acts and gests of *Brutus*, extant at this present day. This young Lady being excellently well seen in Philosophy, loving her husband well, and being of a noble courage, as she was also wise: because she would not ask her husband what he ailed before she had made some proof by her self, she took a little razor such as barbers occupy to pare men's nails, and causing all her maids and women to go out of her chamber, gave her self a great gash withal in her thigh, that she was straight all of a gore blood, and incontinently after, a vehement fever took her, by reason of the pain of her wound. Then perceiving her husband was marvelously out of quiet, and that he could take no rest: even in her greatest pain of all, she spoke in this sort unto him. I being, O *Brutus*, (said she) the daughter of *Cato*, was married unto thee, not to be thy bedfellow and companion in bed and at board only, like a harlot: but to be partaker also with thee, of thy good and evil fortune. Now for thyself, I can find no cause of fault in thee touching our match: but for my part, how may I show my duty towards thee, and how much I would do for thy sake, if I can not constantly bear a secret mischance or grief with thee, which requireth secrecy and fidelity? I confess, that a woman's wit commonly is too weak to keep a secret safely: but yet, *Brutus*, good education, and the company of virtuous men, have some power to reform the defect of nature. And for myself, I have this benefit moreover: that I am the daughter of *Cato*, & wife of *Brutus*. This notwithstanding, I did not trust to any of these things before: until that now I have found by experience, that no pain nor grief whatsoever can overcome me. With those words she showed him her wound on her thigh, and told him what she had done to prove her self. *Brutus* was amazed to hear what she said unto him, and lifting up his hands to heaven, he besought the gods to give him the grace he might bring his enterprise to so good pass, that he might be found a husband, worthy of so noble a wife as *Porcia:* so he then did comfort her the best he could.

[On the Ides of March, the Senate meets
in an assembly room within Pompey's Theater]

Now a day being appointed for the meeting of the Senate, at what
time they hoped *Caesar* would not fail to come: the conspirators
determined then to put their enterprise in execution, because they
might meet safely at that time without suspicion, and the rather, for
that all the noblest and chiefest men of the city would be there. Who
when they should see such a great matter executed, would every
man then set to their hands, for the defense of their liberty. Furthermore, they thought also that the appointment of the place where the
counsel should be kept, was chosen of purpose by divine providence, and made all for them. For it was one of the porches about
the Theater, in the which there was a certain place full of seats for
men to sit in, where also was set up the image of *Pompey*, which the
city had made and consecrated in honor of him: when he did beau-
tify that part of the city with the Theater he built, with divers
porches about it. In this place was the assembly of the Senate
appointed to be, just on the fifteenth day of the month of March,
which the ROMANS call, Idus Martias: so that it seemed some god
of purpose had brought *Caesar* thither to be slain, for revenge of
Pompey's death.

[The aftermath of the assassination:
Antony spared; Brutus speaks to the people]

All the conspirators, but *Brutus*, determining upon this matter,
thought it good also to kill *Antonius*, because he was a wicked man,
and that in nature favored tyranny: besides also, for that he was in
great estimation with soldiers, having been conversant of long time
amongst them: and specially, having a mind bent to great enter-
prises, he was also of great authority at that time, being Consul
with *Caesar*. But *Brutus* would not agree to it. First, for that he said
it was not honest: secondly, because he told them there was hope of
change in him. For he did not mistrust, but that *Antonius* being a
noble minded and courageous man (when he should know that
Caesar was dead) would willingly help his country to recover her
liberty, having them an example unto him, to follow their courage
and virtue. So *Brutus* by this means saved *Antonius* life, who at that
present time disguised himself, and stale away. But *Brutus* & his

consorts, having their swords bloody in their hands, went straight
to the Capitol, persuading the ROMANS as they went, to take their
liberty again. Now, at the first time when the murder was newly
done, there were sudden outcries of people that ran up & down the
city, the which indeed did the more increase the fear and tumult.
But when they saw they slew no man, nether did spoil or make
havoc of any thing: then certain of the Senators, & many of the people emboldening themselves, went to the Capitol unto them. There
a great number of men being assembled together one after another:
Brutus made an oration unto them to win the favor of the people,
and to justify that they had done. All those that were by, said they
had done well, and cried unto them that they should boldly come
down from the Capitol. Whereupon, *Brutus* and his companions
came boldly down into the market place. The rest followed in
troupe, but *Brutus* went foremost, very honorably compassed in
round about with the noblest men of the city, which brought him
from the Capitol, thorough the market place, to the pulpit for orations. When the people saw him in the pulpit, although they were a
multitude of rakehells of all sorts, and had a good will to make
some stir: yet being ashamed to do it for the reverence they bare
unto *Brutus*, they kept silence, to hear what he would say. When
Brutus began to speak, they gave him quiet audience: howbeit
immediately after, they showed that they were not all contented
with the murder.

[Antony rouses the people against the conspirators]

The next day following [the assassination], the Senate being called
again to counsel, . . . they came to talk of *Caesars* will and testament, and of his funerals and tomb. Then *Antonius* thinking good
his testament should be read openly, and also that his body should
be honorably buried, and not in hugger mugger, least the people
might thereby take occasion to be worse offended if they did otherwise: *Cassius* stoutly spoke against it. But *Brutus* went with the
motion, & agreed unto it: wherein it seemeth he committed a second fault. For the first fault he did was, when he would not consent
to his fellow conspirators, that *Antonius* should be slain: And therefore he was justly accused, that thereby he had saved and strength-
ened a strong & grievous enemy of their conspiracy. The second

fault was, when he agreed that *Caesars* funerals should be as *Antonius* would have them: the which indeed marred all. For first of all, when *Caesars* testament was openly red among them, whereby it appeared that he bequeathed unto every Citizen of ROME, 75. Drachmas a man, and that he left his gardens and arbors unto the people, which he had on this side of the river of Tiber, in the place where now the temple of Fortune is built: the people then loved him, and were marvelous sorry for him. Afterwards when *Caesars* body was brought into the market place, *Antonius* making his funeral oration in praise of the dead, according to the ancient custom of ROME, and perceiving that his words moved the common people to compassion: he framed his eloquence to make their harts yearn the more, and taking *Caesars* gown all bloody in his hand, he laid it open to the sight of them all, showing what a number of cuts and holes it had upon it. Therewithal the people fell presently into such a rage and mutiny, that there was no more order kept amongst the common people. For some of them cried out, kill the murderers: others plucked up forms, tables, and stalls about the market place, as they had done before at the funerals of *Clodius*, and having laid them all on a heap together, they set them on fire, and thereupon did put the body of *Caesar*, and burnt it in the middest of the most holy places. And furthermore, when the fire was thoroughly kindled, some here, some there, took burning fire brands, and ran with them to the murderers houses that had killed him, to set them a fire. Howbeit the conspirators foreseeing the danger before, had wisely provided for themselves, and fled.

[The characters and beliefs of Brutus and Cassius]

Now *Cassius* would have done *Brutus* as much honor, as *Brutus* did unto him: but *Brutus* most commonly prevented him, and went first unto him, both because he was the elder man, as also for that he was sickly of body. And men reputed him commonly to be very skillful in wars, but otherwise marvelous choleric and cruel, who sought to rule men by fear, rather then with lenity: and on the other side he was too familiar with his friends, and would jest too broadly with them. But *Brutus* in contrary manner, for his virtue and valliantness, was wellbeloved of the people and his own, esteemed of noble men, and hated of no man, not so much as of his enemies:

because he was a marvelous lowly and gentle person, noble minded, and would never be in any rage, nor carried away with pleasure and covetousness, but had ever an upright mind with him, and would never yield to any wrong or injustice, the which was the chiefest cause of his fame, of his rising, and of the good will that every man bare him: for they were all persuaded that his intent was good. For they did not certainly believe, that if *Pompey* himself had overcome *Caesar*, he would have resigned his authority to the law: but rather they were of opinion, that he would still keep the sovereignty and absolute government in his hands, taking only, to please the people, the title of Consul or Dictator, or of some other more civil office. And as for *Cassius*, a hot, choleric, & cruel man, that would oftentimes be carried away from justice for gain: it was certainly thought that he made war, and put himself into sundry dangers, more to have absolute power and authority, then to defend the liberty of his country. For, they that will also consider others, that were elder men then they, as *Cinna, Marius*, and *Carbo*: it is out of doubt that the end and hope of their victory, was to be Lords of their country: and in manner they did all confess that they fought for the tyranny, and to be Lords of the Empire of ROME. And in contrary manner, his enemies themselves did never reprove *Brutus*, for any such change or desire. For, it was said that *Antonius* spoke it openly divers times, that he thought, that of all them that had slain *Caesar*, there was none but *Brutus* only that was moved to do it, as thinking the act commendable of it self: but that all the other conspirators did conspire his death, for some private malice or envy, that they otherwise did bear unto him.

[An "evil spirit" appears to Brutus]

. . . as they both prepared to pass over again, out of ASIA into EUROPE: there went a rumor that there appeared a wonderful sign unto him. *Brutus* was a careful man, and slept very little, both for that his diet was moderate, as also because he was continually occupied. He never slept in the day time, and in the night no longer, then the time he was driven to be alone, and when every body else took their rest. But now whilst he was in war, and his head ever busily occupied to think of his affairs, and what would happen: after he had slumbered a little after supper, he spent all the rest of the night in dispatching of his weightiest causes, and after he had taken order for them, if he had any leisure left him, he would read some book till the third watch of the night, at what time the Captains, petty Captains and Colonels, did use to come unto him. So, being ready to go into EUROPE, one night very late (when all the camp took quiet rest) as he was in his tent with a little light, thinking of weighty matters: he thought he heard one come in to him, and casting his eye towards the door of his tent, that he saw a wonderful strange and monstrous shape of a body coming towards him, and said never a word. So *Brutus* boldly asked what he was, a god, or a man, and what cause brought him thither. The spirit answered him, I am thy evil spirit, *Brutus:* and thou shalt see me by the city of PHILIPPES. *Brutus* being no otherwise afraid, replied again unto it: well, then I shall see thee again. The spirit presently vanished away: and *Brutus* called his men unto him, who told him that they heard no noise, nor saw any thing at all.[16]

[Omens before Brutus's defeat]

. . . it is reported that the monstrous spirit which had appeared before unto *Brutus* in the city of SARDIS, did now appear again unto him in the self same shape and form, and so vanished away, and said never a word. Now *Publius Voluminius*, a grave & wise Philosopher, that had been with *Brutus* from the beginning of this war, he doth make mention of this spirit, but sayeth: that the greatest Eagle and ensign was covered over with a swarm of bees, and that there was one of the Captains, whose arm suddenly fell a sweating, that it dropped oil of roses from him, and that they oftentimes went about to dry him, but all would do no good. And that before the battle was fought, there were two Eagles fought between both armies, and all the time they fought, there was a marvelous great silence all the valley over, both the armies being one before the other, marking this fight between them: and that in the end, the Eagle towards *Brutus* gave over, and flew away. But this is certain, and a true tale: that when the gate of the camp was open, the first man the standard-bearer met that carried the Eagle, was an AETHIOPIAN, whome the soldiers for ill luck mangled with their swords.

[16]For Cassius's reaction to Brutus's dream, see p. 147–48.

[Brutus's death]

Now, the night being far spent, *Brutus* as he sate bowed towards *Clitus* one of his men, and told him somewhat in his ear, the other answered him not, but fell a weeping. Thereupon he proved *Dardanus*, and said somewhat also to him: at length he came to *Volumnius* himself, & speaking to him in Greek, prayed him for the studies sake which brought them acquainted together, that he would help him to put his hand to his sword, to thrust it in him to kill him. *Volumnius* denied his request, and so did many others: and amongst the rest, one of them said, there was no tarrying for them there, but that they must needs fly. Then *Brutus* rising up, we must fly indeed said he, but it must be with our hands, not with our feet. Then taking every man by the hand, he said these words unto them with a cheerful countenance. It rejoiceth my hart that not one of my friends hath failed me at my need, and I do not complain of my fortune, but only for my country's sake: for, as for me, I think myself happier than they that have overcome, considering that I leave a perpetual fame of our courage and manhood, the which our enemies the conquerors shall never attain unto by force nor money, neither can let their posterity to say, that they being naughty and unjust men, have slain good men, to usurp tyrannical power not pertaining to them. Having said so, he prayed every man to shift for themselves, and then he went a little aside with two or three only, among the which *Strato* was one, with whom he came first acquainted by the study of Rhetoric. He came as near to him as he could, and taking his sword by the hilts with both his hands, & falling down upon the point of it, ran himself through. Others say, that not he, but *Strato* (at his request) held the sword in his hand, & turned his head aside, and that *Brutus* fell down upon it: and so ran himself through, and dyed presently.

[Portia's Death[17]]

And for *Porcia, Brutus* wife: *Nicolaus* the Philosopher, and *Valerius Maximus* do write, that she determining to kill her self (her parents and friends carefully looking to her to keep her from it) took hot burning coals, and cast them into her mouth, and kept her mouth so

---

[17]Plutarch's account of Portia's death ends *The Life of Marcus Brutus.*

close, that she choked her self. There was a letter of *Brutus* found written to his friends, complaining of their negligence, that his wife being sick, they would not help her, but suffered her to kill her self, choosing to dye, rather then to languish in pain. Thus it appeareth, that *Nicolaus* knew not well that time, sith the letter (at the least if it were *Brutus* letter) doth plainly declare the disease and love of this Lady, and also the manner of her death.

Plutarch, from *Life of Marcus Antonius*, trans. Sir Thomas North (1579)

[Antony's family; Antony's riotous youth]

Antonius' grandfather was that famous Orator whom *Marius* slew, because he took *Sylla's* part. His father was an other *Antonius* surnamed *Cretan*, who was not so famous, nor bare any great sway in the common wealth: howbeit otherwise he was an honest man, and of a very good nature, and specially very liberal in giving. . . . His wife was *Julia*, of the noble house and family of *Julius Caesar*, who for her virtue & chastity, was to be compared with the noblest Lady of her time. . . . Now *Antonius* being a fair young man, and in the prime of his youth: he fell acquainted with *Curio*, whose friendship and acquaintance (as it is reported) was a plague unto him. For he was a dissolute man, given over to all lust and insolence, who to have *Antonius* the better at his commandment, trained him on into great follies, and vain expenses upon women, in rioting & banqueting. . . .

[Antony's charisma]

. . . he had a noble presence, and showed a countenance of one of a noble house: he had a goodly thick beard, a broad forehead, crook nosed, and there appeared such a manly look in his countenance, as is commonly seen in *Hercules'* pictures, stamped or graven in metal. Now it had been a speech of old time, that the family of the *Antonii* were descended from one *Anton*, the son of *Hercules*, whereof the family took name. This opinion did *Antonius* seek to confirm in all his doings: not only resembling him in the likeness of his body, as we have said before, but also in the wearing of his garments. For when he would openly show himself abroad before many people, he would always wear his cassock girt down low upon his hips, with a great sword hanging by his side, and upon that, some ill favored cloak. Furthermore, things that seem intolerable in other men, as to boast commonly, to feast with one or other, to drink like a good fellow with every body, to sit with the soldiers when they dine, and to eat and drink with them soldier-like: it is incredible what wonderful love it won him amongst them. And furthermore, being given to love, that made him the more desired, and by that means he brought many to love him. For he would further every man's love, and also would not be angry that men should merrily tell him of those he loved. But besides all this, that which most procured his rising and advancement, was his liberality, who gave all to the soldiers, and kept nothing for himself: and when he was grown to great credit, then was his authority and power also very great, the which notwithstanding himself did overthrow, by a thousand other faults he had.

[Antony offers Caesar a crown; Caesar offers his throat to the people]

Antonius unawares . . . gave *Caesar's* enemies just occasion and color to do as they did. . . . he ran to the Tribune where *Caesar* was set, and carried a laurel crown in his hand, having a royal band or diadem wreathed about it, which in old time was the ancient mark and token of a king. . . . he did put this laurel crown upon his head, signifying thereby that he had deserved to be king. But *Caesar* making as though he refused it, turned away his head. The people were so rejoiced at it, that they all clapped their hands for joy. *Antonius* again did put it on his head: *Caesar* again refused it, and thus they were striving off and on a great while together. As oft as *Antonius* did put this laurel crown unto him, a few of his followers rejoiced at it: & as oft also as *Caesar* refused it, all the people together clapped their hands. And this was a wonderful thing, that they suffered all things subjects should do by commandment of their kings: & yet they could not abide the name of a king, detesting it as the utter destruction of their liberty. *Caesar* in a rage rose out of his seat, and plucking down the choler of his gown from his neck, he showed it naked, bidding any man strike of his head that would. This laurel crown was afterwards put upon the head of one of *Caesar's* statues or images, the which one of the Tribunes plucked off. The people liked his doing therein so well, that they waited on him home to his house, with great clapping of hands. Howbeit *Caesar* did turn them out of their offices for it. This was a good encouragement for *Brutus* & *Cassius* to conspire his death. . . .

[After Caesar's death, Antony seems to make his peace with the conspirators but then rouses the people against them]

The self same day he did bid *Cassius* to supper, and *Lepidus* also bad *Brutus*. The next morning the Senate was assembled, & *Antonius* himself preferred a law that all things past should be forgotten, and that they should appoint provinces, unto *Cassius* and *Brutus*: the which the Senate confirmed, and further ordained, that they should cancel none of *Caesar's* laws. Thus went *Antonius* out of the Senate more praised, and better esteemed, then ever man was: because it seemed to every man that he had cut off all occasion of civil wars, and that he had showed himself a marvelous wise governor of the common wealth, for the appeasing of these matters of so great weight & importance. But now, the opinion he conceived of himself after he had a little felt the good will of the people towards him, hoping thereby to make himself the chiefest man if he might overcome *Brutus*: did easily make him alter his first mind. And therefore when *Caesar's* body was brought to the place where it should be buried, he made a funeral oration in commendation of *Caesar*, according to the ancient custom of praising noble men at their funerals. When he saw that the people were very glad and desirous also to hear *Caesar* spoken of, & his praises uttered: he mingled his oration with lamentable words, and by amplifying of matters did greatly move their hearts and affections unto pity & compassion. In fine to conclude his oration, he unfolded before the whole assembly the bloody garments of the dead, thrust through in many places with their swords, & called them malefactors, cruel & cursed murderers. With these words he put the people into such a fury, that they presently toke *Caesar's* body, & burnt it in the market place, with such tables & forms as they could get together. Then when the fire was kindled, they toke firebrands, & ran to the murderers houses to set them afire, & to make them come out to fight. *Brutus* therefore & his accomplices, for safety of their persons were drive to fly the city.

[Antony's valor and generalship;
Antony does honor to Brutus's corpse]

When [Antony and Octavius] had passed over the seas, and . . .
began to make war, they being both camped by their enemies, to
wit, *Antonius* against *Cassius*, and *Caesar* against *Brutus*. *Caesar*
did no great matter, but *Antonius* had always the upper hand, and
did all. For at the first battle *Caesar* was overthrown by *Brutus*, and
lost his camp, and very hardly saved himself by flying from them
that followed him. Howbeit he writeth himself in his Commentaries, that he fled before the charge was given, because of a dream
one of his friends had. *Antonius* on the other side overthrew *Cassius* in battle, though some write that he was not there himself at the
battle, but that he came after the overthrow, whilst his men had the
enemies in chase. So *Cassius* at his earnest request was slain by a
faithful servant of his own called *Pindarus*, whom he had enfranchised: because he knew not in time that *Brutus* had overcome *Caesar*. Shortly after they fought another battle again, in the which
Brutus was overthrown, who afterwards also slew himself. Thus
Antonius had the chiefest glory of all this victory, specially because
Caesar was sick at that time. *Antonius* having found *Brutus'* body
after this battle, blaming him much for the murder of his brother
Caius, whom he had put to death in MACEDON for revenge of
Cicero's cruel death, and yet laying the fault more in *Hortensius*
then in him: he made *Hortensius* to be slain on his brother's tomb.
Furthermore, he cast his coat armor (which was wonderful rich and
sumptuous) upon *Brutus'* body, and gave commandment to one of
his slaves enfranchised, to defray the charge of his burial. But afterwards, *Antonius* hearing that his enfranchised bondman had not
burnt his coat armor with his body, because it was very riche, and
worth a great sum of money, and that he had also kept back much
of the ready money appointed for his funeral & tomb: he also put
him to death.

The Supernatural:
Divine Signs, Ghosts,
and Prophetic Dreams

The weird sisters of *Macbeth*, Prospero's magic books, the ghost of Hamlet's father, the fairies of *A Midsummer Night's Dream*: the supernatural is a familiar enough feature of Shakespearean drama, but it is still surprising to take stock of how pervasively and powerfully ghosts, prophetic dreams, and wonders suffuse the world of *Julius Caesar*—a world that so often seems dominated by cool political calculation, carefully plotted conspiracies, and Cassius's Epicurean philosophy. Shakespeare found in North's Plutarch the points of departure for his representation of the supernatural: he reproduces many of the signs that foreshadow Caesar's death (see pp. 106–8); expands an account of Brutus's encounter with "an evil spirit" (see pp. 121–22); and transforms a spare dream—"[Calpurnia] dreamed that Caesar was slain, and that she had him in her arms" (see p. 107)—into a rich and complex vision of sacrifice (2.2.76–79). Shakespeare's staging of Roman augury and soothsaying and Roman theories about ghosts and dreams, however, should be understood in a double context: on the one hand, Shakespeare's Roman plays— *Titus Andronicus, Caesar, Antony and Cleopatra,* and *Coriolanus*—suggest a keen interest in Roman culture; on the other hand, Elizabethan beliefs about dreams and ghosts and Elizabethan practices of prognostication—astrology, for example—

must have played a role in Shakespeare's representations of Roman beliefs and practices. Moreover, Roman and Elizabethan modes of divination and prognostication were, in some respects, less divergent than we might expect: pious Romans believed in an extended family of divinities; devout Elizabethans worshipped one God, but more than a few of Shakespeare's contemporaries shared Casca's belief that divine will could be detected in the behavior of birds and thunder and lightning (1.3.1–14).

In the following selections, I have included brief passages from Roman commentaries on the supernatural that many Elizabethan readers and playgoers would have known, but my principal aim is to recover the status of ghosts, dreams, and divine signs in Elizabethan culture—to give the reader a sense both of how Shakespeare may have been assimilating the Roman supernatural to contemporary theories and practices and of the complex contemporary resonances that would have haunted and shaped an Elizabethan audience's experience of the play's supernatural elements. If there is a unifying theme in this section, it is a preoccupation with discerning the future. In Shakespeare's culture, theorizing about prophetic signs and dreams necessarily engaged religious belief: a human being might narrowly predict the future (a physician, for example, might make a learned prognosis about the course of a disease), but only God *knew* the future; thus, harbingers of the future had to be divinely wrought or inspired. Even almanac writers attributed their weather forecasts to the interpretation of divine signs.

In the sixteenth century, Christendom was hardly uniform in its attitude toward the supernatural, and Elizabethan debates about ghosts, dreams, and wonders were shaped by large theological struggles. For example, some Catholics believed that ghosts were souls in Purgatory, but Protestants, who denied the existence of Purgatory, developed an alternative theory of ghosts. Attending to debates about ghosts and the proper interpretation of thunder may seem to lead us to the most peculiar fringes of early modern religiosity, but here, out at its farthest borders, we can engage the complexities of the fundamental fabric of Elizabethan religious culture.

Signs from Heaven: Divining the Future in Caesar's Rome and Shakespeare's England[1]

In ancient Rome, two priestly orders—the *augures* and the *haruspicies*—were charged with the responsibility of divining the will of the gods. The *augures* interpreted the flight of birds, the behavior of birds and other animals, thunder and lightning, and other meteorological events; the *haruspicies* interpreted the entrails of animals that had been ritually sacrificed. In Shakespeare's England, slaughtering animals for the purpose of prognostication would have been deemed a species of witchcraft or paganism, but many Elizabethans accommodated within Christian belief an avid appetite for various practices that promised glimpses of the future. In Elizabethan England, astrology was widely accepted; thousands of men and women had their "nativities" cast; and some almanac writers gathered followings sufficiently devoted to support annual publications over periods of a decade or more. Perhaps we should not be surprised by the Christian assimilation of seemingly pagan modes of divination. Divine signs, after all, are hardly alien to Judeo-Christian culture: the God of the Hebrew Bible sent many signs to His people, and the Book of Revelation gives a detailed account of the harbingers of Christ's second coming. To be sure, many sixteenth-century Christians—especially zealous Protestants—condemned almost all attempts to divine the future: trying to foretell trivial aspects of temporal existence—lucky days for business transactions, good times to plant, the weather—was misguided at best; the only future worth anticipating was the second coming, and Christ himself had so clearly designated the signs of his return as to render human arts of interpretation superfluous.

Sir Thomas North (1535–c. 1603)

See pp. 96–97 for information about Sir Thomas North and about Plutarch as a source for Julius Caesar.

[1]For augury, soothsaying, prodigies, and different attitudes toward divination in *Julius Caesar*, see 1.2.12–24, 1.2.137–39, 1.3.1–78, 2.1.193–202, 2.2.8–51, 5.1.71–100, and 5.1.123–27.

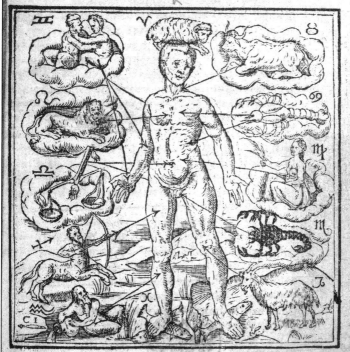

Title page of Leonard Digges' *A Prognostication everlasting of right good effect* (1585), which was reprinted dozens of times.

Plutarch, from *Life of Julius Caesar*, trans. Sir Thomas North (1579)

[Based on his observation of birds, a soothsayer predicts the outcome of Caesar's final battle with Pompey]

Caesar had many signs and tokens of victory before this battle [the Battle of Pharsalia]: but the notablest of all other that happened to him, was in the city of TRALLES. For in the temple of victory, within the same city, there was an image of *Caesar*, and the earth all about it very hard of itself, and was paved besides with hard stone: and yet some say that there sprang up a palm [tree] hard by the base of the same image. In the city of PADUA, *Caius Cornelius* an excellent Soothsayer, (a countryman and friend of *Titus Livius* the Historiographer) was by chance at that time set to behold the flying of birds. He (as *Livy* reporteth) knew the very time when the battle began, and told them that were present, even now they gave the onset on both sides, and both armies do meet at this instant. Then sitting down again to consider of the birds, after he had bethought him of the signs: he suddenly rose up on his feet, and cried out as a man possessed with some spirit, oh, *Caesar*, the victory is thine. Every man wondering to see him, he took the crown he had on his head, and made an oath that he would never put it on again, till the event of his prediction had proved his art true. *Livy* testifieth, that it so came to pass.

Ludwig Lavater (1527–1586)

A Swiss Protestant theologian, Ludwig Lavater studied in Zurich, Strasbourg, Paris, and Lausanne. He was ordained in 1549; by 1550, he was the archdeacon of the great cathedral in Zurich. In 1572, Lavater's De spectris was translated into English by Robert Harrison; Of Ghostes and Spirites, Walking by Night, was reprinted in 1596. Two other works—Book of Ruth Expounded in Twenty Eight Sermons (1586) and Three Christian Sermons (1596)—were popular in Shakespeare's England. Unlike some of his fellow Protestant theologians (see the upcoming selections from Luther and Fulke), Lavater believed that God's revelation of his will did not end with the writing of the Christian Bible; God continued to send signs that presaged the future.

from *Of Ghostes and Spirites, Walking by Night. And of straunge Noyses, Crackes, and sundrie forewarnings, which commonly happen before the death of men: Great slaughters, and alterations of Kingdomes* (1572)[1]

["strange wonders and prognostications . . . sudden noises and cracks . . . are heard before the death of men, before battle, and before some notable alterations and changes"]

Now as concerning other strange things, we must hereafter search what nature they are of: as when one dieth that there is somewhat seen, or some great noise is suddenly heard, but especially that many signs and wonders happen before the death of great Princes. It is well known by histories, what signs went before the death of *Julius Caesar*, amongst the which, a great noise was heard in the night time, in very many places far and near . . . I say flatly, even as I said before concerning spirits, if they be not vain persuasions, or natural things, then are they forewarnings of God, which are sent, either by good Angels, or by some other means unknown unto us, that we might understand that all these things happen not by adventure, without the will and pleasure of God, but that life and death, peace and war, the alteration of Religion, the exchange of Empires, and of other things, are in his power, that we might thereby learn to fear him, and to call upon his name. . . . these things are wrought by God, who only knoweth that they shall come to pass, and they are not only admonishments unto them, whom they especially concern, but also unto them which hear them, and are present at the doing of them.

["Why God doth suffer strange noises, or extraordinary rumblings to be heard before some notable alternations"]

In that there happeneth certain strange things before the death of men, and also before notable alterations, and destructions of countries, as marvelous cracks, and terrible roaring, surely it turneth to good unto the just, and to further damnation to the wicked. For by these means God showeth that nothing cometh to pass by chance, or by adventure, but that the life and death, the prosperous and unfortunate estate of all men, is in the power and hand of God. It is nothing

[1]See pp. 148–51 for Lavater's theories of ghosts.

so as the Epicures affirm, that God hath no regard whether any man live, or be borne, or do well or evil, or otherwise, or whether commonwealths do flourish, or be made waste. Christ himself teacheth us, that not so much as a sparrow falleth unto the ground without the will of God. Solomon and Daniel say that the hearts of kings are in God's hands, and that he appointeth or deposeth kings at his pleasure. Wherefore if we happily do hear any noises or such like, they ought rather to put us in good comfort than to make us afraid. And again, God hereby admonisheth us, that we be not idle and secure, for he hath in all ages stirred up his servants, not only with words, but also with rare and strange apparitions. The very Gentiles accounted these miraculous things, as the admonitions and warnings of their gods, as it may be seen every where, in their histories.

[We sometimes mistake the devil's tricks for divine signs]

But now as concerning other matters, as in case any strange cracks and noises be heard, or any rare and marvelous things happen before the alteration of kingdoms . . . what shall we then do? Surely we must not attribute too much unto such things, for they sometimes, yea and most commonly chance by the deceit of the devil, who hath a great pleasure to have men muse night and day on such matters, and to imagine before their eyes and minds many horrible things, that thereby they may fall into some grievous sickness, and never be at rest. When such things happen indeed, they ought to put us in mind, that we casting from us all these things which displease God, should wholly consecrate ourselves unto God, and so frame our selves, that at what hour soever he come, and please to call us out of this life, we should be ready for him even as he himself teacheth us, and also endure patiently all unfortunate chances, how many soever happen unto us, knowing that they come not by chance, but by the providence of God.

[Pagan attitudes toward divine signs]

Plutarch, albeit he be an Heathen writer, is of a sound judgment (as me seemeth) concerning Monsters and wonders, for writing of *Alexander* the great, in his book *De vitis* [i.e., *The Lives*], he saith; that there happened certain prognostications before his death, which sometimes *Alexander* cared not for, but condemned them, and contrariwise, sometimes he took small and trifling things, as signs of evil luck.

He addeth further, how dangerous a thing it is, to despise tokens and signs sent from God unto men, and on the other side, how pernicious and hurtful it is to be afraid of every trifle, for as in all other things, so is there a measure to be observed herein. . . . True wonders ought to stir us up from sleep. A courageous horse goeth well enough of his own accord, and yet if you do but make sign unto him with a wand, or put spur unto him, he will be more readier and quicker. Even so must we go in the way that leadeth unto heaven so long as we live, but in case we see any foretokens, or some great alteration seem to have over us, we ought to be the more stirred up to give ourselves to prayer, and to exercise godliness. The Gentiles if at any time such forewarnings were showed unto them from heaven, did institute certain solemn prayers and processions to pacify their Gods: how much rather ought all Christian Princes and Magistrates, Doctors and Preachers of our time, to bend themselves wholly herein, when so ever plagues hang over our heads, that all men generally and particularly show forth true repentance?

Abraham Fleming (c. 1552–1607)

Abraham Fleming graduated from Peterhouse, Cambridge, in 1582. He began his writing life as a translator of Greek and Latin texts— everything from Virgil and Cicero to a learned treatise on dogs. Fleming is best remembered as the editor of the 1587 edition of Holinshed's Chronicles of England, Scotland and Ireland, *the great historical work that Shakespeare often had very close at hand when he wrote about England's history and its kings. A Church of England clergyman of some note, Fleming's own works were devotional:* The Diamond of Devotion, Cut and Squared into Six Severall Points *was especially popular, appearing in five editions between 1582 and 1608. Fleming's* A straunge and terrible wunder wrought very late in the parish church of Bongay, a town of no great distance from the citie of Norwich *(1577) belongs to the hugely popular early modern genre of reports of contemporary events. Just as Shakespeare's Casca believes that a "tempest dropping fire" (1.3.10) may be a divine judgment ("the world, too saucy with the gods, / Incenses them to send destruction [1.3.12–13]),*

Fleming interprets the wondrous rain and thunder and other prodigies in Norfolk as signs of God's displeasure.
In his famous A Discoverie of Witchcraft *(1584), Reginald Scot similarly figures heavenly wonders as signs of God's judgment, but rejects more vociferously the notion that the devil, as well as God, can control the elements.*

from *A straunge and terrible wunder wrought very late in the parish church of Bongay, a town of no great distance from the citie of Norwich* (1577)

The Preface to the Reader

God warneth us by signs from heaven, by fiery appearances in the air most terrible, by wonders wrought on earth, strange & unusual, by exinundations of waters beyond their appointed limits, by the removing of senseless trees from the natural place where they were planted, by the great power which the Prince of darkness though Gods permission and sufferance hath recovered, by many late most miserable murders not to be named, much less to be committed among Christians, by insurrections full of danger and detestable treason on this side [of] the seas, by tumults and uproars between Princes of foreign nations, and what should I say more. . . . The occasion that I have wrote this warning (which I would to God I had the grace to follow) was a wonder lately wrought in Norfolk, and so lately wrought, that the terror of the same is at this instance fresh in memory. A spectacle no doubt of God's judgment, which as the fire of our iniquities hath kindled, so by none other means then by the tears of repentance it may be quenched.

[Rain, thunder, and lightning]

Sunday, being the fourth of this August, in the year of our Lord 1577, to the amazing and singular astonishment of the present beholders, and absent hearers, at a certain town called Bongay, not past ten miles distant from the City of Norwich, there fell from heaven an exceeding great and terrible tempest, sudden and violent, between nine of the clock in the morning and ten of the day aforesaid.

This tempest took beginning with a rain, which fell with a wonderful force and with no less violence than abundance, which made the storm so much the more extreme and terrible.

This tempest was not simply of rain, but also of lightning and thunder, the flashing of the one whereof was so rare, and vehement, and the roaring noise of the other so forcible and violent, that it made not only people perplexed in mind and at their wits end, but ministered such strange and unaccustomed cause of fear to be conceived, that dumb creatures with the horror of that which fortuned, were exceedingly disquieted, and senseless things void of all life and feeling, shook and trembled.

[A demonic dog appears in the church]

. . . there appeared in a most horrible similitude and likeness to the congregation then and there present, a dog as they might discern it, of a black color: at the sight whereof, together with the fearful flashes of fire which then were seen, moved such admiration in the minds of the assembly, that they thought doomsday was already come.

This black dog, or the devil in such a likeness (God he knoweth all who worketh all) running all along down the body of the Church with great swiftness, and incredible haste, among the people, in a visible form and shape, passed between two persons, as they were kneeling upon their knees, and occupied in prayer as it seemed, wrung the necks of them both at one instant clean backward, insomuch that even at a moment where they kneeled, they strangely died.

Martin Luther (1483–1546)

In 1517, the nailing of Martin Luther's 95 theses to the door of Wittenberg's castle church launched the Reformation in Germany. In 1511, Luther had been made professor of biblical exegesis at the University of Wittenberg, and the following text, a sermon on Luke 21.25–33, shows him at his professional craft. According to Luther, the signs of the second coming—eclipses, shooting stars, "fires in the air," rainbows, and other phenomena that would not be out of place in Casca's list of prodigies (1.3.1–78)—reveal a crucial difference between Reformed and pagan divination. We can read these signs only because God has anticipated them in scripture: "our Savior Christ [is] of all other the best interpreter and expounder of his word"; "Behold this notable instructor, which knoweth better how to expound signs and tokens of things to come, than any Soothsayer, or Astronomer." Luke's gospel is especially rich in scripturally sanctioned signs of the second coming:

> Nation shall rise against nation, and kingdom against kingdom, And great earthquakes shall be in divers places, and hunger, and pestilence, and fearful things, & great signs shall there be from heaven. (Luke 21.10–11)

> Then there shall be signs in the sun, and in the moon, and in the stars, and upon the earth trouble among the nations with perplexity: the sea and the waters shall roar. (Luke 21.25)

> And he spake to them a parable, Behold, the fig tree, and all trees, When they now shoot forth, ye seeing them, know of your own selves, that summer is then near. So likewise ye, when ye see these things come to pass, know ye that the kingdom of God is near. (Luke 21.29–31)[1]

Anything like a thorough introduction to Luther's theology and its place in Elizabethan religious culture is, of course, beyond the scope of this volume, but we should note that Luther's rejection of astrology and prognostication turns on one of the Reformation's foundational notions: scripture is the revealed will of God; beyond what is revealed in scripture, God's will is inscrutable. The legibility of the signs of the second coming is, then, a warning about the illegibility of any sign not anticipated in scripture. On the other hand, some early modern Christians believed that divine signs had presaged great calamities in pagan history—calamities not mentioned in scripture. Indeed, the anonymous English translator of Luther's sermon on Luke included at the end of his translation his own little treatise about not only the divine forewarnings of the destruction of Jerusalem but also the "signs" and "wonders" that anticipated great events among the pagans. "These few examples I have added in the end of the Sermon," the translator explains in a letter to the reader, "to let men see that before great alterations of changes of Kingdoms and commonweals, God sendeth wonderful tokens thereof, to signify the same before it come to pass." Keep in mind this view—that God sent harbingers of great events not only to the people of Israel and, then, the followers of his Son, but to pagans as

[1] These quotations follow *The Geneva Bible* (1560), the most important Bible for English Protestants in Shakespeare's England.

well—when considering Christian accounts of Roman sign-reading. Brief excerpts from the translator's addenda follow the selections from Luther's sermon.

from *A very comfortable and necessary sermon . . . concerning the comming of our Savior Christ to Judgment and the signs that go before the Last Day* (1570)

[Many of the signs of the second coming have already appeared]

Now to come to my matter, there are two things chiefly to be noted in this Gospel: The one is, that our Savior reckoneth the signs in order which go before the last day, which being fulfilled, we may know for a certainty that the day is even hard at hand. The other note is, that he sayth those signs shall be a consolation and a comfort to his Christian children, so that thereby they may be moved to look for his coming with a merry and cheerful countenance. The first sign (sayth he) shall appear from heaven in the sun . . . [the] moon, and the star: that is to say (as Mathew doth expound it:) *The sun shall be darkened, and the moon shall not give her light, and the star shall fall from heaven. &c.* Moreover upon the earth the people shall be at their wits end through despair, & shall be in such perplexity, that they shall not know whether to go, or where to abide, their hearts shall fail them for fear of those things, which are like to come upon them.

Again, signs shall be seen in the Sea, & in the Waters, so that all creatures, and the powers of heaven shall moue: there shall be such an alteration, that the world shall seem by and by to have an end, and the last day shall seem hard at hand. Here I will not greatly contend with any man, but will leave it to the consideration of my Christian brethren, whether the signs in the sun, the moon, and the stars be already fulfilled, or not. But this is my belief & most certain hope, that the greater part of them have been already seen, and that many other are not here after to bee looked for. For if we will believe, there hath been seen even in our time abundantly both many and great Eclipses or darkening of the sun and moon within few years together, one after an other, besides divers in one year: the like we have not read to have appeared at any time before since the beginning of the world. But he that will not believe the word of

God, will not believe . . . signs, nor take them for signs, but will contemn them, and tread them under his foot, yea although the sun should be daily darkened before his eyes, & the stars should fall by heaps from heaven. Although Astronomers say that such darkening of the sun and moon happen by . . . course of nature (which some of them can tell of before hand) yet they deny not, but they signify some terrible thing to happen on the earth, especially seeing there be so many, & all most every year.

Besides this, contrary to the course of nature, many signs have been seen in the Heavens, many Suns at one time, many Rainbows, many terrible blazing Stars, fires in the air like darts and swords, and divers other prodigious signs, which if they should be written, would fill a whole volume: but all are forgotten, if they be not daily before our eyes, and as soon as they are past, we live securely as though no such thing had ever happened at any time: yea rather the oftener they happen, so much the less we regard them. For we take them for customable things, thinking with our selves that of necessity they must so come to pass, making no more accounts of them afterwards. And true it is, that of necessity they must so come to pass, otherwise they should be tokens in vain, and the world should not bee so soon destroyed, if it being moved thereby, should believe the Gospel. For it might (turning to God by repentance) avoid, or tune away his wrath· or at the least prolong it for a time. But alas, this is rather the chief care of the world, by continuing in wickedness, & most obstinately heaping sin, to hasten Gods wrath, and speedily to procure . . . his own destruction. Thus much as concerning the signs in the Sun, the Moon, and the Stars.

[Christ's prophetic interpretation of the signs of his second coming]

But our Savior Christ of all other the best interpreter and expounder of his word, expoundeth these signs after an other sort, better to our comfort and consolation: showing that those things which seem terrible unto us, are pleasant and beautiful to behold: as if we see the Sun and the Moon darkened, the water and the winds stormy and tempestuous, the mountains overthrown & made equal with the valleys, he teacheth us to say: thanks be to God, for now the pleasant [summer is] . . . at hand, now we see the spring of the leaf in some trees, and other some to shoot out their buds.

No man, no reason, no humane wisdom, could thus interpret these signs, terrible to behold, that redemption and everlasting joy should be signified thereby, which unto reason, & mans wisdom seem rather to prognosticate death and all kind of destruction. But seeing we have learned this interpretation of such a notable schoolmaster, even of him which sendeth them, and therefore knoweth best how to expound them: therefore (I say) let us learn it well, & accustom our selves unto it, that we may print it in our minds the better to our comfort, and that we may behold these signs, and give our judgment of them according to the word of God: and not according to reason and mans wisdom, which is foolish, and full of corruption, which teacheth us to shun and bee afraid of those things, that in deed are pleasant & joyful. It will not gladly suffer us to be hold all things darkened and to look loweringly: thunder & lightening, great storms & tempests, are unacceptable unto it.

The Signs that were given to the inhabitants of Jerusalem, before their destruction

A Whole year before the coming of *Vespas[ian]* to the C[ity] . . . right over it, was seen a blazing Star like unto a sword: which the common people did interpret to be a token of their deliverance out of bondage, into the which they were brought by the *Romans*.

Before the war began, at the feast of unleavened bread, which was then the viii. day of April, there was suddenly seen at nine of the clock at night, for the space of half an hour, such a great light about the Alter, and the Temple, that it seemed to be midday.

At the same feast, a Cow being brought to bee sacrificed, brought forth a Lamb in the midst of the Church.

The [E]ast gate of the Temple, being of brass and shut every night, but not without the strength of twenty men, being locked [and] . . . barred with divers locks and bars, was seen . . . to open itself without the hand of men. This thing was thought of the most part to be a token of good luck, and that the gates of their enemies should open unto them of their own accord. But some that were of th[e] wiser sort, said it was a token that the strength of the Temple should be dissolved without the hand of man, that it might be spoiled of their enemies and destroyed.

Signs, and wonders signifying alteration, or misery and calamity of certain Countries, and Nations, or of great Personages

About the year from the beginning of the world. *3458*. *Tarquinius*, surnamed *Superbus* the seventh King of the *Romans*, was deprived of his kingdom by his subjects, and thrust out by force of arms, and the state of governance altered, from the government of one monarch, unto ii. yearly offices called Consuls: a little before which time in signification thereof (as Historiographers do write) a Dog did speak, and a Serpent [d]id bark.

The year from the beginning of the world. *3538*. the light of the Sun was so taken away by an eclipse seen in *Greece*, that a man might see the Stars as well at midday, as at midnight. Shortly afterwards followed . . . the war of *Peloponnesus* which continued seven and twenty years. *Thucydides*.

William Fulke (c. 1536–1589)

Born to a well-to-do London family, William Fulke attended St. John's College, Cambridge. After a brief legal career, he returned to St. John's to study theology. By 1564, Fulke was a fellow at St. John's, a college preacher, and a vigorous Puritan. Although Fulke's zealotry at times landed him in hot water with college and Church of England authorities, he became the president of St. John's in 1568; however, in the wake of bitter infighting among college factions, Fulke resigned from the college in 1571. In 1578, Fulke became the master of Pembroke College, Cambridge. Fulke played a very prominent role in defending the Church of England against Catholic polemics, and the business of championing the entire Church seems to have softened his Puritanism, though he remained deeply committed to Calvinist theology.

Fulke's Antiprognosticon *(1560) and* A Goodly Gallerye *(1563) simultaneously develop a scientific, rationalist critique of superstition and affirm divine providence: attacking astrologists and almanac makers, Fulke argued both that putatively supernatural phenomena were functions of natural causes and that all events unfolded according to divine providence. Fulke thus dismisses on three grounds human efforts to "divine" the future: the signs—the evidence—adduced by astrologers and other prognosticators are natural rather than divine; even if human beings could predict the future, they could not put such knowledge to use because the future is inalterable and predestined; and human beings do not need to know the future in order to know how they ought to comport themselves in the present—right action depends on right religious belief.*

Fulke may have translated Antiprognosticon, *first published in Latin, at the urging of William Painter, an important man of letters: in a letter published with the 1560 translation, Painter reminds Fulke that "a great number of the busiest and most curious Astrologians in England" and "the common sort" who put their faith in these misguided prognosticators could not read Latin. Painter, then, does not regard prognostication as a matter for academic debate; he wants Fulke's treatise translated into English so that it may reform astrologers and enlighten those who consult them.*

from *Antiprognosticon* (1560)[1]

[A longing to know the future has produced many false arts]

Such is the nature of mankind, earnestly desirous to have knowledge of things to come, that in seeking out & inventing of such arts as might seem to pertain to the certainty thereof, she hath taken great and laborious pains. For travailing to get out a science of Divination, or foreseeing, out of every element, she hath brought forth unto us Pyromancy, which is to for show things by the Fire: Hydromancy, to declare of things to come by the water: Geomancy by the Earth: and divers other arts of this kind, promising the knowledge of hidden and secret matters. . . . These things peradventure might seem somewhat tolerable, so long as mans wit is occupied in matters that are near to him (I mean the elements and such like) if that those false diviners would not draw heaven itself and the stars, to their superfluous rules of Divination, of whom a great number do not this modestly, and as it were devising or

---

[1]*Antiprognosticon that is to saye, an infective agaynst the vain and unprofitable predictions of the astrologians as Nostrodame, [et]c. Translated out of Latine into English. Wherunto is added by the author a shorte treatise in Englyshe, as well for the utter subversion of that fained arte, as also for the better understandynge of the common people, unto whom the fyrst labor seemeth not sufficient. London, 1560.*

guessing; but arrogantly do pronounce their oracles as though they had been given of Apollo Pithyus, the god of foreshowing. It were a small matter if they told only of rain, and weathers, but also they must [fill] the whole world at their pleasure with war, sickness, and rebellion. . . . I thought it worth the labor [to debunk prognosticators], because they so shamefully nowadays do set forth their wares to sell among all men, partly because they so proudly with al their force inveigh against such men as contemn & despise these and such like their predictions. Yea some are not ashamed to commend a necessary use of their divinations. But that only is necessary (if we believe Cicero) without the which we can not live. Then how many thousands of men be there, which not only live, but also live well, and yet never have regard or care so much as ones to see prognostications. Other some there be, which call all men that be desirous of goodly arts and sciences, to their Almanac, as to a storehouse, replenished with all precious jewels. Finally what sign of arrogance or boasting can be named, which in the book of these prophecies may not easily be perceived? Therefore whosoever dare be so bold as ones to open his mouth against these oracles, straight way shall bee called an ignorant person, a detractor, and a sycophant. And this is the cause that so few have taken upon them to detect & open their trifling in prognostications, lest he should incur the reproaches and contumelies of the proud and arrogant rabble of Prognosticators. . . . But I being (as I think) sufficiently armed against all the assaults of all prognosticators, having also gotten convenient leisure (except my tongue or pen do fail me) will endeavor my self utterly to overthrow this tower of Astrology, when's they behold the signification of the planets & stars, that no piece nor parcel thereof that remain.

[Astronomy and astrology distinguished]

Neither let any man slander me, as though I went about to impugn or assault the most beautiful and certain science of Astronomy, as the Prognosticators themselves, (such is their malice) cry out, if any man speak boldly against the vanity of Astrology: But that science as of all human sciences it is the most divine, so would I wish that it should be embraced, learned, & perceived of most men, especially of all such as bear and profess the name of Philosophy. And let not them bee troubled with their proud brag, which say, that their calculation is the end and scope, where unto the noble science of Astronomy doth tend, saying there is no community or fellowship between certainty and uncertainty, neither can truth and feigned falsehood, at any time be coupled and joined together. . . . Lest therefore under the beautiful and glorious cloak of this science of Astronomy, they should any longer proceed to commend their false and hypocritical art, I would wish that this little book were but ones perused and red over of all such as seem to favor this deceit: and except either their willful and perverse affection, or else to gross ignorance did let them, I am assured they would utterly forsake and reject this kind of foreshowing by the stars. For long time under the pretext and colour of Astronomy, this auguration or divination hath been cloaked, in so much that the professors thereof have not doubted openly for Astrologians, to call themselves Astronomers.

[Sound morals and religion, rather than knowledge of the future, must dictate our actions]

What, doth not Paul the apostle of the Gentiles exhort his scholar Titus, that he regard not foolish and superfluous questions of Genealogies and nativities? . . . Likewise he that had rather give credit to the Prognosticators than to saint Paul, should he not having his nativity caste, foresee by it, what good things, and what evil things he should in all his life attain? so shall he devise to avoid the evil, and bring the good things to effect. O blockhead, that must have thy Nativity caste, how dost thou determine to lead thy life, like a brute beast, that thou will suffer all things to work upon thee. Wherefore serveth thy reason which thou dost not use? nay rather which thou dost abuse in such vanities. Knowing thy fortune (they sayest) by thy nativity thou wilt endeavor thy self to seek for good things, and avoid evil things. Why wouldst thou not have done so, although thou hadst never asked counsel of the soothsayer?

[A] short Treatise . . . for the better understanding of the common people

Astrology (lest any man should doubt, because it is no English word) is said to be a knowledge, whereby the practicers of it say, that they can tell of all thing[s] that are not come to pass, before they come to pass, by the course & moving of the stars, or else to describe it more plainly, is it knowledge by which the prognostications be made, that tell of rain and fair weather, sickness and health, war & peace, plenty and dearth, with such like: By which also they cast your nativities, tell you your fortunes, pretend to give you knowledge of things that be lost: and last of all appoint you days and times good or evil, for all things that you have to do.

Ghosts

Ghosts appear on stage in *Macbeth* (3.4.37–72) and *Cymbeline* (5.4.29–124); in *Richard III* 5.2, the stage is so crowded with the ghosts of Richard's many victims—eleven in all—that there is hardly any space left for the living (5.2.71–131).

The proximity of *Caesar* (1599) and *Hamlet* (c. 1601), in which the most famous of all dramatic ghosts plays such a harrowing part, makes the staging of Caesar's ghost in 4.3 especially noteworthy. Brutus's puzzlement over the ghost's ontology is, as we shall see, nicely Protestant: ". . . Who comes here? / I think it is the weakness of mine eyes / That shapes this monstrous apparition. / It comes upon me. —Art thou any thing? / Art thou some god, some angel, or some devil, / That mak'st my blood cold, and my hair to stare?" (4.3.277–82). Protestant theologians such as Ludwig Lavater argued that spirits were not the souls of the dead but good angels, evil angels, or visitations from God himself. Hamlet similarly wonders whether the ghost claiming to be his father is a good or bad angel (1.4.39–41), but he seems to accept the ghost's claim that he is the spirit of Old Hamlet and suffers in purgatory (1.5.8–12). Shakespeare's representations of ghosts, then, stand in a complex relation to the great debate that Protestant and Catholic theologians waged over the nature of spirits and the afterlife.

Sir Thomas North (1535–c. 1603)

For biographical information on North and Plutarch, see pp. 96–97.

Plutarch, from *Life of Marcus Brutus,* trans. Sir Thomas North (1579)

Cassius' opinion of spirits, after the Epicureans' sect

So, being ready to go into EUROPE, one night very late (when all the camp took quiet rest) as he was in his tent with a little light, thinking of weighty matters: he thought he heard one come in to him, and casting his eye towards the door of his tent, that he saw a wonderful strange and monstrous shape of a body coming towards him, and said never a word. So *Brutus* boldly asked what he was, a god, or a man, and what cause brought him thither. The spirit answered him, I am thy evil spirit, *Brutus:* and thou shalt see me by the city of PHILIPPES. *Brutus* being no otherwise afraid, replied again unto it: well, then I shall see thee again. The spirit presently vanished away: and *Brutus* called his men unto him, who told him that they heard no noise, nor saw any thing at all. Thereupon *Brutus* returned again to think on his matters as he did before: and when the day brake, he went unto *Cassius*, to tell him what vision had appeared unto him in the night. *Cassius* being in opinion an EPICUREAN, and reasoning thereon with *Brutus*; spake to him touching the vision thus. In our sect, *Brutus*, we have an opinion, that we do not always feel, or see, that which we suppose we do both see and feel: but that our senses being credulous, and therefore easily abused (when they are idle and unoccupied in their own objects) are induced to imagine they see and conjecture that, which they in truth do not. For, our mind is quick and cunning to work (without either cause or matter) any thing in the imagination whatsoever. And therefore the imagination is resembled to clay, and the mind to the potter: who without any other cause than his fancy and pleasure, changeth it into what fashion and form he will. And this doth the diversity of our dreams show unto us. For our imagination doth upon a small fancy grow from conceit to conceit, altering both in passions and forms of things imagined. For the mind of man is ever occupied, and that continual moving is nothing but an imagination. But yet there is a further cause of this in you. For you being by nature given to melancholic discoursing, and of late continually occupied: your wits and senses having been overlabored, do easily yield to such imaginations. For, to say that there are spirits or angels, and if there were, that they had the shape of men, or such voices, or any power at all to come unto us: it is a mockery. And for mine own part, I would there were such, because that we should not only have soldiers, horses, and ships, but also the aide of the gods, to guide and further our honest and honorable attempts. With these words *Cassius* did somewhat comfort and quiet *Brutus*.

Ludwig Lavater (1527–1586)

Lavater warns his reader that many "ghosts" are figments of the imagination: some men and women hear "the crying of rats, cats, weasels, martins" and "by and by they sweat for fear, supposing some bugs[1] to walk in the dead of night" (49); others "see" ghosts because they are melancholic, mad, excessively timorous, or simply drunk (9–10, 16–17). Lavater attributes other false sightings to the machinations of Papists bent on reconverting Protestants: one wicked priest, he claims, appeared to simple folk in the guise of Mary's ghost—"muffling his face with a thin linen cloth . . . feigning himself with a counterfeit voice, to be the blessed virgin Mary" (42)—and denounced Luther. There are, however, real ghosts: "those Spirits and other strange sights be not the souls of men, but either good or evil Angels, or else some secret and hid operations" of God himself (98). (For a brief biographical sketch of Lavater, see p. 132.)

from *Of Ghostes and Spirites, Walking by Night* (1572)

[False ghosts]

True it is that many men do falsely persuade themselves that they see or hear ghosts: for that which they imagine they see or hear, proceedeth either of melancholy, madness, weakness of the senses, fear, or of some other perturbation: or else when they see or hear beasts, vapors, or some other natural thing, then they vainly suppose, they

---

[1]"An object of terror, usually an imaginary one; a bugbear, hobgoblin, bogy; a scarecrow" (*OED* 1.a).

have seen sights I wot not what, as hereafter I will show particularly by many and notable examples. . . . And . . . it cannot be denied, but that some men which either by dispositions of nature, or for that they have sustained great misery, are now become heavy and full of melancholy, imagine many times with themselves being alone, miraculous and strange things. . . .

[Real ghosts: devils and angels]

No man is able to rehearse all the shapes wherein spirits have appeared, for the devil, who for the most part is the worker of these things, can (as the Poets feign of Proteus) change himself into all shapes and fashions.

* * *

But thou wilt say, I do not yet clearly and plainly understand what manner of things those are, whereof . . . historiographers, holy fathers, and others, make mention . . . which died long ago, appeared unto certain men lying at the point of death, gave them warning, answered unto certain questions, commanded them to do this or that thing: and that some thing is seen and heard at certain times, which not only affirmeth itself to be this or that soul, but also showeth how it may be succored, and afterwards returning again, giveth great thanks unto them of whom it hath received such a benefit: that the husband being dead, came in the night unto his wife now a widow, and that seldom times any notable thing hath happened, which was not foreshadowed unto some man by certain signs and tokens. You will say, I hear and understand very well that these things are not men's souls, which continually remain in their appointed places. I pray you then what are they? To conclude in few words, if it be not a vain persuasion proceeding through weakness of the senses through fear, or some such like cause, or if it be not deceit of men, or some natural thing, whereof we have spoken much in the first part, it is either a good or evil Angel, or some other forewarning sent by God. . . .

* * *

God doth suffer spirits to appear unto his elect, unto a good end, but unto the reprobate they appear as a punishment. And as all other things turn to the best unto the faithful, even so do these also: for if they be good spirits, which appear unto men, warning, and defending them, thereby do they gather the care, providence, and fatherly affection of God towards them. But in case they bee evil spirits, (as for the most part they are) the faithful are moved by occasion of them unto true repentance.

[Prophetic ghosts in classical antiquity]

. . . it is most certain and sure, that all those things which appear unto men are not always natural things, nor always vain terrors to affray men: but that spirits do often appear, and many strange and marvelous things do sundry times chance. For many such things of this sort, are to be read in divers grave and ancient Historiographers: and many men of no small credit, have affirmed, that they have seen spirits both in the day and in the night also. And here I will orderly declare a few histories out of divers allowed authors, touching spirits which have appeared and showed themselves.

* * *

The same author [Plutarch] writteth in the life of Decius Brutus, how when Brutus was determined to transpose his army out of Asia into Europe, being in his tent about midnight, the candle burning dimly, and all the host quiet and silent, as he was musing and revolving with himself, he seemed that he heard one entering the tent into him, and looking back unto the door, he saw a terrible and monstrous shape of a body, which far exceeded the common stature of men, standing fast by him without any words, wherewith he was sore afraid: and yet he ventured to ask it this question. What art thou (saieth he) either a God, or a man? and why commest thou unto me? Whereto the image answered: I am (quoth he) O Brutus, thy evil ghost, at Phillippos thou shalt see me. Then saith Brutus, being nothing amazed: I will see thee. When the sight was vanished, he called his servants, who told him, that they neither saw any such thing, neither heard any noise at all. All that night Brutus could not sleep one wink. In the morning very early he goeth unto Cassius and showeth him his strange vision. Cassius who despised all such things (for he was an Epicure) ascribed the whole matter to natural causes. For his disputation hereof, is yet extant in Plutarch. . . .

* * *

Lucanus as well an excellent Historiographer, as also a most learned Poet, reckoneth up many forewarnings, in his first book of the battle of Pharsalia, which chanced before the great conflict between Julius Caesar, and great Pompeius: and amongst other things, he writteth thus,

> The trumpets blew, and look even as the battle joined apace,
> So did the night with silent shades increase her darkish face.
> And then the ghosts of Sylla fierce, were plainly seen in field
> Thereby declaring evil signs, of blood that should be spilled.
> And by the flood of Anien, the husband did spy
> Great Marius, out of broken grave his head advancing high.

[Ghosts theory and Protestant polemics]

The Papists in former times have publicly both taught and written that those spirits which men sometime see and hear be either good or bad angels, or else the souls of those which either live in everlasting bliss or in Purgatory, or in the place of damned persons. And that diverse of them are those souls that crave aide and deliverance of men.

* * *

[Because of the Catholic doctrine of Purgatory], the common sort were of opinion that those spirits which were seen and heard were the souls of the dead and that whatsoever they did say was without gainsaying to be believed. And so the true, simple, and sincere doctrine of calling upon God in the name of Christ Jesus only: of the confidence in Christ's merits, and redemption from sin and damnation: of the true deeds of Christian charity, was daily more and more impugned and oppressed.

* * *

. . . that all things are possible unto God, we deny it not. We grant then, that God can bring souls out of heaven or hell, and use their travel & service to instruct, comfort, admonish, & rebuke men. But for that no text or example is found in holy scripture, that ever any souls came from the dead, which did so school and warn men: or that the faithful learned or sought to understand anything of the souls deceased, we cannot allow the sequel of their reason.

Dreams[1]

As he embraces his former enemy Coriolanus, Aufidius, his "rapt heart" racing more violently than when he first saw his "wedded mistress" (*Coriolanus*, 4.5.115–16), confesses that in his nightly dreams the two great warriors "have been down together . . . Unbuckling helms, fisting each other's throat" (4.5.124–25); immediately after gently repulsing her beloved Lysander's attempts to seduce her, Hermia dreams that a serpent eats her heart (*A Midsummer Night's Dream*, 2.2.41–162). The richly charged quality of these and many other Shakespearean dreams helps explain why the plays have been such an important terrain for the development of psychoanalysis and psychoanalytic literary criticism. If Shakespeare's interest in the way dreams transfigure unconscious desire and fear into symbolic expression is often strikingly modern, many Shakespearean accounts of dreams emerge from early modern dream theory: in *Cymbeline*, Imogen attributes a dream to the action of indigestion on the brain (4.2.302–3); in *The Merchant of Venice*, Shylock worries that his dream about "money-bags" is a bad omen (2.5.15–19); in *Henry VI, Part 2*, the Duke of Gloucester has a prophetic dream about his downfall at the hands of Cardinal Beaufort (1.2.17–32). If we value dreams as keys to individual psychic life, most Elizabethans dismissed as trivial dreams that merely reflected individual experience and desire; "true dreams," by contrast, came from outside the individual and, properly interpreted, revealed the future.

Virgil (70–19 bce)

The most revered of all Roman poets, Virgil (Publius Vergilius Maro) was born near Mantua in Cisalpine Gaul. The Eclogues *and* Georgics, *published before the poet was 30, were deeply admired and endlessly imitated, but the influence of Virgil's great epic the* Aeneid *on the Renaissance imagination can scarcely be overstated. One very curious aspect of Virgil's enduring fame deserves a brief mention in this section: after the*

---

[1]In Act 2, Caesar recounts Calphurnia's dream and her prophetic interpretation; Decius Brutus offers an alternative interpretation (see 2.2.77–90). Cinna the poet also dreams about Caesar (3.3.1–4).

poet's death, it was thought that one could predict the future by opening his works and choosing a line at random. *During the Civil War, for example, Charles I is reported to have taken a turn at "sortes Virgilianae" (Virgilian lots)—the doomed king's finger landed unpromisingly on Dido's cursing of Aeneas.*
Perhaps the best-known Roman theory of dreams appears in Book 6 of the Aeneid. *At the end of Aeneas's journey to the underworld, where his father Anchises reveals to him the future of the Roman people, Virgil elaborates an etiology of dreams: both true and false dreams are sent to the living by the souls of the dead.*

from *Aeneid*, trans. Thomas Phaer and Thomas Twayne (1573)[1]

Then him of all his wars, and great affairs to come, he told,
Of king Latinus' town, and of his realms and peoples bold,
And how each labour best may voided be, or easily born
Two gates of sleep there be, the one men say is made of horne,
Where through by passage left do spirits ascend with sense right.
That other gate doth shine, and is compact of Ivory bright,
But false deceitful Dreams that way the souls are wont to send.[2]

Thomas Hill (c. 1528–c. 1574)

Thomas Hill's translations of several Italian and Latin treatises played a major role in the dissemination of Paracelsus's theories in England,

---

[1]*The thirteene bookes of Aeneidos. The first twelve being the worke of the divine poet Virgil Maro, and the thirteenth, the supplement of Maphaeus Vegius. Translated into English verse to the first third part of the tenth booke, by Thomas Phaer Esquire: and the residue finished, and now newly set forth for the delight of such as are studious in poetrie: by Thomas Twyne, Doctor in Physicke.* London, 1573. A physician, medical theorist, legal scholar, and man of letters, Thomas Phaer (1510?–60) was nearly finished with his translation when he died; his friend Thomas Twayne (1543–1613) completed the work.

[2]Virgil is following and elaborating Penelope's explanation of dreams in Book 19 of *The Odyssey*: after recounting to the still disguised Odysseus a dream that, properly interpreted, presages the return of her long-lost husband, Penelope remarks that dreams pass through "[t]wo two-leav'd gates; the one of Ivory; / The other, Horne": "Those dreams that *Fantasy* / Takes from the polisht Ivory Port, delude / The Dreamer ever, and no truth include: / Those that the glittering Horn-gate, lets abroad, / Do evermore, some certain truth abode" (ll. 784–98; George Chapman, *The Odysses of Homer* in *The Whole Works of Homer*. London, 1616).

but he was, perhaps, best known in his own time for his many almanacs, the very popular A Briefe Treatyse of Gardening *(1560) and* The Moste pleasaunte Arte of the Interpretacioun of Dreams *(1567). The title of Thomas Hill's dream treatise certainly tempts us to draw comparisons with Freud's epochal* The Interpretation of Dreams *(1900), but Hill cares most about a category of dream that psychoanalysis does not recognize: prophetic dreams inspired by God. To be sure, most dreams, Hill argues, are merely human, merely natural: caused by perturbations of the body (disease, humoral imbalances, indigestion, and so on), their content is either drawn from the dreamer's recent experiences or expresses his or her waking desires or fears. Some dreams, however, are divinely wrought: in the Book of Joel, Hill reminds his readers, "God sayeth I will breathe down my spirit on all the earth so that your sons and daughters shall Prophecy and your old men dream dreams, and your young men see visions. Also in sundry places of the new testament we read how that the Apostles and other holy men were taught and warned by dreams" ("The Epistle Dedicatory"). Hill consistently figures the interpretation of "true dreams" as divination, though his catalogue of dreams "which were reported to have been proved" includes a few visions that seem anything but divinely inspired (for example, a penis that eats bread; see p. 158).*

Hill's discussion of dreams that spring from personal experiences, anxieties, and longings might be brought to bear on many Shakespearean dreams (e.g., Hermia's serpent dream), but Calpurnia's dream in Julius Caesar *(see 2.2.76–79) seems to be, on Hill's terms, a "true dream," a divine warning that, when properly interpreted, reveals the future. Plutarch mentions only in passing that Calpurnia "dreamed that Caesar was slain"; Shakespeare gives her a complex dream that produces two distinct—if closely related—interpretations and predictions (2.2.75–90).*

from *The Moste pleasaunte Arte of the Interpretacioun of Dreams* (1576)[1]

The Preface to the Reader

If it be superstitious (gentle Reader) and therefore denied of some men, to have a foresight and judgment in things to come, why is not then denied to learned Physicians, skillful warriors, weary husband-

[1] *The Moste pleasaunte Arte of the Interpretacioun of Dreames, whereunto is annexed sundry Problems with apte aunsweares neare agreeing to the matter, and very rare examples, not the like extant in the English tongue.* 1567; rpt. London, 1576.

men, and politic Captains, to have knowledge in the Arts of divination: if they be condemned which bee of such antiquity, so generally received, and so often confirmed by the sundry works of learned men, who then shall dare presume to open the secretes of dreams, wherein is contained so high and so many mysteries. But great pity it were that so noble knowledge, so necessary to all men bee trod under foot, and so lightly esteemed. Al Arts of foreknowledge hath been of longtime had in great price and estimation. In times past the noble warriors, the grave Senators, the mighty Princes, & almost every private man, did direct all their doings, and weighty affairs, by conjectures and divinations.

The worthy Romans, seldom took any great matter in hand, before their soothsayers or wise men brought them good or bad tidings. . . . many bent their minds to invent more such studies, which as they increased in number, so were their operations diverse, and their judgments several. Of the which number many may worthily by cut off, some as most detestable and wicked, some as vain and frivolous and many as mere[ly] foolish, only those are so reserved and excepted wherein any wit, wisdom, or reason is contained, among this sort, the divination of dreams doth occupy as a Mistress one of the chiefest rooms. . . .

It is a wonderful thing and almost incredible that dreams should have such virtue in them, were it not that God hath revealed it unto us: When he himself, as a mean, often used them, to open unto his people of Israel his secrete wit and pleasure. Were it not that we have read of the wonderful chances in old time foretold by them: and were it not again that we daily see the effect of dreams. But alas, our ignorance maketh us so blind, that we know them not, until they be paste. For a man beholding in his sleep the top or end of an house falling down, hearing a dog to bark or howl, seeing a hare to chase a hound, or a bird to fly without wings will seek no further, but esteem it as a vain dream, laughing at his own conceit, having more regard to the present spectacle, than to the circumstances to come making no more account of them, than of things casual, natural, or impossible. For a house to fall down is casual, a dog to bark natural, the hare to persecute the hound, is against nature, and a fowl to fly without wings soundeth impossible. Yet all these by circumstances signify such events, as may be for the profit or hindrance of the dreamer. It seemeth a thing against nature, & a thing most strange for a woman to be delivered of a firebrand: if Hecuba had left here, and sought no further, then had she not known how her son Paris with whom she then went, should be the destruction of his own country Troy.[2] It is monstrous for a vine to spring out of a woman's bowels, and for the Branches to cover or shadow the great country of Asia, yet this foreshowed Astiages, that of his daughter should bee borne such a child, as should grow to a mighty Prince and unnaturally should drive him out of his kingdom.

. . . These few examples, gentle Reader, of an infinite number, I have set forth to show thee what notable destinies, changes of fortune, notable ill luck, and notable good luck, what honour, what shame, what singularity in learning and wisdom, have in ancient times by dreams signified and foreshowed. And in this my treatise . . . I will manifest such strange haps[3] have chanced in later years, and also teach thee further how thou maist use and behave thyself in expounding such as hereafter are to come, And gentle Reader . . . use good discretion, . . . believe nothing rashly, nor . . . pronounce any thing without good judgment but first . . . practice it with thy self secretly and then if thy judgments fall out right, thou maist the bolder communicate it with others; if not, condemn it not, but leave it to their judgments, whose learning being more profound, or knowledge more perfect can better and more sincerely interpret the same.

[The causes of dreams]

[Dreams] are either bodily or not bodily, and both also are either new, or before wrought. So that it must needs ensue, that there be four kinds of dreams. Now the new and bodily causes, are meat and drink, like as the heads of Garlic, the Colewort, the Onions . . . and whatsoever ascend to the head, and especially those which engender melancholy. Further yellow choler doth cause to appear in sleep, both fires & lightning, and Melancholy causeth to appear in sleep clay, mire, or dirt, Burials, graves, imprisonment, and fear. . . . But the uncorporate causes precedent [not bodily,

---

[2] While she was pregnant with Paris, Hecuba dreamed that she gave birth to a firebrand; the firebrand sparked a fire that consumed Troy. In *Henry IV, Part 2*, an insufficiently educated page attributes the dream to Althea (2.2.72–75).

[3] Events.

not new] are cares cogitations, matters as committed to memory, fear, hope, gladness, heaviness or sadness or mind hatred and love. But the new and those which frame the superior cause come unto the soul. For all the other members all the causes of the divisions do so agree that many endeavor to place this last under some of the three aforesaid. And it behooveth first to seek out which may be of every kind, & therefore which true and which false, for that none do show matters to come, but those which are sent from the superior causes, and those also which are caused of humors.

[Vain dreams]

The causes of all dreams bee on this wise, first those which are caused of meats and drinks. . . . sleep is the rest of the spirits, and . . . waking [is] the vehement motion of them, and the vain dream is a certain trembling and imperfect motion of them. Therefore all are vain dreams caused through the spirits [lightly] moved. Whereof whiles we soundly sleep, we then dream nothing at all.

. . . the matter of [vain dreams] is the remembrance of the seen and heard, for no vain dreams are caused but through them. As like for example, when a man in his sleep thinketh to see a monster with three heads, which he either heard of by description of some or saw painted in the like sort, which heads he remembered to be in this wise, as the one like a Lyon, the other a serpent or Dragon & the other a Goat. . . . [And] if any other strange matter also a man shall see in his sleep, or some unknown thing, or deformed Plant, then are those none other than imperfect things or transposed.

. . . But sometimes they think to kill a man, and sometimes that they themselves are dead, because the fantasy doth imagine that which either it conveyeth or feareth.

[True dreams come more frequently to princes]

For that by nature men see true dreams, which dream but seldom, and false dreams which daily dream. Also such as be occupied in great actions, and businesses, and greatly abstain from meat and drink not are troubled with fear nor sadness, do see and have true dreams. . . . And for that cause the dreams of Princes are commonly true.

Of those Dreams which were reported to have been proved

If he, which is in love with a woman, dreameth to have found a bird's nest, and that he reaching or putting his hand into the nest, feeleth it cold, it is a token of hasty or sudden sadness, and sorrow, for she shall either marry to another man, or else shall dye, and he shall depart soon from that city or abiding place, into another town. For the nest signified & is in the place of birth, and coldness expresseth death.

To dream that he seeth one coming and casting stones against him, declareth that shortly after he shall bee damaged and wrong done to him by words, or that some man shall go about or endeavor to do him injury. . . .

And a certain man dreamed that he thought he fed his privy member with bread and cheese like as it wear a certain beast, who after died shamefully. For the meat which he should have offered to the mouth, he did give to the privy member as it were darkly signifying and in a figure, that he should have neither mouth not face. And a certain woman dreamed that she thought that out of her breast sprang ears of wheat, and that the ears after burst open into her nature to be drowned again. Which woman after by certain hap unknown to her, did lie with her own son, and after slew herself, and so died unhappily. For the ears signified the son, and the drowning of them into her nature signified the coupling. But the death of her signified the seeds sprung out of her body: because that out of the earth, and not out of living bodies they spring up.

And one thought in his dream that he has a mouth in his fundament, and great and fair teeth, and to speak by it, and to eat meat, and whatsoever also are wont to be done by the mouth, it to have all like: who after through his light and foolish talk, fled his country, & was banished for a long time after. . . .

And one thought in his sleep that he saw himself drowned in the water, and that he minded to refrain from swimming the day following. Who on the morrow forgetting his dream, went to swimming and there was drowned the day.

[Dreams and ghosts]

A certain man being the Son of a philosopher, after his fathers death sought a certain book of his, and could not find the same for which he became very sad. After which in a certain night his father appeared to him in a sleep, who showed to him the place where the book lay hid. Who awaking in the morning sought the book there and there as he showed him he found it, that by the same help, the book might come and serve unto all ages hereafter.

* * *

Before the battle against the Philippians, a certain soldier thought in his sleep that Julius Caesar spake to him, saying show . . . unto Octavius that he shall fight the happier and luckier, if . . . he take some of these things with him, which I, whiles I was head governor, was accustomed to wear and carry about me. Which Octavius understanding, got after the ring to wear, with the which Caesar had accustomed to seal letters, and the same he wear not only before the battle, but many times afterward.

Republicanism, Popular Politics, and the Rhetoric of Liberty in 1599

Dramatists before and after Shakespeare have expected their audiences to recognize the crises and personalities of their own cultures in plays set in distant times or places: Arthur Miller's *The Crucible* (1953) doubles as a tragedy about the persecution of witches in seventeenth-century Massachusetts and a contemporary critique of McCarthyism; in *The Trojan Women* (415 BCE), Euripides reached back to the distant Greek triumph over Troy to warn the Athenians of 415, fresh on the heels of their conquest of Melos, that imperialism had brutal and unsavory consequences. Shakespeare's contemporaries could also see in dramas about far-off places and the dusty past veiled, displaced representations of their own culture. Sometimes the veils were not thick enough. In the early 1590s, for example, the Master of the Revels, the Crown official charged with censoring dramatic performances, ordered that a representation of the 1517 popular uprising against foreigners be removed from *Sir Thomas More*, a play to which Shakespeare contributed several scenes; the staging of the uprising, he feared, would exacerbate a current wave of (sometimes violent) resentment against foreign workers among London's citizens and craftsmen.

Would the first audiences of *Julius Caesar* have "applied" the play to their own world? The political struggles at the center of *Julius Caesar* seem very far removed from late-Elizabethan England: the conspirators hope to preserve a 300-year-old republic against the innovation of monarchy; in the Elizabethan historical consciousness, the inhabitants of the island had been ruled by monarchs from time immemorial, and there was no movement to introduce republicanism or any other alternative to monarchy. Put another way, Elizabeth isn't a very neat fit for the role of Caesar, and it is very hard to cast any of her subjects in the roles of Brutus and Cassius. To be sure, Elizabeth survived her share of murderous conspiracies, but her enemies—mostly Catholics who dreamed of reuniting England and Rome—did not aim to alter *the form* of English government; rather, they wanted to set another great noble such as Elizabeth's Catholic cousin Mary on the throne. Some of the challenges to Elizabeth's authority were motivated by ambition rather than religious conviction: by the time *Caesar* was first performed in 1599, Robert Devereaux, the Earl of Essex, had begun to bristle under Elizabeth's rule, but the (rather puny) rebellion that Essex would lead in 1601 was hardly revolutionary. Essex had no quarrel with monarchy; he just wanted to be a king rather than a mere earl. Essex won't fit into Brutus's or Cassius's sandals unless we believe that one of those conspirators hid monarchic ambition under the rhetoric of republican freedom.

The stark struggle between republicanism and monarchism that dominates *Caesar* has no convincing parallel in Shakespeare's England; nevertheless, for many Elizabethans republican Rome was not a distant, exotic culture, and Shakespeare's representation of the demise of Roman republicanism stands in a complex relation to the political culture of late sixteenth-century England. According to many early modern commentators, the special genius of the English state was its reconciliation of monarchy and (updated) versions of republican Rome's Senate (the House of Lords) and popular tribunate (the House of Commons). England was a "mixed-estate" rather than an absolute monarchy: the monarch enjoyed many powers that he or she could exercise unilaterally, but Parliament—defined by early modern political writers as the monarch, the House of Lords, and the House of Commons—was the sovereign legislative authority. The English people were governed by a powerful monarch, but, unlike their European counterparts, they could claim to be free subjects because Elizabeth could levy certain kinds of taxes and enact certain kinds of law only with the consent of both the Lords and the Members of the House of Commons. Thus, Brutus and Cassius's rhetoric—their pervasive celebrations of "freedom" and "freemen," disparagement of "bondage" and "bondmen," and horror of "tyranny"—may well have resonated in complex ways for a culture in which the common subject's "ancient freedoms" were a cornerstone of political discourse and national identity. Brutus and Cassius, of course, equate monarchy and tyranny; for Shakespeare's contemporaries, defending the subject's freedom did not constitute an attack on monarchy but instead an attempt to keep monarchic power within traditional boundaries. Thus, the distinctly English notion that monarchs became tyrants when they ignored legal limitations on their authority—when, for example, they acted unilaterally in matters requiring the consent of Parliament—strikes some sparks when we rub it against *Julius Caesar*: in the minds of many Elizabethans, Parliament protected the subject's liberty against the threat of excessive monarchic power, and, by 1599, it had become commonplace to draw analogies between Parliament and the political institutions of republican Rome.

Freedom and English Identity

According to many Elizabethan and Jacobean historians, literary artists, legal theorists, and politicians, the English were different from—and happier than—the people of other nations because they were freer and abhorred slavery. As the following selections show, "slave," "bondage," "freedom," and "liberty" were extraordinarily important and common terms in early modern English discourse.

William Harrison (1535–1593)

William Harrison flourished at Oxford—he graduated from Christ Church in 1557 and became a fellow of Merton College in 1557—but left the university after he was ordained in 1558. An active and vigorous Protestant, Harrison held several clerical positions, but he is now best remembered as a historian. The Description of England *first appeared in 1577, but the revised text found its way to a much wider audience when John Hooker included it in the second edition of Holinshed's* Chronicles of England *(1587), the great historical work that Shakespeare consulted so often. In the following excerpt, Harrison describes the social ladder of England from top to bottom; the absence of "slaves and bondmen," he claims, defines England's difference from other countries.*

from *The Description of England* (1587)

We in England divide our people commonly into four sorts, as gentleman, citizens or burgesses, yeoman, and artificers or laborers. Of gentleman the first and chief (next the King) be the prince, dukes, marquises, earls, viscounts, and barons, and these are called gentlemen of the greater sort, or (as our common usage of speech is) lords and noblemen; and next unto them be knights, esquires, and, last of all, they that are simply called gentlemen. . . . Citizens and burgesses have next place to gentleman, who . . . are to serve the commonwealth in their cities and boroughs, or in corporate towns where they dwell. And in the common assembly of the realm, wherein our laws are made. . . . which assembly is called the High Court of Parliament. . . . In this place also are our merchants to be installed, as amongst the citizens. . . . Yeoman are those which by our law are called *legales hominess*, freemen born English. . . . This sort of people have a certain preeminence, and more estimation then laborers and the common sort of artificers. . . . The fourth and last sort of people in England are day laborers, poor husbandmen, and some retailers (which have no free land), copyholders, and artificers, as tailors, shoemakers, carpenters, bricklayers, masons, etc. As for slaves and bondmen, we have none; nay, such is the privilege of our country by the especial grace of God and bounty of our princes that if any come hither from other realms, so soon as they set foot on land they become so free of condition as their masters, whereby all note of servile bondage is utterly removed from them, wherein we resemble (not the Germans, who had slaves also, though such as in respect of the slaves of other countries might well be reputed free, but) the old Indians and the Taprobanes, who supposed it a great injury to Nature to make or suffer them to be bound whom she in her wanted course doth produce and bring forth free.

James Morice (1539–1597)

James Morice came from a family of courtiers, members of Parliament, and government officials. He entered the Middle Temple in 1558. In his work as a jurist and legal scholar, Morice argued that unless a monarchy was bound in some measure by legal codes, "hateful Tyranny, and Insolent oppression" would always threaten the subject.[1] Morice was a prominent member of Parliament; in the speech below, Morice describes as "blessed" a relation between subject and monarch that preserves the subject's freedom.

from a Speech in the House of Commons (February 27, 1593)[2]

. . . among all sorts and kinds of government, the monarchy is preferred as the best; and worthily as I think. Behold with us the sovereign authority of one, an absolute prince, great in majesty, ruling and reigning, yet guided and directed by principles and precepts of reason which we term the law. No Spartan king, or Venetian duke, but free from account and coercion of any, either equal or superior; yet firmly bound to the commonwealth by the faithful oath of a Christian prince, bearing alone the sharp sword of justice and correction, yet tempered with mercy and compassion; requiring tax and tribute of the people, yet not causeless, nor without common assent.

We again the subjects of this kingdom are born and brought up in due obedience, but far from servitude and bondage, subject to lawful authority and commandment, but freed from licentious will and tyranny; enjoying by limits of law and justice our lives, lands, goods and liberties in great peace and security, this our happy and blessed estate.

Sir Christopher Yelverton (c. 1536–1612)

While studying law at Gray's Inn, Sir Christopher Yelverton tried his hand at poetry and even wrote the odd scene for a play, but he soon dedicated himself to what became a fabulously successful career in law

---

[1]Qtd. in the *Oxford Dictionary of National Biography*.

[2]T. E. Hartley, ed. *Proceedings in the Parliaments of Elizabeth I. Volume III: 1593–1601*. London: Leicester University Press, 1995, p. 35.

and politics. Although his puritan leanings occasionally put him at odds with Elizabeth, he served his queen well as a lawyer, prosecutor, judge, and member of Parliament. Yelverton was a renowned orator, and in 1597 he was made Speaker of the House of Commons. At the close of every session of an early modern Parliament, the Speaker made an oration to the monarch and requested that he or she sign the bills passed by both the House of Lords and the House of Commons.

from a Speech to Elizabeth I at the Closing of Parliament (February 9, 1598)[1]

If that common wealth (most sacred and most renowned Queen) was reputed in the world to be the best-framed, and most likely to flourish in felicities, where the subjects had there freedom of discourse, and there liberty of liking, in establishing the laws that should govern them; then must your Majesty's mighty, and most famous realm of England (by your most gracious benignity) acknowledge it self the most happy of all the nations under heaven, that possesseth this favour in more frank and flowing manner than any kingdom doth besides. Singular was the commendation of Solon that set laws among the Athenians; passing was the praise of Licurgus that planted laws among the Lacdemonians and highly was Plato extolled that devised laws for the Magnesians: but neither yet could the inconveniences of the state by so providently foreseen, nor the reason of laws be so deeply searched into, were they never so wise, nor the course of them be so indifferent, or so plausible; nor the people be so willing to put themselves under the duty of them, as when the people themselves be agents in the framing of them.

And where the rules of government in some common wealths have been settled only by some few magistrates, there divers varieties of mischief have also many times befallen them. . . . According therefore to your Majesty's most wide and princely command anent, and according to ancient and well-ruled freedom of the subjects of England, hath the whole state of your kingdom (represented here by Parliament) assembled, consulted, and resolved upon some few petitions, thought fit for laws to them by your Majesty to be established.

* * *

[1]T. E. Hartley, ed. *Proceedings in the Parliaments of Elizabeth I. Volume III: 1593–1601.* London: Leicester University Press, 1995, pp. 197–98, 198–99.

The picture of Pygmalion, though by art it were never so curious and exquisite, and that in all the lineaments (almost) it had overcome nature and enticed the artisan himself, through the fineness of the features, to be fondly enamored with his own creature, yet it had not the delight of life until Jupiter, assuming some pity of his woeful state and travail, inspired breath into it.

So these our petitions, how fit soever they be framed, and how commodious soever they be imagined for your kingdom, yet be they but empty and senseless shadows until your Majesty taking compassion on the common wealth . . . shall instill your most high and royal assent, to give full life and essence unto them.

Parliament and Liberty

Yelverton figures Parliament as a foundation of the subject's freedom and felicity: the English are "the happiest of all the nations under heaven" because it is the subject's "ancient . . . freedom" to consent to taxes and laws not in his own person but through his representatives in the House of Commons. We should not mistake the early modern House of Commons for the House of Representatives or the modern House of Commons: Parliament met only when called by the monarch;[1] many elections to the House of Commons were uncontested because powerful men (and occasionally women) had settled among themselves who would stand for places; and the franchise was limited to approximately one third of the adult male population. However, many thousands of relatively humble men did vote and played a role in returning more than 450 "knights" (the members of Parliament who represented shires) and "burgesses" (the members of Parliament who represented boroughs); those members frequently claimed to speak for "the people of the realm" and often attributed their power to their status as representatives; the Crown and the Lords could not enact statutes without the consent of the Commons; and the Elizabethan and early Jacobean Commons, while hardly a revolutionary body, did

[1]During Shakespeare's life (1564–1616), Elizabeth and James called 12 parliaments, which met, collectively, for roughly 60 months.

on many occasions assert itself on matters of religious and economic policy. The following selections treat the House of Common's role in English governance.

John Hooker (c. 1527–1610)

John Hooker (alias Vowell) studied law at Oxford and Cologne and theology at Strasbourg. After a brief period of employment by Miles Coverdale, the bishop of Exeter, Hooker served in a variety of important secular offices and positions: chamberlain of Exeter; legal advisor in Ireland to Sir Peter Carew; Member of the Irish House of Commons; and Member of the English House of Commons. A member of the Society of Antiquaries, Hooker was an important historian of Ireland, Devon, and the English Parliament. In 1571, he published The Order and usage of the keeping of a Parlement in England *along with a translation of the* Modus Tenendi Parliamentorum, *a medieval treatise on Parliament. Hooker included* The Order and usage *in the 1587 edition of Holinshed's* Chronicle, *which he helped to edit. The Order and usage played an important role in the development of parliamentary practices and was, by leaps and bounds, the best-known early modern treatise on the subject.*

from *The Order and usage of the keeping of a Parlement in England* (1571)

The King, who is God's anointed, being the head and chief of the whole Realm and upon whom the government and estates thereof do wholly and only depend, hath the power and authority to call and assemble his Parliament, and therein to seek & ask advice, council and assistance of his whole Realm, and without . . . his authority no parliament can properly be summoned or assembled.

* * *

The Parliament is the highest, chiefest, and greatest Court that is or can be within the Realm, for it consisteth of the whole realm, which is divided into three estates—that is to wit, the King, the Nobles, and the Commons, every of which estates are subject to all such orders as are concluded and established in Parliament.

These three estates may jointly and with one consent or agreement establish and enact any Laws, orders, & statutes for the common wealth, but being divided, and one swerving from the other, they can do nothing, for the King, though he be the head, yet alone cannot make any Law. . . .

* * *

. . . every [member of the House of Lords] doth represent but his own person, & speaketh in the behalf of himself only. But in the Knights, Citizens, and Burgesses are represented the Commons of the whole realm, and every one of these giveth not consent only for himself but for all those also for whom he is sent.

Sir Thomas Smith (1513–1577)

Sir Thomas Smith was a star student at Cambridge and attained the position of Regius Professor of Civil Law before he was 30. A legal and political theorist of vast erudition, Smith was also a man of action who served as a member of Parliament, clerk of the privy council, and secretary of state. Smith wrote De Republica Anglorum *in the early 1560s; when it was finally published in 1583, Smith's treatise quickly became one of the most important and frequently invoked accounts of English political and legal institutions.*

from *De Republica Anglorum* (1583)

The . . . degree of Lords doth answer to the dignity of the Senators of Rome, and the title of our nobility to their *patricii*. . . . When the Romans did write *senatus populusque Romanus*, they seemed to make but two orders, that is of the Senate and of the people of Rome, and so in the name of people they contained *equites* and *plebem*: so when we in England do say the Lords and the commons, the knights, esquires & other gentlemen, with citizens, burgesses & yeomen be accounted to make the commons. In ordaining of laws, the senate of Lords of England is one house, where the Archbishops and Bishops also be, and the king or Queen for the time being as chief; the knights and all the rest of the gentlemen, citizens and burgesses which be admitted to consult upon the greatest affaires of the Realm be in an other house by themselves, and that is called the house of the commons, as we shall more clearly describe when we speak of the parliament.

* * *

The most high and absolute power of the realm of England, consisteth in the Parliament. For as in war where the king himself in person, the nobility, the rest of the gentility, and the yeomanry are the force and power of England: so in peace & consultation where the Prince is to give life, and the last and highest commandment, the Barony for the nobility and higher; the knights, esquires, gentlemen and commons for the lower part of the common wealth, the bishops for the clergy bee present to advertise, consult and show what is good and necessary for the common wealth, and to consult together, and upon mature deliberation every bill or law being thrice read and disputed upon in either house, the other two parts first each a part, and after the Prince himself in presence of both the parties doeth consent unto and alloweth. That is the Princes and whole realms deed: whereupon justly no man can complain but must accommodate himself to find it good and obey it.

That which is done by this consent is called firm, stable, and *sanctum*, and is taken for law. The Parliament abrogateth old laws, maketh new, giveth orders for things past, and for things hereafter to be followed, changeth rights, and possessions of private men, legitimates bastards, establisheth forms of religion, altereth weights and measures, giveth forms of succession to the crown, defineth of doubtful rights, whereof is no law already made, appointeth subsidies, tailes, taxes, and impositions, giveth most free pardons and absolutions, restoreth in blood and name as the highest court, condemneth or absolveth them whom the Prince will put to that trial: And to be short, all that ever the people of Rome might do either in *Centuriatis comitijs* or *tributis*,[1] the same may

---

[1] In the margins, Smith glosses "*Centuriatis comitiis* or *tributes*" as "*Tribunitiis.*" In *The Description of England*, Harrison's description closely follows Smith's: "To be short, whatsoever the people of Rome did in their *centuriatis* or *tribunitiis comitiis*, the same is and may be done by authority of our Parliament House, which is the head and body of all the realm and the place wherein every particular person is intended to be present, if not by himself, yet by his advocate or attorney" (149–50).

be done by the parliament of England, which representeth & hath the power of the whole realm both the head and the body. For every Englishman is intended to bee there present, either in person or by procuration and attorneys, of what preeminence, state, dignity, or quality soever he be, from the Prince (be he King or Queen) to the lowest person of England. And the consent of the Parliament is taken to be every man's consent.

Anonymous Member of the House of Commons; Speech on Succession

In 1566, a Member of the House of Commons—unfortunately, contemporary records do not identify the speaker—rose to urge Elizabeth I to name a successor. Elizabeth was only 33 at the time, but her subjects were wary: neither of Elizabeth's half-siblings, Edward VI (reigned, 1547–1553) and Mary I (reigned 1553–1558), had produced an heir, and Elizabeth was the last surviving child of Henry VIII. Many of Elizabeth's counselors and subjects hoped that she would soon marry and have children. While they waited, they worried that if Elizabeth died suddenly without having first established the succession, England would be vulnerable to civil war and foreign meddling. When Parliament met in 1566, members of both the House of Lords and the House of Commons pressed Elizabeth to settle the succession; Elizabeth told them such matters were her business and far too weighty for the likes of them. Our anonymous member boldly disagreed. In the beginning of his speech, he acknowledged that Elizabeth was, of course, the supreme head of the nation, but he also argued that the House of Commons was an important supplement to the Queen—she was just one person; the 400 plus members of the Commons could inform the monarch of the needs and desires of her entire realm. At the end of the speech, he speaks for "all England" and entreats Elizabeth to protect her realm by naming a successor.

from a Speech in the House of Commons (October [?] 1566)

The office of the head consisteth in these two pointes: first, carefully to devise and put in execution all things most commodious for the whole body and every member thereof; then, wisely to foresee and prevent the evils that may come to any part thereof. . . . This king, this head, with the consent of the whole body and through the providence of God, weighing that his eye and ear cannot be in every corner of his kingdom and domains at one instant to view and hearken out the benefits or inconveniences that might grow to the head, body, or any member thereof, hath established this honorable council of every part of the same absent from the king's eye and ear, the which is termed a parliament.

* * *

I speak for all England, yea, and for the noble English nation. . . . Therefore noble England, being now in great distress (as is before said) it crieth out in most soulful wise by me, the poor and simple advocate thereof, saying: "Help, o yee my noble, faithful counselors and subjects' inheritors, help this my feeble and weak estate that I may long live and be preserved to your use"—Mr. Speaker, oh that noble England should entreat us here to perform it to our own uses—"for I have no means to help me but you, and to that you were especially born; and there is no time and place to heal my sickness but this."

Republican Rome in the Elizabethan Political Imagination

The analogies that Thomas Smith draws between the political institutions of republican Rome and the political institutions of Elizabethan England—between the Senate and the House of Lords, between the tribunate and the House of Commons—were commonplace in early modern England. In *Romes Monarchie* (1596), a long verse history, an anonymous poet first describes the scene of Caesar's death as the "senate" and then as "parliament"; Member of Parliament Dudley Carlton referred to Christopher Yelverton as "the old Tribune of the House"; the anonymous authors of *A Lamentable Complaint of the Commonality, by way of supplication to the High Court of Parliament, for a learned ministry* (1585) called the Parliament a "Godly . . . Senate"; in 1606, James I scolded some members of Parliament for acting like "Tribunes of the people"; in 1601, Member of Parliament Robert Carey suggested that the Speaker of the House of Commons was analogous to the consuls of the Roman republic.[1] For most commentators, the similarities between the Roman republic and England's mixed-estate were merely formal, but John Hooker suggested that parallels between republican institutions and English institutions derived from a historical relation between Roman institutions and the House of Commons.

John Hooker (c. 1527–1610)

For biographical information on Hooker, see p. 167.

from *The Order and usage of the keeping of a Parlement in England* (1571)

. . . by the ancient orders and prescribed laws of this land, only such are to be elected and to have place [in the House of Commons] as for gravity, wisdom, knowledge and experience, are reputed and known to be the most chosen and principal personages of the whole land and Realm. . . . The order (therefore) among the Romans was that none should be received or allowed to be of their Senate house: unless he were grave in years, and well experienced in common affaires of the public wealth. . . . The like order also was and is within this Realm, the same being derived and taken chiefly from among the Romans, among whom and under whom: divers of the old and ancient Kings, have been bred and brought up.

These good Kings and Princes (I say) finding this land by disordered life, lawless liberty, and loose behavior to be brought to an utter ruin, decay, and desolation . . . after many devices, consultations and attempts for redress, [determined that] no way could be found so good, no remedy son present, nor help so

[1]Anon., *Romes Monarchie*; qtd. in David Harris Wilson, ed., *The Parliamentary Diary of Robert Bowyer, 1606–1607*, Minneapolis, MN, 1931, p. 123, n. 1; *A Lamentable Complaint*, London, 1585, sig. D1; Wilson, p. 42; qtd. in Jennifer Loach, *Parliament under the Tudors*, Oxford, 1991, p. 155. As even these few examples suggest, efforts to weave analogies between England's mixed-estate and the late Republic were often vexed: if, for example, the Speaker of the House is like a consul, the Lords like the Senate, and the members of Parliament like tribunes, what is the monarch like?

speedy as to erect and establish a Senate of the most grave, wise, and expert personages of the whole Realm, called by the name of a Parliament. . . . Wherefore according to the good and profitable and ancient orders of the Romans and the Israelites, these good Kings do erect a Senate or Parliament. . . . the benefit thereof grew so much in short time, that there was as it were a Metamorphoses of the state of the public weal on those days, for what Sedition and contention had disordered: good order and concord recovered. What looseness and dissoluteness of life had marred: honest behavior restored. What disobedience had decayed: loiable obedience amended. And finally what soever by any disorder was amiss: was by these means reformed and redressed . . . as that the people being better governed. . . . Lo, such are the fruits which grew of the Parliaments.

John Northbrooke (flourished 1567–1589)

Persecuted during the reign of Mary, Northbrooke quickly found favor when Elizabeth I became queen and restored the Protestant faith. He thrived as a preacher in Devon, where he held a series of important positions at St. Mary Radcliffe. Northbrooke was an active theologian and occasionally articulated positions at odds with Elizabethan church orthodoxy, though he seems to have been shrewd and amiable enough to steer clear of trouble. The following passage neatly illustrates how familiar the Roman Republic was to Elizabethans. Northbrooke is not writing about history or politics; he is trying to explain the role Christ plays in salvation. Northbrooke suggests an analogy between the way Christ mediates between God and the sinner and the way the Roman tribunes mediated between the common people and the patricians. It is worth remarking, of course, that this analogy casts a very favorable light on the tribunate and the Republic.

from *Spiritus est vicarius Christi in terra. A breefe and pithie summe of the Christian faith made in fourme of a confession* (1571)

When we say, then, that Christ maketh intercession for us, our meaning is, that he doth by the merits of his death, passion, and blood shedding, let or stop the wrath and vengeance of God, that it be not poured upon us for our filthy sins and offences. Again we say, that he maketh intercession for us, when he suffereth not the ears of the father to be stopped unto our prayers, but causeth them to be heard and accepted. And it is a manner of speaking borrowed of the ancient Romans. For, when the Consuls and Senators of Rome went about to make any decree or law that did seem to be prejudicial and hurtful unto the common weal, then the officers of the people, called *Tribunes*, were wont to let that decree or law . . . not go forward, and thereof did come, *intercessio Tribunorum*, that is to say: a let or prohibition of the *Tribunes*, that some matter might not go forward.

Even so: that almighty and most righteous God, the father of savior Jesu Christ, hath every day, and every hour, a most just occasion by reason of our detestable enormities, to destroy us both bodies and souls, and by his determinate decree and sentence, to condemn us, to the everlasting punishments of hell fire. But we have in the Senate house of heaven, a most mighty advocate, which doth continually appear before the face of God for us, that so he may by his omni-sufficient intercession, stop this determinate decree and sentence of that righteous judge, that it do not proceed and go forward against us.

But what if any man besides the *Tribunes*, had taken upon him, or presumed in the old Senate house of Rome, to prohibit, let, or stop any decree or law that the Consuls and Senators went about to make, should not he have been taken as a traitor, because that he had contrary to the order of the common weal, presumptuously taken that thing upon him, that did only appertain to the office of the *Tribunes*?

Samuel Daniel (1562–1619)

Daniel went up to Magdalen Hall, Oxford in 1581; after three years, he left before taking a degree. Daniel was a versatile literary artist: Delia, a sonnet sequence much admired in its own day, was published in 1592; his plays—especially The Tragedy of Cleopatra *(1594)—influenced Shakespeare and other playwrights; and* A Defence of Rhyme *(1603) ranks among the most important early modern treatises on poetry.*

Daniel published The First Foure Bookes of the Civile Wars between the Two Houses of Lancaster *and* Yorke *in 1595;* The Civil Wars Between the Two Houses of Lancaster *and* York, *a revision with many additions, was published in 1609. Daniel's verse history treats the War of the Roses, the great dynastic struggle between the House of Lancaster and the House of York that bedeviled England from 1455 to 1485. The same conflict is dramatized by Shakespeare in* Henry VI, *Parts 1, 2, and 3 and* Richard III. *In the following passage, Daniel asks his muse to help him represent the bloody Battle of Towton, in which the Yorkist army routed the Lancastrian forces; Daniel draws a comparison between Towton and the Pharsalia, where Julius Caesar defeated Pompey and the Senate. As he elaborates the comparison between the two civil wars, Daniel seems to prefer the Roman Republic to the English monarchy: Henry VI and Richard, Duke of York fight only for personal gain and glory—whatever the outcome, the English will remain in servitude to a king. By contrast, in the struggle between Caesar and Pompey, Pompey, Cato, and the Senate fight for freedom and the common good.*

from *First Foure Bookes of the Civile Wars between the Two Houses of* Lancaster *and* Yorke (1595)

Show, how our great Pharsalian Field was fought
At *Towton* in the North; the greatest day
Of ruin, that dissension ever brought
Unto this Kingdom: where, two Crowns did sway
The work of slaughter; two Kings[1] Causes wrought
Destruction to one People, by the way
Of their affections, and their loyalties;
As if one, for these ills, could not suffice.

Where *Lancaster* and that courageous side
(That noble constant Part) came furnished
With such a Power, as might have terrifi'd
And over-run the earth; had they been led
The way of glory, where they might have tri'd
For th'Empire of all *Europe*, as those did
The Macedonian[2] led into the East;
Their number being double, at the least.

---

[1]Henry VI and Richard, Duke of York both claimed to be the rightful king of England.
[2]Alexander the Great.

And where brave *York* comes as completely manned
With courage, valor, and with equal might;
Prepar'd to try with a resolved hand,
The metal of his Crown, and of his Right:
Attended with his fatal fire-brand
Of War, *Warwick*; that blazing star of fight,
The Comet of destruction, that portends
Confusion, and distress, what way he tends.

What rage, what madness, *England*, do we see?
That this brave people, in such multitude
Run to confound themselves, and all to be
Thus mad for *Lords*, and for mere Servitude.
What might have been, if (Roman-like, and free)
These gallant Spirits had nobler ends pursu'd,
And strain'd to points of glory and renown
For good of the Republic and their own?

But, here no *Cato* with a Senate stood
For Common-wealth: nor here were any sought
T'emancipate the State, for public good;
But only, headlong, for their faction wrought.
Here, every man runs on to spend his blood,
To get but what he had already got.
For, whether *Pompey*, or a *Cæsar* won,
Their state was ever sure to be all one.

John Higgins (c. 1544–1602)

Higgins may have attended Christ Church, Oxford; he certainly picked up a great deal of learning somewhere, as he became an admired translator of French and Latin texts. Higgins is now best remembered as the author of The First Parte of the Mirour for Magistrates *(1574), a supplement to William Baldwin's influential* A Mirour for Magistrates *(1559); in 1587, Higgins's text and Baldwin's were combined in a single work that was closely studied, by among many others, Shakespeare and Christopher Marlowe. Higgins's poem, like Baldwin's, is a species*

of the *Mirror for Princes* genre, in which the falls of the great serve as
cautionary tales and as occasions for the poet's meditations on government and governors. Higgins figures both Caesar and his republican
enemies as self-interested: Brutus and Cassius are motivated by frustrated ambition; Caesar is vain and power hungry.

from *A Mirour for Magistrates* (1587)

My glory did procure me secret foes,
Because above the rest I bare the sway.
By sundry means they sought my deep decay.
For why, there could no *Consuls* chosen be,
No *Praetor* take the place, no sentence have decree,
Unless it liked me first, and were approved by me.

'Tis they envied that sued aloft to clime,
As *Cassius*, which the *Praetorship* did crave,
And *Brutus* eke his friend which bare the crime
Of my dispatch, for they did first deprave
My life, mine acts, and sought my blood to have,
Full secretly amongst them selves conspired, decreed
To be attempters of that cruel bloody deed,
When *Caesar* in the *Senate* house from noble hart should bleed.

* * *

You Princes all, and noble men beware of pride,
And careful will to war for Kingdome's sake:
By me, that set my self aloft the world to guide,
Beware what bloodsheds you do undertake.
Ere three & twenty wounds had made my hart to quake,
What thousands fell for *Pompey's* pride and mine?
Of *Pompey's* life that cut the vital line,
My self have told what fate I found in fine.

Full many noble men, to rule alone, I slew,
And some themselves for grief of hart did slay:
For they ne would mine Empire stay to view.
Some I did force to yield, some fled away
As loath to see their Countries quite decay.
The world in *Aphrike, Asia*, distant far,

And *Europe* knew my bloodsheds great in war,
Recounted yet through all the world that are.

But since my whole pretence was glory vain,
To have renown and rule above the rest,
Without remorse of many thousands slain,
Which, for their own defense, their wars addressed:
I deem therefore my stony heart and breast
Receiv'd so many wounds for just revenge, they stood
By justice right of *Jove*, the sacred sentence good,
That who so slays, he pays the price, is blood for blood.

Roman Tyranny in Elizabethan Context

If Shakespeare's contemporaries were in the habit of thinking of their Parliament as not unlike the Roman Senate and tribunate, they certainly never mistook themselves for republican subjects: that every man and woman was the monarch's subject went without saying. The discourse of tyranny in Shakespeare's England was, not surprisingly, very different from the discourse of tyranny in late republican Rome. Some Catholic polemicists figured Elizabeth as a tyrant because she suppressed freedom of conscience. Invocations of domestic tyranny in Elizabethan and Jacobean England, however, were typically prompted by an attempt by the monarch to limit free speech in Parliament or to impose taxes in the absence of the subject's consent. Such concerns may seem very remote in the Rome of *Caesar*, where Brutus and Cassius strive to prevent monarchy rather than limit its powers, but we should remark the depth of English feeling about the subject's "freedom" and juxtapose it with the conspirators' anxieties about what Caesar would do were he to become king.

Sir William Fitzwilliam (1526–1599)

Much of Sir William Fitzwilliam's career was spent in Ireland; he was Elizabeth's Lord Deputy of Ireland for most of the last thirty years of her reign. His stint as a member of Parliament in 1584–85 came during an interruption in his term as Lord Deputy. We know little of Fitzwilliam's activities in the House of Commons, but he gives a vivid account here of how seriously his fellow members of Parliament regarded Elizabeth's attempts to limit their speech. Freedom of speech was routinely figured as a cornerstone of "the liberty of Parliament"; "the liberty of Parliament," in turn, was the necessary condition of the subject's liberty and felicity. In the following selection, John Puckering, the Speaker of the House, has just informed the Commons in 1585 that Elizabeth has insisted that they cease debating religious matters; the distraught members of Parliament identified this attack on their freedom of speech as an attack on the people's liberty.

from Sir William Fitzwilliam's Parliamentary Diary (1584–1585)[1]

With this message the House found them selves so greatly moved and so deeply wounded as they could not devise which way to cure themselves again, for so their case stood, as either they must offend their gracious sovereign towards whom, in respect of their singular benefits that they received by her most blessed and happy government, they durst not so much as lift up one evil thought or imagination, or else to suffer the liberties of their House to be infringed, whereby they should leave their children and posterity in thralldom and bondage, they themselves by their forefathers being delivered into freedom and liberty.

Richard Martin (1570–1618)

While studying law at the Middle Temple in the early 1590s, Richard Martin joined a circle of poets and intellectuals that included Ben Jonson, Fulke Greville, and Lionel Cranfield. A very successful lawyer and politician, Martin was sympathetic to some of Elizabeth I's and James I's parliamentary initiatives, but he opposed the Crown's positions on many occasions. In the following selection, Martin deplores Elizabeth's use of monopolies as a form of patronage; granting monopolies to favorites, Martin argues, oppresses the poor subject.

---

[1]T. E. Hartley, ed. *Proceedings in the Parliaments of Elizabeth I. Volume II: 1584–1589.* London: Leicester University Press, 1995, p. 183.

from a Speech in the House of Commons (November 20, 1601)[1]

I do speak *for* a town that grieves and pines, *for* a country that groaneth and languisheth under the bur-then of monstrous and unconscionable [monopolies] . . . of starch, tin, fish, cloth, oil, vinegar, salt and I know not what. . . . If these blood-suckers be still let alone to suck up the best and the principalest commodities, which the earth there hath given us; what shall become of *us*, from whom the fruits of *our* own soil, and the commodities of *our* own labor, which with the sweat of *our* brows (even up to the knees in mire and dirt) *we* have labored for, shall be taken from *us* by warrant of supreme authority, which the poor subject dares not gainsay.

Sir Thomas Hetley (c. 1570–1637)

Sir Thomas Hetley (also known as Hedley) was a lawyer of considerable distinction and an important member in several parliaments. Hetley frequently opposed initiatives near and dear to James I's heart: the union of England and Scotland, and the proposal to naturalize all Scots born after 1603. In the following selection, Hetley argues passionately against James's practice of levying impositions; this alienation of the subject's property "without the assent of parliament," he claims, will transform England into a slave state.

from a Speech in the House of Commons (June 8, 1610)[1]

But it is not so much to lose all a man's wealth as the power of holding it, for that is nothing else but bondage, or the condition of a villein, whose lands and goods are only in the power of his lord, which doth so abase his mind . . . that he is neither fit to do service to his country in war nor peace, for the law enables him not so much as to serve in a jury, and the wars design him but to the galleys or the gallows. So if the liberty of the subject be in this

[1]T. E. Hartley, ed. *Proceedings in the Parliaments of Elizabeth I. Volume III: 1593–1601.* London: Leicester University Press, 1995, pp. 197–98, 198–99.

[1]Elizabeth Read Foster, ed. *Proceedings in Parliament, 1610*, vol. 2. New Haven, CT, 1966, pp. 185–86, 191.

point impeached, that their lands and goods be any way in the king's absolute power to be taken from them, then they are (as it hath been said) little better than the king's bondmen, which will so discourage them and so abase and deject their minds, that they will use little care or industry to get that which they cannot keep and so will grow both poor and base-minded like to the peasants in other countries, which be no soldiers nor will be ever made any, whereas every Englishman is as fit for a soldier as the gentleman elsewhere.

* * *

But once take this ancient liberty from the commons, so that they perceive their lands and goods not absolutely their own but in the absolute power and command of another, they will neither have care for that wealth and courage that now they have, but a drooping dismayedness will possess and direct them or deliver them up to desperate resolutions; for seeing their liberty and condition no better than the bondmen or peasants in other places, their courage will be no better than theirs; for it is not the nature of the people or climate, though I know they are not utterly without their operation and influence, that makes this difference; but it is the laws, liberties, and government of this realm.

Performance History

On September 21, 1599, Thomas Platter, a visitor from Switzerland, did what any good tourist in England today would do: he took in a play at the Globe (the original, of course): "I . . . saw," he wrote in his diary, "the tragedy of the first Emperor Julius with at least fifteen characters very well acted."[1] Platter's happy night at the theater has since been shared by millions: *Caesar* has, with very few interruptions, been enormously popular for more than 400 years. Our records of performances during James I's and Charles I's reigns are rather thin, but many poems and plays of the period refer to *Caesar*; if the play was not being staged during this period, it was certainly being read. During the Civil War and the Interregnum (1642–60), the public theaters were closed, but *Caesar* was back on the boards just three years after the Restoration of Charles II in 1660 and was revived several times before the turn of the century. During the first half of the eighteenth century, "only five years were without at least one *Julius Caesar* revival" (Ripley 23).[2] The play's popularity suffered a modest decline during the second half of the century, but John Philip Kemble's 1812 Covent Garden revival, with famous actors in the leading roles, sparked a fifty-year vogue for *Caesar*, and, just when the play seemed to be passing from theatrical memory, Beerbohm Tree's 1898 revival, much remarked for its visual impact, launched *Caesar* into the twentieth century, when its popularity never flagged. Americans have found *Caesar* deeply compelling from before the Revolutionary War. The first production was staged, appropriately enough, in Philadelphia, at

---

[1]Qtd. in E. K. Chambers. *The Elizabethan Stage*, vol. 2. Oxford, 1923, p. 365.

[2]This entire paragraph relies on Ripley's very thorough study.

the Southward Theater in 1770; the play was a mainstay of nineteenth-century American theater; and, thanks perhaps to the play's secure place in the high school English curriculum, *Caesar* remained throughout the twentieth century and remains today one of Shakespeare's most frequently staged plays.

Among the dozens of interesting twentieth-century performances of the play, I have chosen three—two famous, one obscure—for extended discussion: Orson Welles's path-breaking 1937 production in New York; the 1953 M-G-M film starring John Gielgud and Marlon Brando; and a 1916 outdoor performance in Beachwood Canyon, California. Each of these incarnations of the play tells us something important about *Caesar*, in particular, and about Shakespeare's afterlife in modernity.[3]

Shakespeare in Hollywood, Part I: The Hollywood Carnival Association Production of 1916

In 1916, The Hollywood Carnival Association and the Actors' Fund of America, with the support of the Los Angeles County Board of Supervisors, produced an astonishing, one-night-only, open air performance of *Caesar* to mark the tercentenary of Shakespeare's death and to benefit the Fund, which helped struggling actors. For months before the performance on May 19, local papers reported the progress of this massive undertaking: a 400-acre section of Beachwood Canyon—future site of the Hollywood Bowl—was cleared; hilltops were leveled; huge teams of carpenters and painters reproduced a gladiatorial arena, Antony's house, Brutus's house, Caesar's house, the Forum, and the Capitol; roads, lined with columns, were built to connect the various sites; a cast of 5,000 rehearsed in a vast warehouse; the General Electric Company installed huge batteries of flood lights; construction crews built access roads to connect parking areas and the seating and viewing

---

[3]Ripley discusses the Welles production at some length (pp. 222–32) but mentions only in passing the 1916 Beachwood Canyon event and the M-G-M film.

areas; a 75-piece orchestra was assembled. The performance, attended by 40,000 spectators, generated, after expenses, $15,000 for the Actors' Fund; even though the actors, director, and many of the companies and individuals involved in construction donated their services, the production still cost $20,000.

The Beachwood Canyon *Caesar* and its reception were shaped, in part, by the rapid growth of the film industry. On the one hand, in headlines such as "Los Angeles to Outdo World in Tribute to the Bard of Avon" and assurances that "experts" regarded the production "as the most spectacular Shakespearean pageants ever undertaken," we can feel a still young city's anxious claim to legitimacy.[1] In the Los Angeles of 1916, of course, civic pride and civic inferiority complexes were bound in the film industry's status in American culture, and the Beachwood Canyon *Caesar* was very much a Hollywood enterprise. Most of the leading actors—Tyrone Power (Brutus), Frank Keenan (Cassius), Theodore Roberts (Caesar), Charles Gunn (Octavius), William Farnum (Antony), Sarah Truax (Portia), and Constance Crawley (Calphurnia)—and the director Raymond Wells were, by 1916, best known to the public for their work in motion pictures. The frontier city of Los Angeles and the upstart film industry, the organizers of the event seemed determined to show, could put Shakespeare on the boards with the best of them. On the other hand, the production itself and its reception reflect a bold, even arrogant confidence in the superiority of film to stage. The production seemed oddly devoted to demonstrating theater's deficiencies: a cast of 5,000 playing on a 400-acre stage was not going to become standard theatrical practice; the combined forces of Hollywood could stage such a spectacle, but, unlike a movie, this *Caesar* would not be visiting your town. The performance had, moreover, all the trappings of a Hollywood film premier: "Roman soldiers will vise [sell] the tickets. Roman sentries will guide the visitors to their seats."[2] Finally, and most remarkably, the sheer scale of the production seemed to assimilate the phenomenology of theater-going to the phenomenology of movie-going. When the anonymous reviewer for the *Los Angeles Times* praises the performance because it "required no effort on the part of the spectators to imag-

---

[1] *Los Angeles Times*, April 16, 1916, p. II1; *Los Angeles Times*, April 23, 1916, p. II1.
[2] *Los Angeles Times*, April 23, 1916, p. II1.

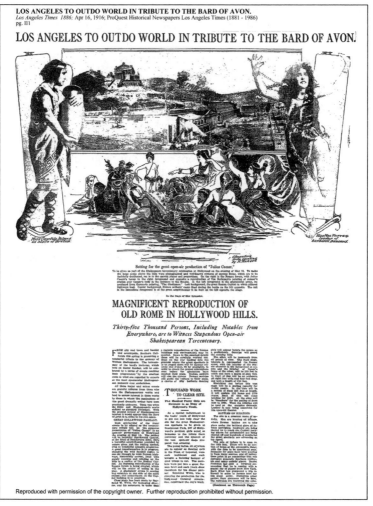

"Los Angeles to Outdo World in Tribute to the Bard of Avon."
Los Angeles Times, April 16, 1916.

ine themselves in Rome," we seem worlds away from the exhortations of the Chorus of *Henry V* (1599):

> But pardon, gentles, all,
> The flat unraised spirits that hath dared
> On this unworthy scaffold to bring forth

So great an object. Can this cock-pit hold
The vasty fields of France? Or may we cram
Within this wooden O the very casques
That did affright the air at Agincourt?
O pardon: since a crooked figure may
Attest in little place a million,
And let us ciphers to this great account,
On your imaginary forces work.
....
Piece out our imperfections with your thoughts:
Into a thousand parts divide one man,
And make imaginary puissance.

                       (Prologue, 8–18, 23–25)

"Imaginary forces" and "thoughts" could be left at home, our reviewer suggests: no need to "divide one man" into "a thousand"; the battle scenes involved 3,000 actors.[3] The director Raymond Wells suggested that only an even more extravagant approach could save Shakespeare for the modern theater: "It is Mr. Wells's belief that Shakespeare's plays would be acceptable today if they were produced on a stage four miles square, employed 20,000 people in the cast, and were presented before an audience of 50,000. . . . Mr. Wells is seriously considering having the title character make his first entrance in an aeroplane."[4] By 1916, film epics such as D. W. Griffith's *Birth of a Nation* (1915) had wowed the country; perhaps Mr. Wells's zany ideas did not seem so zany to those who worried that the theater would be eclipsed by film.

from "Forty Thousand See Rome's Mighty Tragedy Re-enacted," *Los Angeles Times* (May 20, 1916)

Seated in a vast amphitheater fashioned by nature in beauty and grandeur, 40,000 people looked upon old Rome. . . . There, with perfect setting, with nothing to destroy the illusion, unhampered

---

[3] Although I am emphasizing the emergence of the film industry as the shaping context for this production, participants also were keenly aware of the World War (see, e.g., the excerpts from the March 30 and April 27 editions of the *Los Angeles Times* in this Contexts section).

[4] *Los Angeles Times*, May 14, 1916, p. II14.

by the confining walls of a stage, 5,000 actors presented 'Julius Caesar' as it never was played before. Batteries of great floodlight projectors with a capacity of 6,000,000 candle power brought the actors in sharp relief in the Forum, the arena and even on the distant hills, where the battling forces of Mark Antony and Cassius played their part in the drama, which was unfolded by stellar Shakespearean actors.

It required no effort on the part of the spectators to imagine themselves in Rome, witnesses in verity of the great tragedy of history. Inspired by the realism of the setting and the absorbed attention of the great audience, the actors became for the hour, Romans, indeed, and lived their parts with every gesture and utterance.

It was more than a play. It was production, realistic, Gargantuan. It was more than a stage, for the actors had 400 acres of space.

* * *

The spectacle opened with all the lights on. The audience was given a glimpse of old Rome, its populace, its forum, its arena, Capitol Hill and the distant hills and ravines. Then all was dark. Briefly the light was projected on the arena on the hill at the left. There two gladiators were engaged in mortal combat. Above them the Roman populace, excited by the vigor of the fighting, encouraged their favorites.

When the light was shifted the gladiators were still fighting. Then, in the foreground of the forum, their faces weirdly distorted by green light, fifty barbaric dancers, girls, gyrated madly, clad only in leopard skin robes. Faster and more madly became the dance until the dancers sank in utter exhaustion, with staring eyes and disheveled hair to the ground.

* * *

After Caesar and his wife had crossed the forum Mark Antony and the senators were disclosed conferring in groups, as they might have done in Rome itself. Cleopatra's entry with Egyptian girls was a striking and gorgeous pageant.

In the second act new surprises were given the audience. The fountain playing near Antony's house scintillated with color. . . . The climax was inspiring. Glimpses of great armies, thousands of men, were given on the hills with the tents of Cassius' army on a hillside in the distant left. . . . Then Antony's forces put those of

Cassius to rout, applied the torch to the tents and they were consumed in a great blaze.

Nothing like this scene was ever staged before.

from an Advertisement in the *Los Angeles Times* (March 30, 1916)

A CALL TO ARMS
WANTED VOLUNTEERS WANTED
—All—
Public Spirited Citizens and Boosters
—of—
THE GREAT CITY OF LOS ANGELES, CAL.
GENTLEMAN:

Your Presence is desired on Friday, March 31st, at 1 P.M., at Beachwood Park, Hollywood, to assist—

The Honorable Charles Sebastian, Mayor of L.A.

Honorable City Council of L.A.

Board of Supervisors of L.A.

City Engineers of L.A.

Board of Trade of Hollywood

Commercial Club of Hollywood

Bring your overalls and assist in the turning of the first spade of earth for The Great Shakespearean Festival. . . . Greatest open-air production ever staged in America, presenting Shakespeare's masterpiece, "Julius Caesar." . . . Supported by a picked cast of 5,000 actors, and every citizen of the State of California.

Forward March. Citizens, be on hand Friday, March 31st, at 1 P.M.

from "Conscription: 'Julius Caesar' and 'Brutus' Enlist Armies in High Schools," *Los Angeles Times* (April 27, 1916)

Los Angeles will have its first touch of conscription today, when Capt. Louis R. Ball, U.S.A., descends upon the Lincoln High School, accompanied by Theodore Roberts [the actor who played Caesar], and enlists every boy in the school over five feet ten for the Roman army which is to battle in the Beachwood natural amphitheater on May 19. Julius Caesar, in the person of Mr. Roberts, will first deliver a plea for the best blood of Lincoln High to join the army, and then the entire male portion of the school will be lined up and Capt. Ball will put the measuring stick on them, and every one measuring the required height will be requested to report at once for the cause of Southern California.

Julius Caesar and the Political Crisis of the Twentieth Century: Orson Welles's Mercury Theater Production of 1937

Long before the rise of Mussolini, Hitler, Stalin, and other twentieth-century autocrats, the potential of *Caesar* as political theater flourished: in 1706, John Dennis staged the play as a cautionary tale about the ambitious French "tyrant" Louis XIV; advertisements for the 1770 production in Philadelphia urged George III's subjects—many of whom bristled under his rule—to come watch "The noble struggles for Liberty by that renowned patriot Marcus Brutus";[5] and some commentators saw an 1870 production in New York as a celebration of the fall of Napoleon III, who had been deposed just days before the first performance. Orson Welles's 1937 Mercury Theater production in New York, however, enjoys pride of place among overtly political stagings of the play: journalists, theater critics, and editorial writers from around the country made the play the cultural event of the late 1930s; the New York run topped 150 performances; and imitators quickly followed in Welles's footsteps.[6] Many aspects of Welles's dramaturgy, it should be noted, were bold and innovative: the striking use of a bare stage and unusual lighting techniques made a deep impression on American theatrical culture. Welles's assimilation of Shakespeare's Caesar to Mussolini was, however, the most widely remarked aspect of the production. Welles's political commitments were deeply felt, as a remarkable anecdote reveals. In an April performance, Welles (Brutus) accidentally stabbed Joseph Holland (Caesar); although Holland had to be hospitalized, Leonard Lyons of *The Washington Post* reported that the company would continue to use real knives. An item about Welles's

[5]Qtd. in Ripley (100).

[6]In a 1938 BBC television production, the leading male characters wore Italian military uniforms; the 1939 Embassy Theater production in London was also overtly anti-fascist. It is hard to exaggerate the excitement Welles's *Caesar* generated. In his column for *The Washington Post* ("The Post's New Yorker"), Leonard Lyons mentions Welles's production 17 times in 1937 and 1938.

accidental stabbing of Joseph Holland, the Caesar, reported: "From the very start, Mercury officials have refused to use the rubber imitation daggers—because they're marked 'Made in Japan.'"[7] The social and political resonances that Welles created made his *Caesar* something considerably more complicated than an indictment of Mussolini: as many commentators noted, the production also revealed a fascination with American gangsters and the dangers of "the mob."

from Mark Barron, "'Julius Caesar' Given New Fire on N.Y. Stage," *The Washington Post* **(November 21, 1937)**

Not only have the Mercury Theater players staged an extraordinary, clear production of this somewhat confusing play, but they have done it in such a manner that Shakespeare seems to be directing his remarks and conclusions at the present day dictatorships.

Their "Julius Caesar" is a thrilling document that directs its emphasis upon the movement and temper of crowds, the ironic threats rather than the poetry of Shakespeare's speech. It is played without scenery, but with lights picking out and emphasizing scenes or else giving a dazzling background in such a manner that scenery probably would only be superfluous.

The actors are attired in modern clothes, but they all wear the same colored shirts, a sort of greenish hue. Not only does this attire suggest the sameness of fascist costume, but in the way the manuscript has been cut and emphasis placed on certain scenes, the performance gives a definite mood that Shakespeare is commenting upon world politics today. Too, Joseph Holland, who plays Julius Caesar so well, has a strong physical resemblance to Mussolini.

* * *

Where Shakespeare believed character most important this production makes "Julius Caesar" seem more concerned with action and revolution, with movements of the multitude rather than thoughts and beliefs of individuals.

[7]*The Washington Post*, April 16, 1938, p. X16.

from "Only 'Caesar' Lives," *Chicago Daily Tribune*
(November 23, 1938)

The accent is entirely on the play as an agelessly significant story.
"Here a fascist dictator is struck down by an alliance of his foes,
and never once does it seem to you," wrote Mr. Watts in the Herald
Tribune, "that anything new is written into Shakespeare's original
intent. You cannot escape the feeling that, with the clairvoyance of
genius, he was predicting for us the caldron of modern Europe."

from Burns Mantle, "Shakespeare Revivals Are Called Queer,"
Chicago Daily Tribune (November 21, 1937)

This . . . is a stunt rather than a production, and as a stunt, generally
effective and sometimes thrilling. With Caesar standing as defiantly
as any dictator and giving the Fascist salute to crowds of milling
men shadowed in the darkness, the audience has such awareness of
a boiling modern Europe that the softly spoken Shakespearean text,
breaking into familiar phrases, comes often as a shock.

　　Going so far in the modernization I cannot see why they should
not have gone the whole way and rewritten the text. A Clifford
Odets could have revised Shakespeare in a gangland vernacular that
might have made this an exciting and truly thrilling propaganda
play aimed at present-day dictatorships.

　　However, we must take it as it is, and as it is it is interesting
because it gives an indication of what a new public is willing to accept
as Shakespearean drama.

from Charles Collins, "Orson Welles Stages 'Julius Caesar' as
Parable of Fascism," *Chicago Daily Tribune* (March 20, 1938)

The intention of this treatment of Shakespeare's tragedy is to point
out a historical parallel. By the use of Fascist uniforms, modern
civilian clothing, and certain attitudes and gestures said to be char-
acteristic of contemporary political movements in central Europe,
this unorthodox interpretation of a classic text emphasizes the fact
that the history of ancient Rome throws its shadow into the present.
A pattern of life and political thought is repeating itself. . . . It is a
mere "stunt," of course, and as such may be slightly deprecated by
those who prefer Shakespeare's plays as written: but it is a "stunt"
with a special sanction in scholarship.

Shakespeare in Hollywood, Part II:
Metro-Goldwyn-Mayer's *Julius Caesar* of 1953

Metro-Goldwyn-Mayer's 1953 film *Julius Caesar* assembled some of America's and Britain's most exalted theatrical and cinematic stars: John Houseman (producer and presiding genius), Joseph Mankiewicz (director), John Gielgud (Cassius), Marlon Brando (Antony), James Mason (Brutus), Greer Garson (Calpurnia), and Deborah Kerr (Portia). The reception of the film, however, suggests that the Hollywood of 1953 was perhaps more anxious about the aesthetic legitimacy of commercial films than the Hollywood of 1916. Nearly forty years after the Beachwood Canyon *Caesar* showed off what Hollywood talent and ambition could do when it turned its attention to theater, the reviewers of the M-G-M *Caesar* seem giddy that Hollywood has produced commercially viable art. However, beneath the notes of triumph, we can still hear rumbling anxieties about the superiority of the stage and about Britain's special relation to Shakespeare.[8]

from Bosley Crowther, "Julius Caesar," *New York Times* (June 14, 1953)

. . . the inevitable initial inquiry is how this motion picture version of the familiar Shakespeare play stacks up against the previous movie versions of "Hamlet" and "Henry V." This is a reasonable question, since those popular films of Laurence Olivier set exquisite and elevated standards for the picturing of Shakespeare on the screen. . . . Though perhaps not as moving as "Hamlet" or as vivid and thrilling as "Henry V," there is a rare sort of intellectual violence in this bold "Julius Caesar."

from Philip K. Scheuer, "'Julius Caesar' Faithful to Play and Finely Acted," *Los Angeles Times* (November 11, 1953)

"Julius Caesar" is a prestige picture—Shakespeare first and a movie second. Its rectitude in following the classic line is extraordinary for

[8]At the end of the year, the National Board of Review of Motion Pictures named *Julius Caesar* the Best Picture of 1953 because, as the board's chair explained, "it was not merely an able transfer of a stage play to the screen, but an unusually skillful portrayal of a historic event" (*The Washington Post*, Dec. 21, 1953, p. 8).

Hollywood; only a few years ago such a procedure would have spelt "box office poison." Today it should find a more widely appreciative audience, though I do not think this is the one that will break down the barrier separating the theater-art lover from the rank-and-file fan.

from Mae Tinee, "Shakespeare's 'Julius Caesar' Made into a Magnificent Movie," *Chicago Daily Tribune* (December 25, 1953)

And so, here is a magnificent motion picture of Shakespeare's political tragedy, presented in a form which gives it life and depth, and makes it available to millions. Except to the student, this cunning story of historic upheaval, the clash of ambition with ideals and the vanity which often comes with high office, is but vaguely familiar and seldom noted.

* * *

Metro-Goldwyn-Mayer can well be proud of this stunning production, as can the entire industry. The film proves that Shakespeare is not the exclusive property of the British stage and screen. The Bard has been interpreted in moving and memorable fashion here, to see this film is both a privilege and a pleasure. Merry Christmas!

Reception

Some schools of Shakespearean criticism are closely associated with or even founded on the interpretation of a particular play or plays—psychoanalytic critics return again and again to *Hamlet*; feminist critics to *Titus Andronicus*, *Othello*, *Macbeth*, and *Antony and Cleopatra*; scholars of gender identity to the cross-dressing in *As You Like It* and *Twelfth Night*—but no great critical edifice rests on *Caesar*. *Caesar*, of course, is central to all studies of the Roman plays, and it often figures in studies of Shakespeare's tragic vision; but the play's greatest claim to being a Shakespearean touchstone lies in its politics (or, perhaps, its putative politics). Scholars, directors, and readers searching for evidence of Shakespeare's attitude toward the common people often turn to the Act 1 confrontation between the people and their tribunes, the Forum scene, and the murder of Cinna the poet; in the representation of Caesar, they discern Shakespeare's views on monarchy and tyranny; and Brutus and Cassius are exhibit A for studies of Shakespeare's relation to republicanism. The following selections will give the reader some sense of the diversity of opinion about not only the political import of *Caesar* but also the play's aesthetic quality. Few of Shakespeare's mature works have so divided his readers.[1]

Thomas Rymer (1641–1713)

As a neo-classicist, Thomas Rymer abhorred Shakespeare's departures from Aristotelian principles of dramatic art. For Rymer, Shakespeare's refusal to respect the unities of time and space—to limit, that is, the

[1]I found many of the materials assembled here by way of Brian Vickers' *Shakespeare: the Critical Heritage*. 6 vols. London: Routledge and Kegan Paul, 1974–81.

action of a play to a single day and place—and his breaches of decorum (mixing genres, making kings and clowns share the same stage) radically undermined his achievement.

from *A Short View of Tragedy* (1693)[1]

[Julius Caesar] sins not against Nature and Philosophy only but against the most known History and the memory of the Noblest Romans, that ought to be sacred to all Posterity. He might be familiar with *Othello* and *Iago*, as his own natural acquaintance: but *Caesar* and *Brutus* were above his conversation. To put them in Fools Coats, and make them Jack-puddens in the Shakespeare dress, is a *Sacrilege.* . . . The Truth is, this authors head was full of villainous, unnatural images, and history has only furnish'd him with great names thereby to recommend them to the World, by writing over them *this is* Brutus, *this is* Cicero, *this is* Caesar.

Joseph Addison (1672–1719)

Joseph Addison was a distinguished statesman, an important literary critic, a successful playwright, and, with Richard Steele, the founder of the Spectator—*perhaps the most influential periodical ever circulated in England. The following selection appeared in the* Tatler, *a precursor to the* Spectator *edited by Steele.*

from the *Tatler* 53 (August 10, 1709)

In the Tragedy of *Julius Caesar*, [Shakespeare] introduces his Hero in Night-Gown. He had at that Time all the Power of *Rome*. *Depos'd* Consuls, subordinate Generals, and Captive Princes might have preceded him; but this Genius was above such Mechanick Methods of showing Greatness. Therefore he rather presents this great Soul debating upon the Subject of Life and Death with his intimate Friends, without endeavoring to prepossess his Audience with empty Show and Pomp. When those who attend him talks of the many Omens which had appear'd that Day, he answers:

[1]*A Short View of Tragedy, Its original excellency and corruption, with some reflections on Shakespeare and other practitioners for the stage.* London, 1693.

Cowards die many Times before their Deaths;
The Valiant never talk of Death but once.
Of all the Wonders that I yet have heard,
It seems to me most strange that Men should fear;
Seeing that Death, a necessary End,
Will come, when it will come.

When the Hero has spoken this Sentiment there is nothing that is great which cannot be expected from one whose first Position is the Contempt of Death to so high a Degree, as making his *Exit* a Thing wholly indifferent, and not a Part of his Care, but that of Heav'n and Fate.

Nicholas Rowe (1674–1718)

Nicholas Rowe enjoyed considerable success as a playwright and translator, but he is now best known as Shakespeare's earliest modern editor: his six-volume edition of the plays appeared in 1709, and many of Rowe's editorial decisions—for example, his divisions of the plays into acts and scenes—have been preserved by generations of subsequent editors.

from *Some Account of the Life, etc, of Mr. William Shakespeare* (1709)[1]

Had *Shakespeare* read either *Sallust* or *Cicero* how could he have made so very little of the first and greatest of Men, as that *Caesar* should be but a Fourth-rate Actor in his own Tragedy? How could it have been that seeing *Caesar*, we should ask for *Caesar*? That we should ask, where is his unequall'd Greatness of Mind, his unbounded Thirst of Glory, and that victorious Eloquence with which he triumph'd over the Souls of both Friends and Enemies, and with which he rivall'd *Cicero* in Genius as he did *Pompey* in Power? How fair an Occasion was there to open the Character if *Caesar* in that first Scene between *Brutus* and *Cassius*! For when *Cassius* tells *Brutus* that *Caesar* was but a Man like them, and had

[1]Rowe's *Account* served as the preface to his edition of the plays.

the same natural Imperfections which they had, how natural had it been for *Brutus* to reply that *Caesar* indeed had their Imperfections of Nature but neither he nor *Cassius* had by any means the great Qualities of *Caesar*. . . . if *Brutus*, after enumerating all the wonderful Qualities of *Caesar*, had resolv'd in spite of them all to sacrifice him to publick Liberty, how had such a Proceeding heighten'd the Vertue and Character of *Brutus*! But then indeed it would have been requisite that *Caesar* upon his Appearance should have made all this good.

Lewis Theobald (1688–1744)

Lewis Theobald's 1733–34 edition of Shakespeare's plays remains a landmark in Shakespearean scholarship.

from *The Censor* 70 (April 2, 1717)

Of all the Plays, either Ancient or Modern, the Tragedy of *Julius Caesar*, written by Shakespeare, has been held in the fairest Esteem and Admiration. I don not reckon from the Vulgar, tho' they, where their Passions are concern'd, are certainly no ill Judges, but from the establish'd Rules of Dramatic Poetry and the Opinion of the best Poets. As to particular Irregularities it is not to be expected that a Genius like Shakespeare's should be judg'd by the Laws of Aristotle and other Precscribers to the Stage. It will be sufficient to fix a Character of Excellence to his Performances if there are in them a Number of beautifull Incidents, true and exquisite Turns of Nature and Passion, fine and delicate Sentiments, uncommon Images, and great Boldness of Expression.

In this Play of our Countryman's I think I may affirm, tho' against the Opinion of untasting Criticks, that all these Beauties meet, and if I were to examine the Whole it would be no great Difficulty to prove the Truth of my Assertion. But I have singled out only one Scene to be the subject of my present *Lucubration*. Omitting the incomparable Speeches of Brutus and Mark Antony (of which those of the latter were perhaps never equall'd in any Language) the Scene I have chose is the Quarrel and Reconciliation of Brutus and Cassius. . . .

Voltaire (1694–1778)

Voltaire—the famous alias of François-Marie Arouet—was the founding father of Enlightenment poetry, drama, criticism, and philosophy. Voltaire's relationship to Shakespeare is complicated: on the one hand, he, like Rymer, recoiled from Shakespeare's "barbaric" disregard for classical rules of art; on the other hand, he recognized Shakespeare's genius and was clearly captivated by Julius Caesar, which he saw performed in 1726 in London while in exile. In 1731, Voltaire wrote La Mort de César, a reworking of Shakespeare's play; he translated nearly half the play in 1764; and he returned to it again and again in his meditations on dramatic art.

from *Discours sur la tragédie, à milord Bolingbroke* (1731)[1]

With what pleasure did I see in London your tragedy of *Julius Caesar*, which for 150 years, has delighted your nation! I certainly do not pretend to approve of the barbarous irregularities of which it is full; it is astonishing only that one does not find more of them in a work composed in an age of ignorance, by a man who himself did not know Latin, and who had no master other than his own genius. But, in the midst of so many gross faults, with what ravishment I beheld Brutus, still holding a dagger dripping with Caesar's blood, assemble the Roman people, and speak to them thus from the height of the rostrum:

[Voltaire quotes 3.2.13–48 (Brutus's speech and its ecstatic reception by the people)]

After this scene, Antony comes to move to pity these same Romans, whom Brutus had inspired with his rigor and his barbarity. By means of an artificial speech, Antony turns these superb spirits [the people] about, without their even being aware of it; and when he sees that they have softened, he shows them the body, and, making use of the most pathetic rhetoric, he excites them to vengeance. Perhaps the French would not have permitted one to represent a chorus of artisans and plebeians on their stage, nor the bloody corpse of Caesar to be exposed there to the eyes of the people, nor the people exhorted to revenge from the rostrum: custom, which is the

[1]Printed with *Le Brutus*. Paris (London), 1731. The translation is my own.

queen of this world, changes the taste of nations and turns into pleasure objects of our revulsion.

Edward Capell (1713–1781)

Edward Capell's timing was dreadful: he published his ten-volume edition of Shakespeare's plays in 1768, three years after Samuel Johnson had issued his famous edition. However, Capell's approach to editing Shakespeare was novel and vastly influential; he established his texts for the plays by thoroughly comparing the First Folio versions and Quarto versions.

from *Notes and Various Readings to Shakespeare* (1779)[1]

[On Brutus's speech to the people]

Every true admirer of Shakespeare has good cause for wishing that there had been some authority to question this speech's genuineness. But editions afford it not; and it has the sanction besides of many likenesses to other parts of his work. . . . The truth is, his genius sunk in some measure beneath the grandeur of Roman characters; at least in this play, which we may judge from thence to have been the first he attempted. His Caesar is more inflated than great, and the oratory of this speech has no resemblance whatever to that which Brutus affected, which was a nervous and simple laconism. . . . he either could not come up to it [Brutus's oratorical style], or judg'd it improper, or else sacrificed this and his other weaknesses to the bad taste of the people he writ for.

Elizabeth Montagu (1720–1800)

A leading figure in the Blue Stocking Circle, a floating salon active during the second half of the eighteenth century, Elizabeth Montagu attracted the admiration of Dr. Johnson, David Garrick, Fanny Bur-

[1]3 vols. London, 1779–80.

ney, and many others. An Essay *was a hit in England and France (despite its vigorous dressing down of Voltaire).*

from An Essay on the Writings and Genius of Shakespeare (1769)[1]

The principal object of our poet was to interest the spectator for Brutus; to do this he was to shew that his temper was the furthest imaginable from any thing ferocious or sanguinary, and by his behavior to his wife, his friends, his servants, to demonstrate that out of respect to public liberty he made . . . [was a] difficult a conquest over his natural disposition. . . . The victories of Alexander, Caesar, and Hannibal, whether their wars were just or unjust, must obtain for them the laurel wreath which is the ambition of conquerors. But the act of Brutus in killing Caesar was of such an ambiguous kind as to receive its denomination from the motive by which it was suggested; it is that which must fix upon him the name of patriot or assassin. Our author, therefore, shews great judgment in taking various opportunities to display the softness and gentleness of Brutus. The little circumstance of his forebearing to awaken the servant who was playing to him on the lute is very beautiful, for one cannot conceive that he whose tender humanity respected the slumber of his boy Lucilius would from malice or cruelty have cut short the important and illustrious course of Caesar's life.

* * *

As it was Shakespeare's intention to make Brutus his hero he has given a disadvantageous representation of Caesar, and thrown an air or pride and insolence into his behaviour which is intended to create an apprehension in the spectator of his disposition to tyrannize over his fellow-citizens.

[1]*An Essay on the Writings and Genius of Shakespeare, Compared with the Greek and French Dramatic Poets, with Some Remarks Upon the Misrepresentations of Mons. de Voltaire.* London, 1769.

Samuel Taylor Coleridge (1772–1834)

Author of three seminal long poems ("Kubla Kahn," "The Rime of the Ancient Mariner," and "Christabel"), Samuel Taylor Coleridge enjoys an even greater stature in literary history as the co-author, with Wordsworth, of Lyrical Ballads, *the foundational text of Romanticism. Coleridge's lectures on poetry and drama are among the most important works in the history of literary criticism.*

from *Lectures and Notes on Shakespeare and Other English Poets* (1811)[1]

[On Brutus's contemplation of Caesar's ambition (2.1.10–28)]

This speech is singular;—at least, I do not at present see into Shakespeare's motive, his rationale, or in what point of view he meant Brutus' character to appear. For surely— (this, I mean, is what I say to myself, with my present quantum of insight, only modified by my experience in how many instances I have ripened into a perception of beauties, where I had before descried faults;) surely, nothing can seem more discordant with our historical preconceptions of Brutus, or more lowering to the intellect of the Stoico-Platonic tyrannicide, than the tenets here attributed to him—to him, the stem Roman republican; namely,—that he would have no objection to a king, or to Cæsar, a monarch in Rome, would Cæsar but be as good a monarch as he now seems disposed to be! How, too, could Brutus say that he found no personal cause—none in Caesar's past conduct as a man? Had he not passed the Rubicon? Had he not entered Rome as a conqueror? Had he not placed his Gauls in the Senate?— Shakespeare, it may be said, has not brought these things forwards—True;—and this is just the ground of my perplexity. What character did Shakespeare mean his Brutus to be?

---

[1]Coleridge delivered his lectures in 1811–12, but they were not published until 1897; I quote here from *Lectures and Notes on Shakespeare and Other English Poets*. London, 1914.

William Hazlitt (1778–1830)

Critic, painter, essayist, and political radical, William Hazlitt was one of the great literary titans of the nineteenth century; his prose style and his evaluations of poetry, drama, politics, and philosophy helped to shape English literary culture for generations. Coleridge is his only rival among nineteenth-century commentators on Shakespeare.

from *Characters of Shakespear's Plays* (1817)

Julius Caesar was one of three principal plays by different authors, pitched upon by the celebrated Earl of Hallifax to be brought out in a splendid manner by subscription, in the year 1707. The other two were the King and No King of Fletcher, and Dryden's Maiden Queen. There perhaps might be political reasons for this selection, as far as regards our author. Otherwise, Shakespear's *Julius Caesar* is not equal as a whole, to either of his other plays taken from the Roman history. It is inferior in interest to *Coriolanus*, and both in interest and power to *Antony and Cleopatra*. It however abounds in admirable and affecting passages, and is remarkable for the profound knowledge of character, in which Shakespear could scarcely fail. If there is any exception to this remark, it is in the hero of the piece himself. We do not much admire the representation here given of Julius Caesar, nor do we think it answers to the portrait given of him in his Commentaries. He makes several vapouring and rather pedantic speeches, and does nothing. Indeed, he has nothing to do. So far, the fault of the character is the fault of the plot.

The well-known dialogue between Brutus and Cassius [1.2.25–214], in which the latter breaks the design of the conspiracy to the former, and partly gains him over to it, is a noble piece of high-minded declamation. Cassius's insisting on the pretended effeminacy of Caesar's character, and his description of their swimming across the Tiber together, "once upon a raw and gusty day," are among the finest strokes in it. But perhaps the whole is not equal to the short scene which follows, when Caesar enters with his train. We know hardly any passage more expressive of the genius of Shakespear than this. It is as if he had been actually present, had known the different characters and what they thought of one another, and had taken down what he heard and saw, their looks, words, and gestures, just as they happened.

* * *

Shakespear has in this play and elsewhere shown the same penetration into political character and the springs of public events as into those of everyday life. For instance, the whole design of the conspirators to liberate their country fails from the generous temper and over-weaning confidence of Brutus in the goodness of their cause and the assistance of others. Thus it has always been. Those who mean well themselves think well of others, and fall a prey to their security. That humanity and honesty which dispose men to resist injustice and tyranny render them unfit to cope with the cunning and power of those who are opposed to them. The friends of liberty trust to the professions of others, because they are themselves sincere, and endeavour to reconcile the public good with the least possible hurt to its enemies, who have no regard to anything but their own unprincipled ends, and stick at nothing to accomplish them. Cassius was better cut out for a conspirator. His heart prompted his head. His watchful jealousy made him fear the worst that might happen, and his irritability of temper added to his inveteracy of purpose, and sharpened his patriotism. The mixed nature of his motives made him fitter to contend with bad men. The vices are never so well employed as in combating one another. Tyranny and servility are to be dealt with after their own fashion: otherwise, they will triumph over those who spare them, and finally pronounce their funeral panegyric, as Antony did that of Brutus.

* * *

The truth of history in *Julius Caesar* is very ably worked up with dramatic effect. The councils of generals, the doubtful turns of battles, are represented to the life. The death of Brutus is worthy of him—it has the dignity of the Roman senator with the firmness of the Stoic philosopher. But what is perhaps better than either, is the little incident of his boy, Lucius, falling asleep over his instrument, as he is playing to his master in his tent, the night before the battle. Nature had played him the same forgetful trick once before on the night of the conspiracy. The humanity of Brutus is the same on both occasions.

George Bernard Shaw (1856–1950)

In the 1890s, before he established himself as a great playwright, George Bernard Shaw was the most important music and theater critic in England. During this crucial moment in theater history, Shaw championed Ibsen, Strindberg, and a socially engaged, intellectually ambitious approach to drama.

from a Review of Beerbohm Tree's 1898 Production of *Julius Caesar, The Saturday Review* (January 29, 1898)

It is when we turn to *Julius Caesar,* the most splendidly written political melodrama we possess, that we realize the apparently immortal author of *Hamlet* as a man, not for all time, but for an age only, and that, too, in all solidly wise and heroic aspects, the most despicable of all the ages in our history. It is impossible for even the most judicially minded critic to look without a revulsion of indignant contempt at this travestying of a great man as a silly braggart, whilst the pitiful gang of mischief-makers who destroyed him are lauded as statesmen and patriots. There is not a single sentence uttered by Shakespear's Julius Caesar that is, I will not say worthy of him, but even worthy of an average Tammany boss. Brutus is nothing but a familiar type of English suburban preacher: politically he would hardly impress the Thames Conservancy Board. Cassius is a vehemently assertive nonentity. It is only when we come to Antony, unctuous voluptuary and self-seeking sentimental demagogue, that we find Shakespear in his depth; and in his depth, of course, he is superlative. Regarded as a crafty stage job, the play is a triumph: rhetoric, claptrap, effective gushes of emotion, all the devices of the popular playwright, are employed with a profusion of power that almost breaks their backs. No doubt there are slips and slovenliness of the kind that careful revisers eliminate; but they count for so little in the mass of accomplishment that it is safe to say that the dramatist's art can be carried no further on that plane. If Goethe, who understood Caesar and the significance of his death— "the most senseless of deeds" he called it—had treated the subject, his conception of it would have been as superior to Shakespear's as St. John's Gospel is to the Police News; but his treatment could not have been more magnificently successful. As far as sonority, imagery, wit, humor, energy of imagination, power over language, and a whimsically keen eye for idiosyncrasies can make a dramatist, Shakespear was the king of dramatists. Unfortunately, a man may have them all, and yet conceive of high affairs of state exactly as Simon Tappertit did.[1]

August Strindberg (1849–1912)

August Strindberg's Master Olof *(1872–77),* Miss Julie *(1888),* The Dance of Death *(1901),* A Dream Play *(1902), and* The Ghost Sonata *(1907) were crucial to the advent of modern drama and remain key works in theater history. The Intimate Theater of Stockholm, with which Strindberg was very closely involved, opened in 1907; several of Strindberg's plays were staged there before the Theater closed in 1910.*

from *Open Letters to the Intimate Theater* (1909)[1]

When I used *Julius Caesar* as a textbook in English in 1869 (although I could hardly pronounce the sounds of that difficult language), the play has been selected because the English in it was easy and the play did not contain anything course. We youngsters, who were highly critical, commented at once that the play should have been called Brutus, since Caesar fades away in Act III; and we found that the world's greatest hero, whom we knew from world history and his own *De bello gallico*, had been badly depicted; a wretch who believed in signs and apparently was henpecked so that he wanted to stay at home from the senate because his wife had had bad dreams and had asked him—a general—to be careful. These major criticisms from twenty-year olds have certainly been made before and since by famous commentators, but now, when at the age of sixty I reread my *Julius Caesar*, which because of the commentaries I know best of Shakespeare's plays, these same weaknesses came to mind.

---

[1]In Dickens' *Barnaby Rudge* (1841), Simon Tappertit, a onetime locksmith's apprentice, is well out of his depth when he becomes a leader of an anti-Catholic mob.

---

[1]Trans. Walter Johnson. Seattle and London: Reprinted by permission of the University of Washington Press.

When I again examined Caesar's role in detail as I had done before, I again found a certain weakness if his characterization, which must not be called a merit just because one likes Shakespeare.

* * *

So far as the central character of Brutus goes, he is an ideal figure related to Hamlet, who was created in about the same way. Brutus philosophizes about everything he undertakes and speculates about his destiny and the problems of existence. Brutus has no flaws, but commits a big mistake when he interferes with the plans of Providence and murders Caesar; it is this act that causes his fall after it has dawned on him what a rabble he had been working with and what the men who succeeded the tyrant were like. Antony tampers with Caesar's will; Cassius is avaricious and accepts bribes; Lepidus is an ass. The people who on scene 1 of Act I have been cheering for Caesar had shortly before "climb'd up to walls and battlements" to shout for Pompey; after Caesar's death they cheer for Brutus, shortly afterward for Antony, and then for Caesar again when his will is opened. Brutus has sacrificed his friend's life for the fickle mob; on the altar of abstract freedom of the people he has liquidated the abstract concept of tyrant, which is simply a bad translation of ruler.

Yves Bonnefoy (1923–)

A major poet for more than fifty years, Yves Bonnefoy's French translations of Hamlet, King Lear, Julius Caesar, *and the* Sonnets *have made him one of France's great champions of Shakespeare.*

from *Shakespeare and the French Poet* (2004)[1]

I can remember my first encounter since it was one of those moments that are not experienced in an especially powerful way at the time but that later come to dominate your thinking and to influ-

---

[1]*Shakespeare and the French Poet*, ed. and trans. John T. Naughton (© 2007 The Johns Hopkins University Press). This excerpt is reproduced with the kind permission of the Press.

ence your choices. I was in school, and in the book of readings we were using to study English there was the most famous scene in *Julius Caesar*: "Friends, Romans, countrymen, lend me your ears," and that whole speech in which Mark Antony captivates his listeners, winning them over with cynical skill but at the same time speaking with such nobility and emotion about Caesar's remains. It's a great moment, not just of rhetoric but also of the lyrical essence of poetry. "'Twas on a summer's evening in his tent"—that whole passage that causes the "gracious drops" to flow.

Why did I find this scene so striking, more striking at the time than any other passage of English poetry, with the exception of *The Rime of the Ancient Mariner*? It was certainly because of the beauty and intensity I've mentioned, but today I think it was also because that superb English harbored a great deal of our own approach to poetry: the grand words of Latin origin, but also, and even more important, something of that resonant space that French poetry often maintains between words to allow their range of meaning a wider scope. In this case, the connection was somewhat closer than usual, and it allowed me to measure all the more fully the distance between these two paths of poetry, English and French.

I think I was also struck, though of course somewhat subconsciously, or, at least, in a not yet fully informed way, by the manner in which Shakespeare seems to consciously and deliberately bring together in this scene the aims and methods of rhetoric on the one hand, and poetry on the other. In a word, Antony's speech shows poetry in various kinds of relation to something other than itself. And this can help us to understand that poetry doesn't spring forth in a single bound from the depths of one's mind and spirit, but must free itself from various obstacles that are a function of the particular nature of language or cultural tradition. For someone like me, who wanted very much to devote himself to poetry, it was obviously important to understand this. I could almost convince myself that poetry is born in a more ordinary way in our lives and in our poems than I would have thought from reading Latin poets like Virgil, whose words seemed suggestive of an absolute; these poets were mysterious and seemed almost from another world because I understood Latin rather poorly, and there's no better way to find its words and phrases unsettling!

Need I add that these thoughts I had about Shakespeare were in an embryonic form? I had no particular capacity or knowledge or points of reference to develop them more fully. Let's just say that I thought a great deal about those speeches of Brutus and of Mark Antony; I wanted to translate them and, in fact, did many years later. *Julius Caesar* was the first play I translated, along with *Hamlet,* which I undertook at the same time—with the feeling of a very important rendez-vous with myself.

Further Reading

Shakespeare's Roman Plays

Brower, Reuben A. *Hero and Saint: Shakespeare and the Graeco-Roman Heroic Tradition.* New York: Oxford University Press, 1971.

James, Heather. *Shakespeare's Troy: Drama, Politics, and the Translation of Empire.* Cambridge: Cambridge University Press, 1997.

Kahn, Coppélia. *Roman Shakespeare: Warriors, Wounds, and Women.* New York: Routledge, 1997.

Kayser, John R., and Ronald J. Lettieri. "The Last of All the Romans: Shakespeare's Commentary on Classical Republicanism." *Clio* 9 (1980): 197–227.

Leggatt, Alexander. *Shakespeare's Political Drama: The History Plays and the Roman Plays.* 989; rpt. London: Routledge, 1992.

MacCallum, Mungo William. *Shakespeare's Roman Plays and Their Background.* London: Macmillan, 1910.

Martindale, Charles, and Michelle Martindale. *Shakespeare and the Uses of Antiquity: An Introductory Essay.* London: Routledge, 1990.

Miola, Robert S. *Shakespeare's Rome.* Cambridge: Cambridge University Press, 1983.

Platt, Michael. *Rome and Romans According to Shakespeare.* 1976; rev. New York: University Press of America, 1983.

Spencer, T. J. B. *Shakespeare: The Roman Plays.* London: Longmans, Green & Company, 1963.

Thomas, Vivian. *Shakespeare's Roman Worlds*. New York: Routledge, 1989.

Traversi, Derek. *Shakespeare: The Roman Plays*. Stanford, CA: Stanford University Press, 1963.

Julius Caesar

Blits, Jan H. *The End of the Ancient Republic: Essays on Julius Caesar*. Durham, NC: Carolina Academic Press, 1982.

Booth, Stephen. "The Shakespearean Actor as Kamikaze Pilot." *Shakespeare Quarterly* 36 (1985): 553–70.

Brower, Reuben A. "The Discovery of Plutarch." In *Hero and Saint: Shakespeare and the Graeco-Roman Heroic Tradition*. New York: Oxford University Press, 1971.

Burt, Richard A. "'A Dangerous Rome': Shakespeare's *Julius Caesar* and the Discursive Determinism of Cultural Politics." In *Contending Kingdoms*, ed. Marie-Rose Logan and Peter L. Rudnytsky. Detroit, MI: Wayne State University Press, 1991, 109–30.

Drakakis, John. "'Fashion it thus': *Julius Caesar* and the Politics of Theatrical Representation." *Shakespeare Survey* 44 (1992): 65–73.

Garber, Marjorie. "A Rome of One's Own." In *Shakespeare's Ghost Writers: Literature as Uncanny Causality*. New York and London: Methuen, 1987.

Girard, René. *A Theater of Envy: William Shakespeare*. New York: Oxford University Press, 1991.

Goldberg, Jonathan. *James I and the Politics of Literature*. 1983; rpt. Stanford, CA: Stanford University Press, 1989.

Halpern, Richard. *Shakespeare Among the Moderns*. Ithaca, NY: Cornell University Press, 1997.

Holmes, Christopher. "Time for the Plebs in *Julius Caesar*." *Early Modern Literary Studies: A Journal of Sixteenth- and Seventeenth-Century English Literature* 7 (2001).

Kewes, Paulina. "*Julius Caesar* in Jacobean England." *The Seventeenth Century* 17 (2002): 155–86.

Kezar, Dennis. "*Julius Caesar* and the Properties of Shakespeare's Globe." *English Literary Renaissance* 28 (1998): 18–46.

Knight, G. Wilson. "The Eroticism of Julius Caesar." In *The Imperial Theme: Further Interpretations of Shakespeare's Tragedies, Including the Roman Plays*. Rev. ed. Oxford: Oxford University Press, 1951.

Liebler, Naomi Conn. "'Thou Bleeding Piece of Earth': The Ritual Ground of *Julius Caesar*." *Shakespeare Studies* 14 (1981): 175–96.

McGowan, Margaret M. "Caesar's Cloak: Diversion as an Art of Persuasion in Sixteenth-Century Writing." *Renaissance Studies* 18 (2004): 37–48.

Parker, Barbara L. "'A Thing Unfirm': Plato's Republic and Shakespeare's *Julius Caesar*." *Shakespeare Quarterly* 44 (1993): 30–43.

Pechter, Edward. "*Julius Caesar* and *Sejanus*: Roman Politics, Inner Selves, and the Powers of the Theatre." *Shakespeare and His Contemporaries: Essays in Comparison*, ed. E. A. J. Honigmann. Manchester: Manchester University Press, 1986, 60–78.

Rabkin, Norman. "Structure, Convention, and Meaning in *Julius Caesar*." *Journal of English and Germanic Philology* 63 (1964): 240–54.

Rebhorn, Wayne A. "The Crisis of the Aristocracy in *Julius Caesar*." *Renaissance Quarterly* 43 (1990): 75–111.

Ripley, John. *Julius Caesar on Stage in England and America, 1599–1973*. Cambridge: Cambridge University Press, 1980.

Rose, Mark. "Conjuring Caesar: Ceremony, History, and Authority in 1599." *English Literary Renaissance* 19 (1989): 291–304.

Spotswood, Jerald W. "'We Are Undone Already': Disarming the Multitude in *Julius Caesar* and *Coriolanus*." *Texas Studies in Literature and Language* 42 (2000): 61–78.

Stirling, Brents. *The Populace in Shakespeare*. New York: Columbia University Press, 1949.

Velz, John W. "Undular Structure in *Julius Caesar*." *The Modern Language Review* 66 (1971): 21–30.

Wilson, Richard. "'Is this a holiday?': Shakespeare's Roman carnival." In *Will Power: Essays on Shakespearean Authority*. Detroit, MI: Wayne State University Press, 1993.

The Supernatural: Divine Signs, Ghosts, and Prophetic Dreams

Brown, Peter, ed. *Reading Dreams: The Interpretation of Dreams from Chaucer to Shakespeare.* Oxford: Oxford University Press, 1999.

Curry, Patrick. *Prophecy and Power: Astrology in Early Modern England.* Princeton, NJ: Princeton University Press, 1989.

Marshall, Peter. *Beliefs and the Dead in Reformation England.* Oxford: Oxford University Press, 2002.

Schumaker, Wayne. *The Occult Sciences in the Renaissance: A Study in Intellectual Patterns.* Berkeley: University of California Press, 1972.

Sondheim, Moriz. "Shakespeare and the Astrology of His Time." *Journal of the Warburg Institute* 2 (1939): 243–59.

Thomas, Keith. *Religion and the Decline of Magic: Studies in Popular Beliefs in Sixteenth and Seventeenth Century England.* London: Weidenfeld & Nicolson, 1971.

Republicanism, Popular Politics, and the Rhetoric of Liberty in 1599

Arnold, Oliver. *The Third Citizen: Shakespeare's Theater and the Elizabethan House of Commons.* Baltimore, MD: The Johns Hopkins University Press, 2007.

Collinson, Patrick. "The Monarchical Republic of Queen Elizabeth I." In *Elizabethan Essays.* London: Hambledon Press, 1994, 31–58.

Elton, G. R. "Parliament." In *The Reign of Elizabeth I*, ed. Christopher Haigh. Athens: The University of Georgia Press, 1987, 79–100.

Hadfield, Andrew. "Shakespeare and Republicanism: History and Cultural Materialism." *Textual Practice* 17 (2003): 461–83.

Haigh, Christopher, ed. *The Reign of Elizabeth I.* Athens: The University of Georgia Press, 1987.

Hartley, T. E. *Elizabeth's Parliaments: Queen, Lords, and Commons, 1559–1601.* New York: Manchester University Press, 1992.

Hexter, J. H., ed. *Parliament and Liberty from the Reign of Elizabeth to the English Civil War.* Stanford, CA: Stanford University Press, 1992.

Kahn, Victoria. *Machiavellian Rhetoric: From the Counter-Reformation to Milton.* Princeton: Princeton University Press, 1994.

Miola, Robert S. "Julius Caesar and the Tyrannicide Debate." *Renaissance Quarterly* 38 (1985): 271–89.

Neale, J. E. *The Elizabethan House of Commons.* 1949; rpt. Harmondsworth, Middlesex: Penguin Books, 1963.

Patterson, Annabel. *Shakespeare and the Popular Voice.* Cambridge: Basil Blackwell, 1989.

Peltonen, Markku. *Classical Humanism and Republicanism in English Political Thought, 1570–1640.* Cambridge: Cambridge University Press, 1995.

Sacks, David Harris. "Parliament, Liberty, and the Commonweal." In *Parliament and Liberty from the Reign of Elizabeth to the English Civil War,* ed. J. H. Hexter. Stanford, CA: Stanford University Press, 1992, 85–121.

Sommerville, Johann P. "Parliament, Privilege, and the Liberties of the Subject." In *Parliament and Liberty from the Reign of Elizabeth to the English Civil War,* ed. J. H. Hexter. Stanford, CA: Stanford University Press, 1992, 56–84.